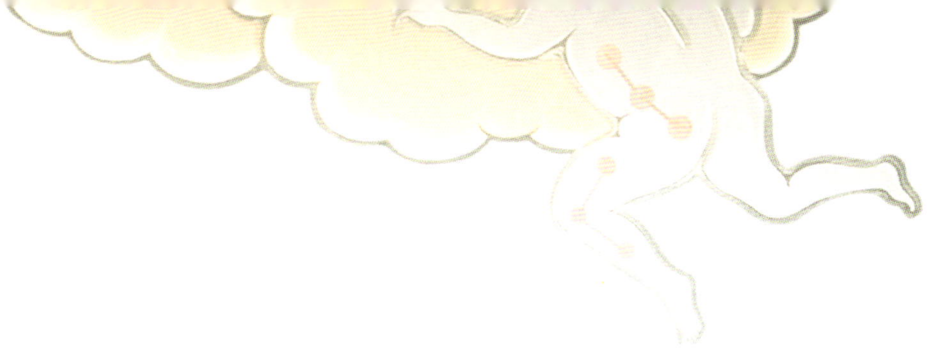

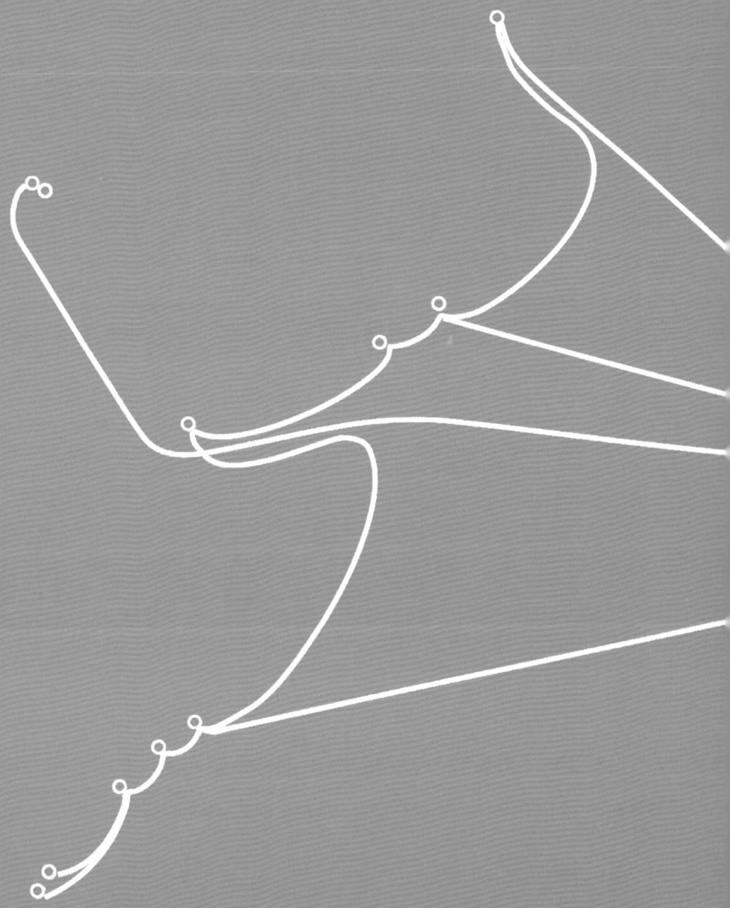

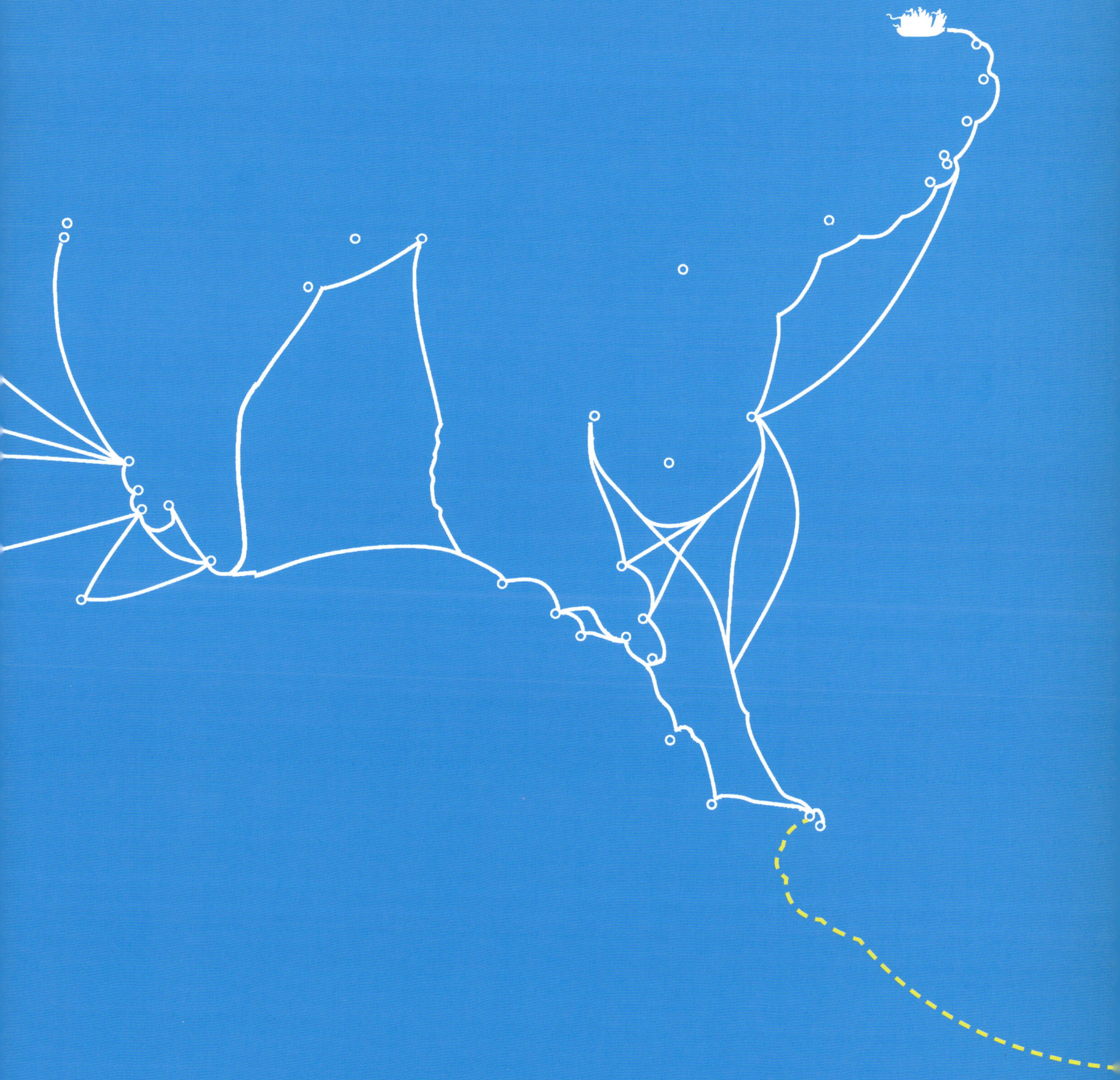

Other Histories

GUAN WEI'S FABLE FOR A CONTEMPORARY WORLD
DOCUMENTATION OF AN EXHIBITION

另一种历史 关伟的一个现代寓言 从方案文件到展览实现

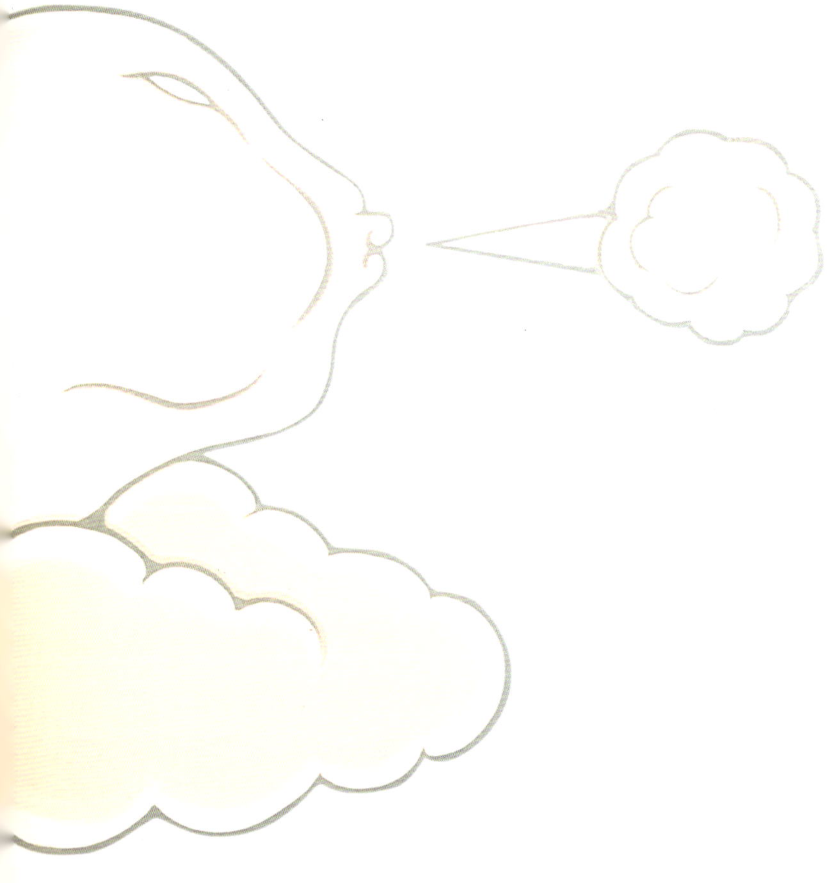

Other Histories

GUAN WEI'S FABLE FOR A CONTEMPORARY WORLD
DOCUMENTATION OF AN EXHIBITION

Edited by Claire Roberts

Published by **Wild Peony** Pty Ltd

In association with powerhouse museum science + design

With the support of ANU THE AUSTRALIAN NATIONAL UNIVERSITY

Song Ya Feng Culture & Art Center Beijing

ARTRON
Beijing Artron Colour Printing Co Ltd

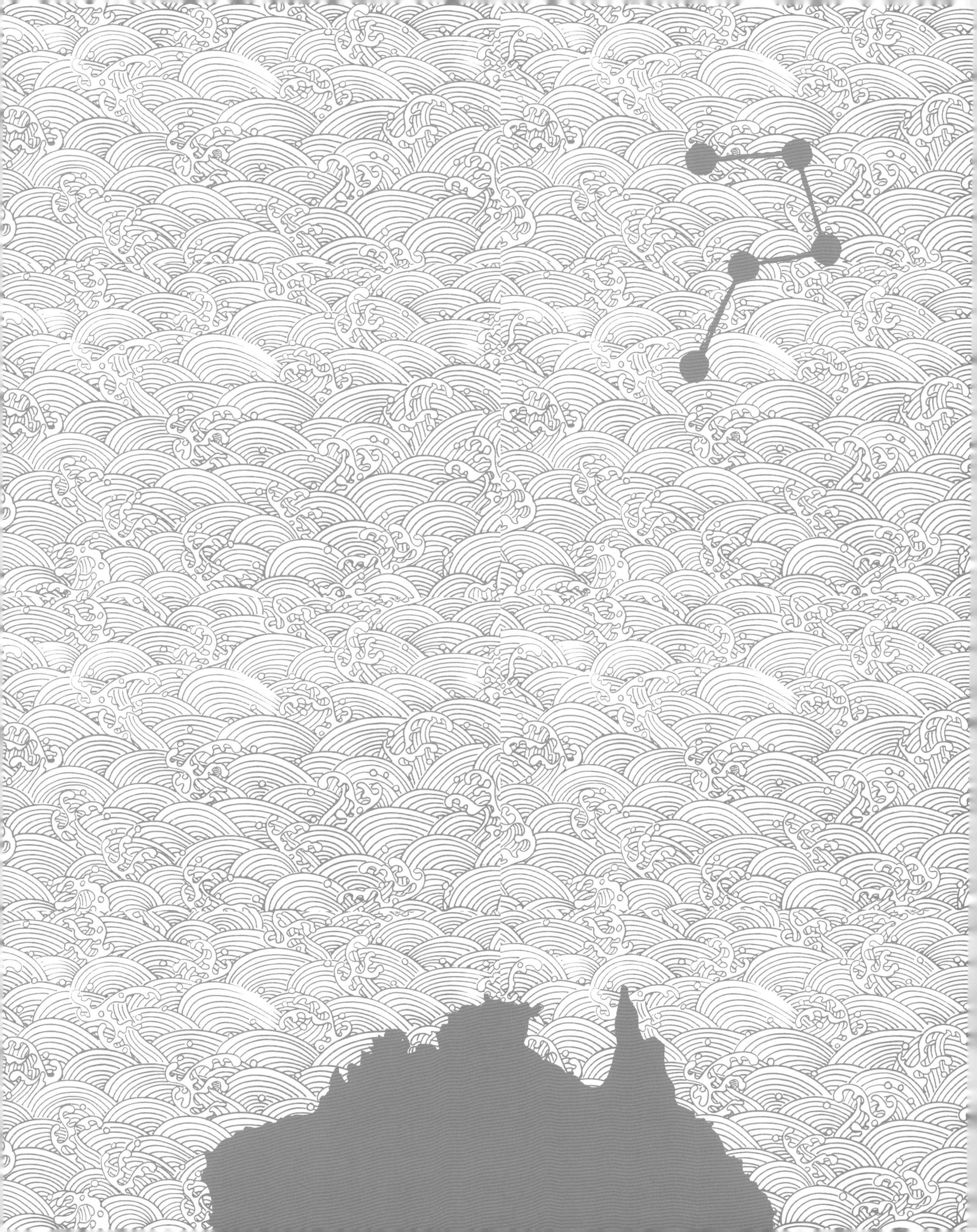

Published by Wild Peony Book Publishers PO Box 636 Broadway (Sydney) NSW 2007 Australia in association with Powerhouse Museum PO Box K346 Haymarket (Sydney) NSW 1238 Australia www.powerhousemuseum.com following the exhibition 'Other Histories: Guan Wei's Fable for a Contemporary World', Powerhouse Museum, Sydney, 11 October 2006–22 April 2007 and with the support of 'Beijing as Spectacle', a Federation Fellowship Project led by Geremie R. Barmé of The Australian National University and funded by the Australian Research Council.

International Distribution:
University of Hawaii Press
2480 Kolowalu Street
Honolulu, Hawaii 96822, USA
Fax: 1 808 988-6052
http://www.uhpress.hawaii.edu

First Published 2008

ISBN: 978-1-876957-11-7 (hard-cover edition)

Editor: Claire Roberts
Liaison Manager: Jin Sha
Production Manager: Liu Zheng
Project Team: Claire Roberts, Mabel Lee, A. D. Syrokomla-Stefanowska, Guan Wei, Jin Sha, Sang Ye, Geremie R. Barmé
Copy Editing: Mabel Lee, A. D. Syrokomla-Stefanowska, Sang Ye, Maxine McArthur
Design: Wang Zi, Zhao Fang, Song Ya Feng Culture & Art Center Beijing
Production: Song Ya Feng Culture & Art Center Beijing
Powerhouse Museum Photography: Jean-François Lanzarone, Marinco Kojdanovski
Printing: Beijing Artron Colour Printing Co. Ltd

Contents

Foreword

'Other Histories: Guan Wei's Fable for a Contemporary World' is the result of a unique collaboration between Guan Wei and the Powerhouse Museum, Sydney. Over the course of one month in late 2006, together with a team of assisting artists and museum staff, Guan Wei created an installation of large-scale mural paintings and museum objects that transformed the Museum's Asian Gallery into a 'floating poetic corridor in which history and memory, fact and fiction are blurred'. Crossing the threshold of the gallery, visitors entered into the fantasy world of Guan Wei, one inspired by the voyages of Ming dynasty admiral Zheng He (1371–1432) and the artist's own journey of migration to Australia. Guan Wei assigned new meanings to museum objects so that they substantiated the assumed history of the artistic realm he and his collaborators created. He also included in the display contemporary, imitation and found objects as well as paintings of ancient navigational maps and exotic plants and animals that Zheng He's men had encountered on their voyages that were 'on loan' from a fictitious Museum of Australian East Asian Art.

The Powerhouse Museum is Australia's leading museum of history, science, design and decorative arts. Established in 1880 following the success of the 1879 Sydney International Exhibition it has developed a large and important collection that reflects human ingenuity and creative practice in Australia and other parts of the world. The Museum has a significant collection of Chinese objects acquired since the late-nineteenth century that reflects the history of Chinese migration to Australia. Working with Claire Roberts, the Senior Curator of Asian Decorative Arts and Design, Guan Wei had access to the Museum's collection, and together they selected objects that could be 'borrowed' to add authenticity to his narrative. Guan Wei's fable for a contemporary world began during the Ming Empire and took visitors on an ocean voyage to the Australian goldfields of the 1850s where large numbers of Chinese came to seek their fortune, many of whom then stayed.

Guan Wei was born in Beijing and first came to Australia in 1989. Since then he has participated in numerous solo and group exhibitions including the Asia-Pacific Triennial of Contemporary Art, Brisbane (1999), the Kwangju Biennial (2000) and the Adelaide Biennial (2008). Today, Guan Wei is one of Australia's leading contemporary artists with key works held in national and state museums as well as in private and corporate collections in Australia and East Asia. It is the cartoon-like simplicity of Guan Wei's art together with his playful sense of humour and infectious idealism in dealing with serious matters such as the environment, the plight of refugees, race relations and the 'War on Terror' that has endeared him to viewers. As an artist who grew up during the Cultural Revolution (1966–1976) Guan Wei understands the power of art to communicate with people and create a lasting resonance. He approaches his practice with a social conscience, and a belief in the interconnectedness of humanity.

'Other Histories' was an unconventional museum exhibition because it was not based on factual research but on history and speculation, storytelling, personal experience and fantasy. Working within a museum environment and incorporating museum objects in showcases and in-house text panels and labels, Guan Wei's installation functioned as an inventive intervention, prompting visitors to question what was being presented as a record of the past, both in his installation and by other historical narratives. Guan Wei also hoped that those who experienced the exhibition would initially be disoriented, and then relax and reflect on and rejoice in the common ground that we all share as human beings. In the exhibition brochure he explained: 'We, who come from different cultural backgrounds, need to better understand one another, connect with one another and seek friendship with one another. It is imperative that we find a shared set of values to ensure our survival.'

It was an honour for the Powerhouse Museum to have worked with Guan Wei in presenting 'Other Histories'. Published in the months leading up to the Beijing Olympic Games, this book documenting the exhibition seeks to acquaint more people with the abiding value of Guan Wei's work and with this bold, whimsical and thought-provoking installation.

Jennifer Sanders
Acting Director, Powerhouse Museum

Introduction

Guan Wei is a storyteller who uses images to attract our attention and challenge our cultural bearings. He combines fact and fantasy, asking us to leave behind narrow definitions of who and what we are so that we may be led into a realm where new narratives are possible. His art is connected to current themes and yet offers whimsical and unexpected ways forward. It transcends national boundaries, seeks cross-cultural understanding and promotes hope for a better world.

'Other Histories' is Guan Wei's most ambitious project to date. It is a large-scale art installation in a museum setting that uses wall paintings, museum and other objects to explore an imaginary history based on the voyages of the Ming dynasty admiral Zheng He (1371–1432) and Guan Wei's own encounter with Australia. This volume documents the development and realisation of the 'Other Histories' exhibition at Sydney's Powerhouse Museum in 2006–7. Included is an artist statement and working drawings by Guan Wei, a curatorial perspective, and photographs by Powerhouse Museum photographer Jean-François Lanzarone of Guan Wei and his assisting artists Frank Hope, Jin Sha, Yang Xifa and Zhao Baokang at work. Essays by Geremie R. Barmé, a leading historian and Sinologist specialising in China's cultural and intellectual history, and by award-winning novelist Alexis Wright, a member of the Waanyi nation of the southern highlands of the Gulf of Carpentaria, offer different insights on Guan Wei's project.

Guan Wei's art has developed within a complex set of cultural frames that reflect his equally complex life experience. It acknowledges his Chinese-ness, or rather his Manchu-ness as a descendent of a noble line of Manchu bannermen, the officials who ruled China under the Manchu-Qing dynasty (1644–1911). Yet it declares an Australian-ness: he migrated to Australia in 1990 following a series of artist-in-residence programs that began in early1989. Guan Wei's art is imbued with a confidence that may be accounted for by his maturity as an artist as well as the growing international status of contemporary Chinese art.

In the late 1980s, before relocating to Australia, Guan Wei would regularly meet with his Beijing artist friends at one or other of their homes to discuss life and to make art. Conditions were cramped and the works they produced were small, playful and largely non-commercial. They were made in a collective

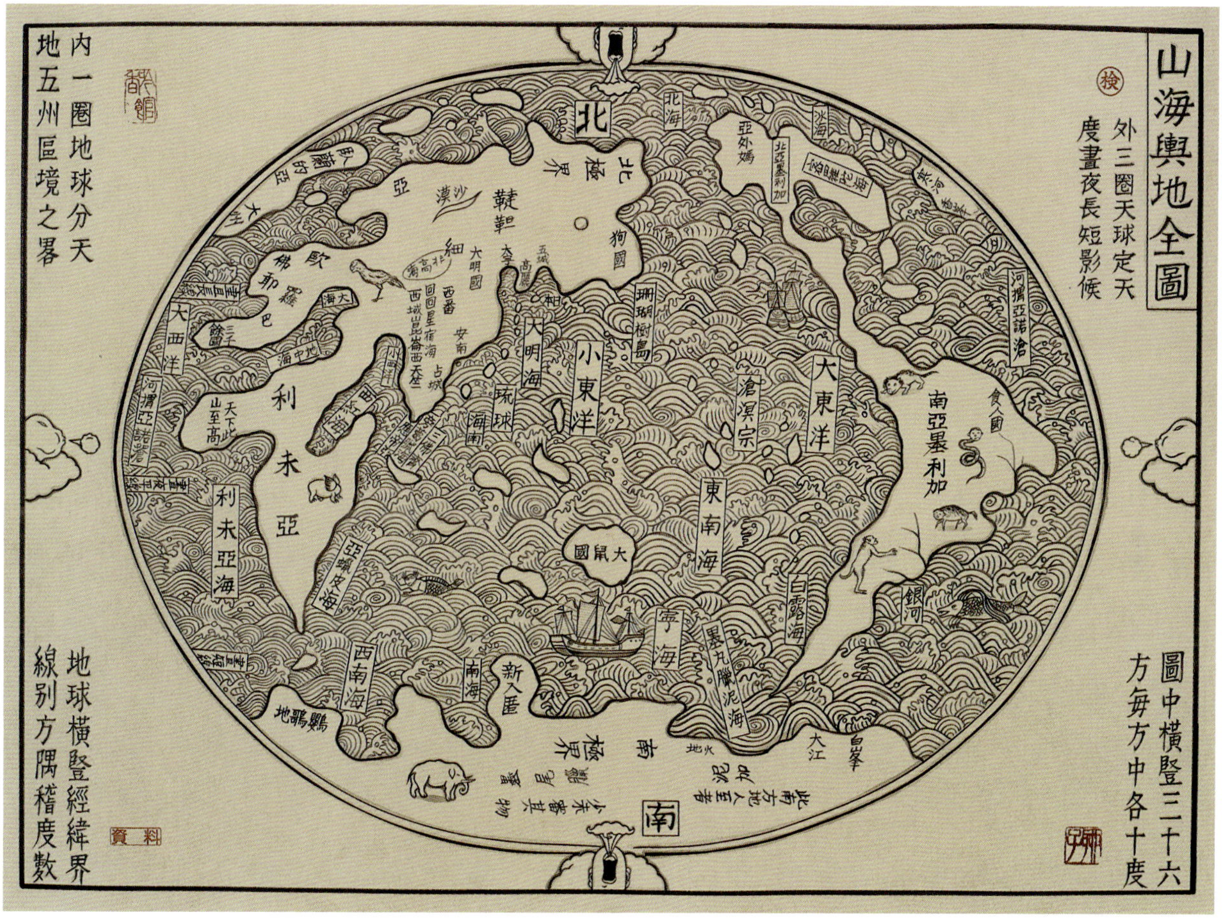

'Chinese Map of the World (1433)', work on paper by Guan Wei. Photograph: courtesy Powerhouse Museum, Sydney.

environment of camaraderie and shared difficulties. The art was gritty, experimental and created using cheap materials that were readily available. There were no studios and few opportunities to exhibit anything other than officially sanctioned work. Art was made for self-expression, self-satisfaction and the amusement of friends. The making and sharing of art largely happened at home.

Guan Wei was one of the many Chinese artists lured to the West in search of freedom of expression and a different way of life. Early in 1989 he travelled to Australia at the invitation of the Tasmanian School of Art, where he was artist-in-residence for three months. He was fascinated by the idea of the Great Southern Land, referred to in mysterious terms in ancient Chinese texts and understood by his compatriots as a place that was sparsely populated, but had strange animals and brilliant sunlight. In Tasmania he experienced the novelty of living on an island, of being surrounded by water, as if floating in a vast ocean of nothingness, alone. Tasmania was a microcosm of Australia: a place that was exotic, detached and with dark secrets of its own. Over time he became interested in Australian history and our troubled and contested past. In his paintings he expressed the need for Indigenous and non-Indigenous people to live in peace and harmony. He depicted boat people in distress, adrift on vast and forbidding oceans, referring to the Australian Government's treatment of refugees: a category that could easily have included Guan Wei had his fate been different. The landscape of Australia came to feature prominently in his paintings too: a vast landmass, brilliant blue ocean, bright light and heightened colour. In recent years his focus has shifted to the 'War on Terror'. Silhouettes of gun-toting soldiers scour the Australian landscape in search of the long-dead bushranger Ned Kelly, but with the aid of helicopters and warships, alluding to the persistent climate of fear created following 9/11 and the subsequent American invasion of Iraq in 2003, supported by Australia.

Guan Wei is celebrated as one of Australia's leading contemporary artists. He was the subject of a ten-year retrospective at Sydney's Museum of Contemporary Art in 1999 and was one of eight artists selected to produce a limited edition of fine art prints for the Sydney 2000 Olympic poster program. He has also won a number of prestigious commissions including the cover design of the *Sydney Morning Herald* newspaper on Australia Day 2001, as well as an 18-metre artwork for the foyer of the Bureau of Meteorology in Melbourne in 2004, said to be the largest wall painting in the southern hemisphere. Guan Wei's art works have been collected by major national and state art institutions, and Sherman Galleries in Sydney, one of Australia's leading commercial galleries represented him from 1991 to 2007.

Since Guan Wei's departure from China in 1989 there have been dramatic changes in the Chinese art world. Art making and exhibiting is now big business, part of the global economy. Brian Wallace, the Australian who in 1986 founded Red Gate Gallery, the first foreign-run commercial art space to operate in Beijing, and who represents Guan Wei in China, now has competition from many overseas galleries and art foundations seeking a share in China's lucrative art market. Today, Chinese artists are regular participants in international biennales and triennales. Their works are eagerly sought by local and international galleries as well as auction houses, which play an increasingly significant role in the art market.

Over the past ten years many expatriate artists have returned to China, lured by the opportunities that have accompanied China's dramatic economic development. These artists have returned with savvy new ideas for art creation and promotion that has injected new energy into the Beijing art world and accelerated its integration into the international art community. The most successful have spacious studios on the outskirts of Beijing and employ assistants to work on ambitious projects for local and international exhibitions. Many have bought houses and studios and divide their time between Beijing and elsewhere, living and working where and when they choose. It is the kind of life that was impossible to imagine twenty years ago.

From 2008, Guan Wei will increasingly divide his life between Beijing and Sydney. He has rented a large studio space on the outskirts of Beijing where he can be part of the energy and excitement of the Beijing art world and engage assistants for creating large-scale works. Against this background, 'Other Histories: Guan Wei's Fable for a Contemporary World' can be interpreted as a parable of Guan Wei's own life experience, presented as a one-way journey about cross-cultural understanding and misunderstanding, migration and settlement. Will Guan Wei's future works depict a triumphant homecoming or a narrative of return, or will he evoke the exoticism of China from an Australian perspective? One thing seems certain: no matter where Guan Wei is located, he will be attuned to the geopolitical dimension of China's growing importance on the world stage, as well as the strong personal bonds that link him with Australia.

Claire Roberts

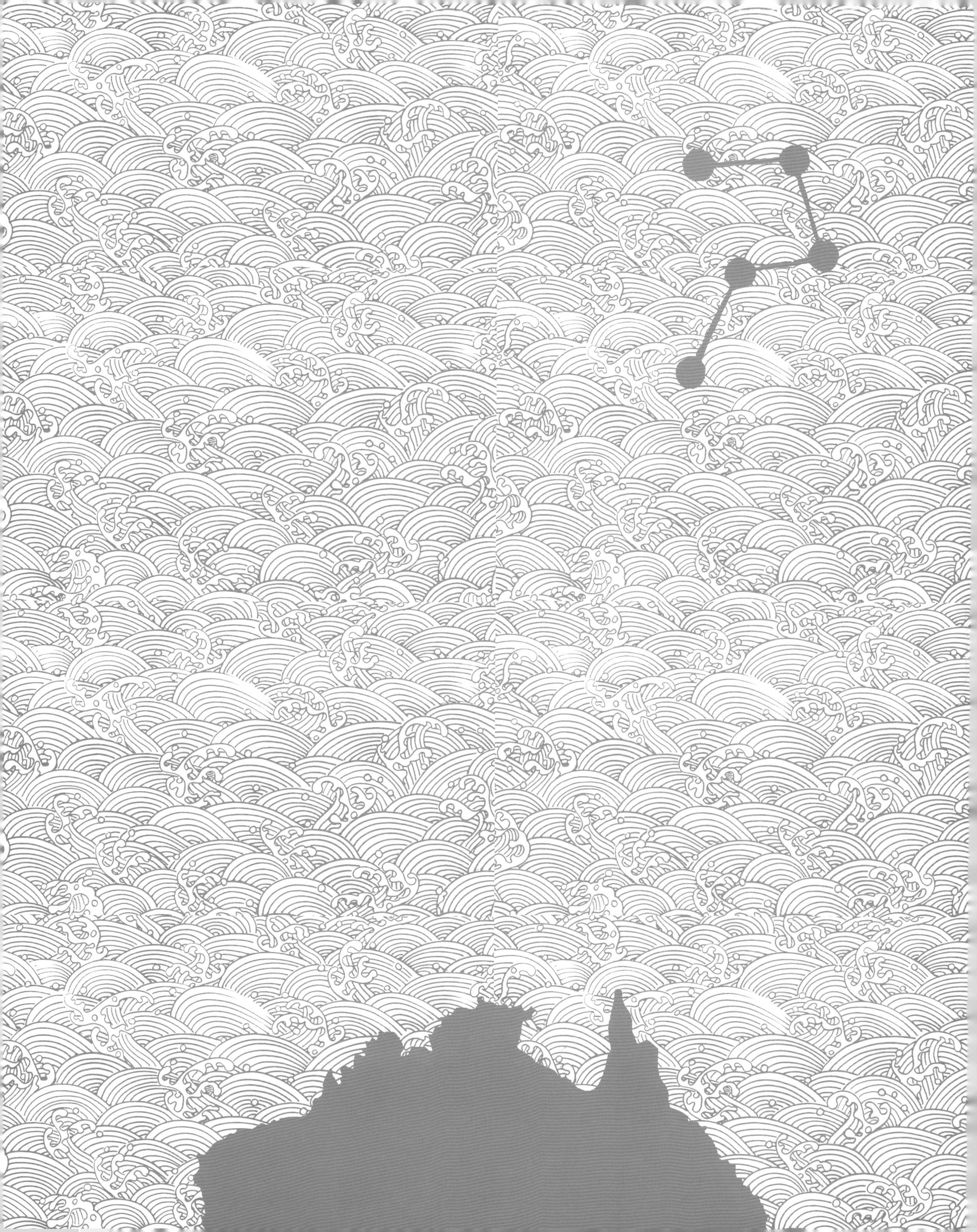

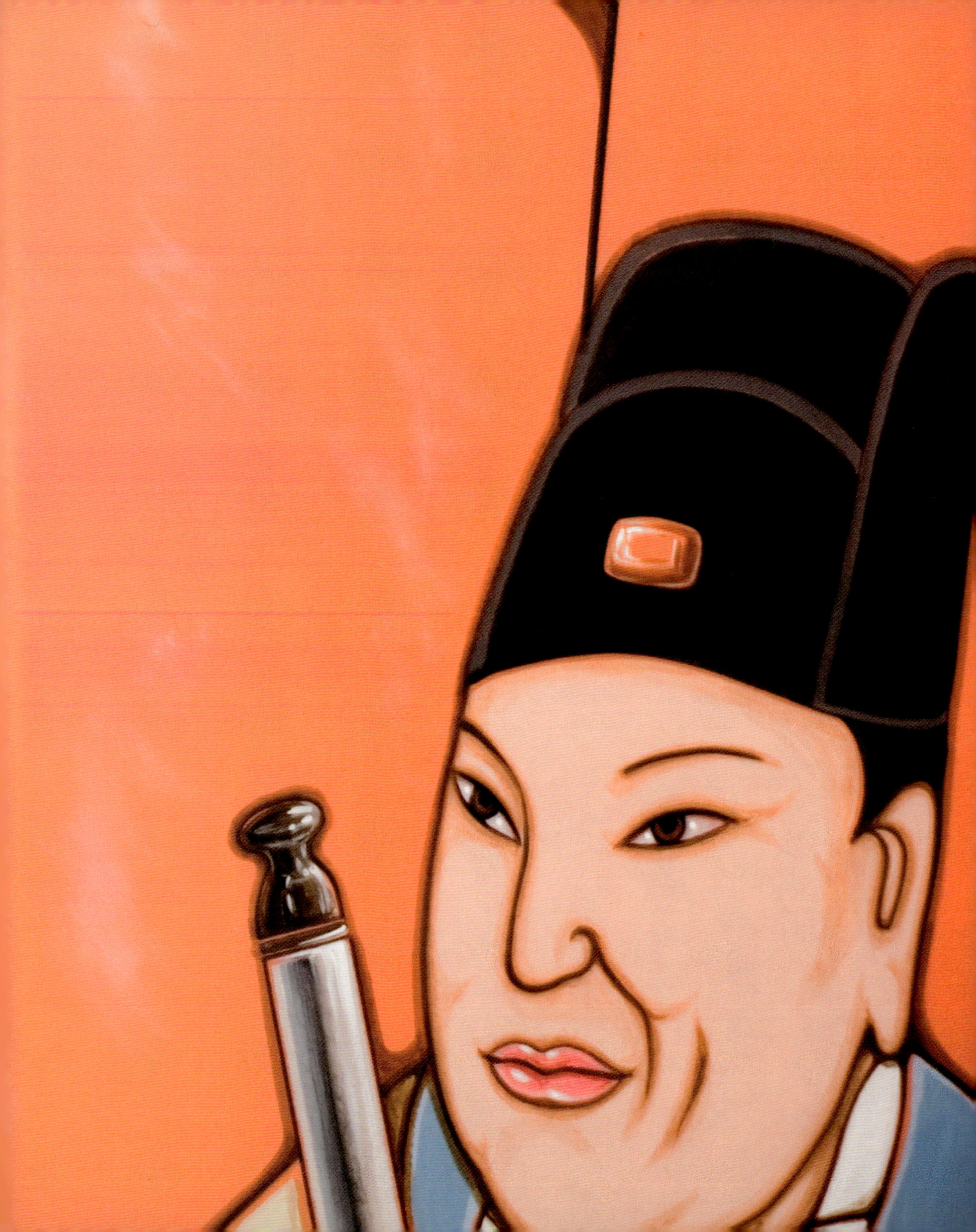

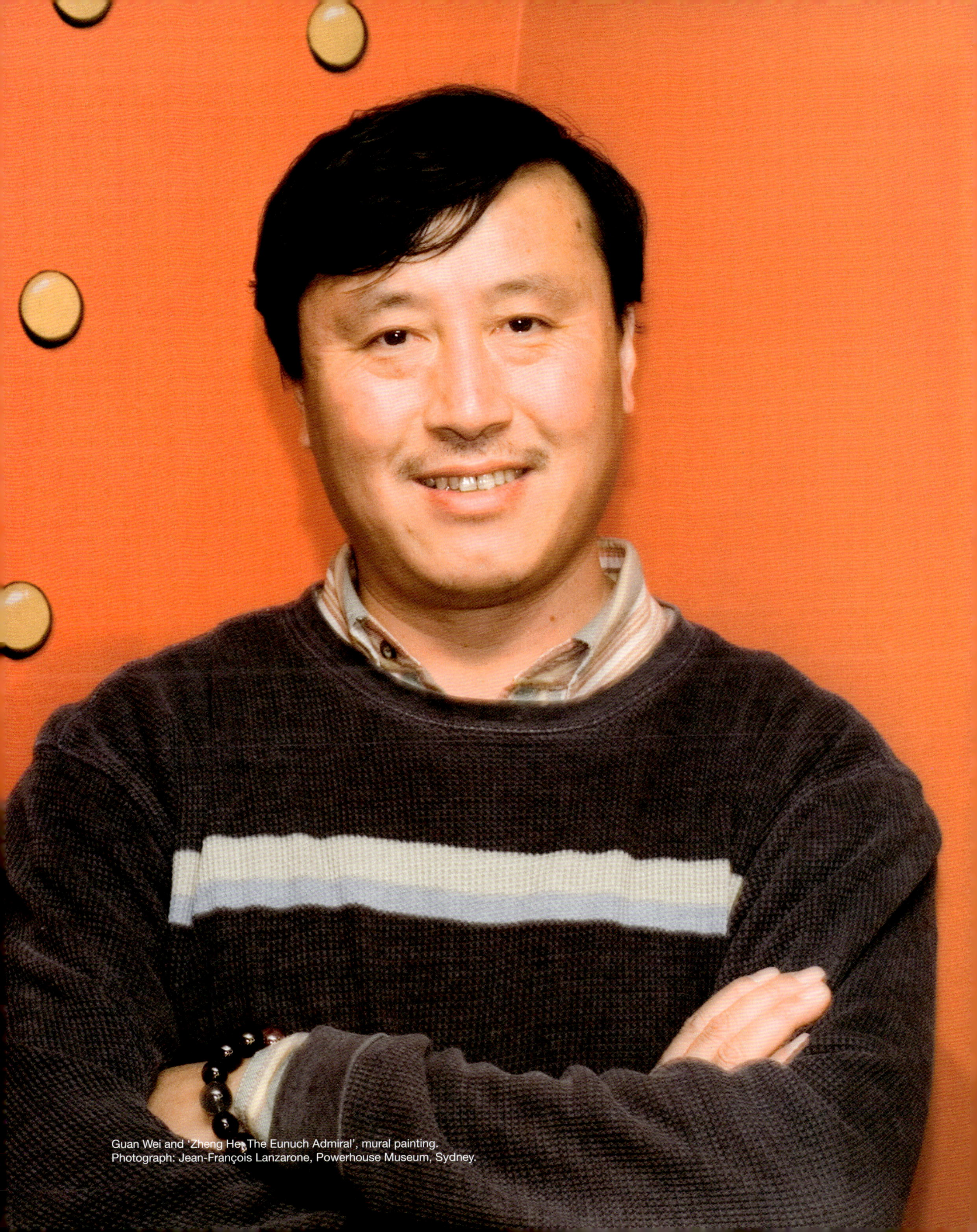

Guan Wei and 'Zheng He, The Eunuch Admiral', mural painting.
Photograph: Jean-François Lanzarone, Powerhouse Museum, Sydney.

'Other Histories': Origins and Creative Lessons

Guan Wei

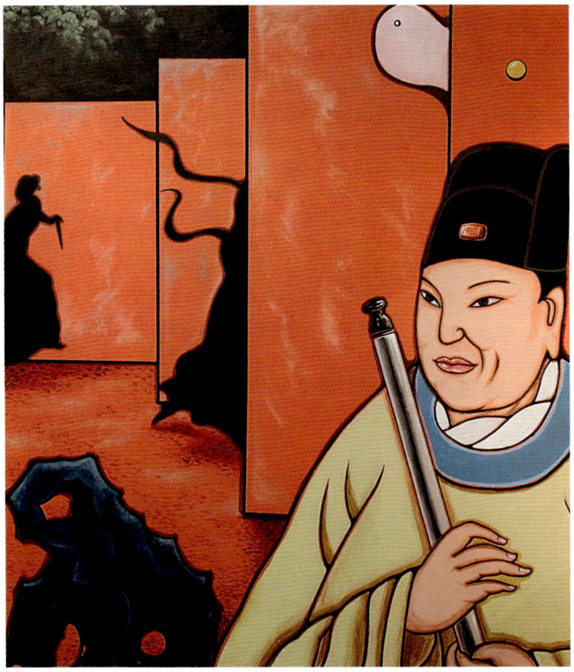

Detail of 'Zheng He', mural painting.
Photograph: Marinco Kojdanovski, Powerhouse Museum, Sydney.

My large-scale mural installation 'Other Histories: Guan Wei's Fable for a Contemporary World' was developed over a period of two years and opened at Sydney's Powerhouse Museum in October 2006. In the exhibition I brought together a variety of artistic media to present another history—the fantasy journey of the great Chinese mariner Zheng He and his men, who almost six hundred years ago arrived on this vast landmass that we now call Australia.

Following the orders of the Yongle Emperor (r. 1403–1424) of the Ming dynasty, Zheng He led some 27,000 men in an armada of massive sailboats to explore the world. Over a period of 28 years he made seven voyages covering a distance of more than 70,000 nautical miles, the equivalent of circumnavigating the world three times. During those voyages he visited many countries and regions, traded and had contact with local people, and in the process established and strengthened understanding between those places and China. Zheng He's first voyage began on 11 July 1405, 87 years before Christopher Columbus (c. 1451–1506) discovered America, 92 years before Vasco da Gama (c. 1460–1524) passed the Cape of Good Hope, 114 years before Ferdinand Magellan (1480–1521) began his circumnavigation of the world, and 350 years before James Cook (1728–1779) arrived on the shores of Australia.

In March 2002, the retired submarine commanding officer of the British Royal Navy Gavin Menzies announced the findings of his research in London: that the Chinese were the first to draw a maritime map of the world, that Zheng He and his men had arrived on the American subcontinent before Columbus, and that Zheng He was the first person to circumnavigate the world. That same year he published *1421: The Year China Discovered America*, which was then renamed *1421: The Year China Discovered the World* and re-printed. In his book Gavin Menzies says that Zheng He was the first person to discover America and Australia, and that close to 600 years ago Zheng He had already set foot on Australian soil and established colonies in Australia and New Zealand. In support of the above assertions Gavin Menzies revealed a navigational map, a compass and a few other relics that were the fruits of his research over more than a decade. It is a fascinating problem that there are few objects and there are disputes over whether those objects can be used to corroborate his account of this history.

Nonetheless, as an artist, I can legitimately draw on the research of historians and archaeologists in viewing their work as part of the process of decoding and encoding objects. The analysis and authentication by researchers of newly discovered objects is part of the process of deciphering their secret codes. Historians and archaeologists have bestowed meaning and significance on objects that are placed in museum displays to reflect that status, but in actual fact they are placed within an historical chronology that was fixed long ago and accepted by most people. As a result, when viewers are drawn to look at objects on display and are prompted to think about a particular historical period and reflect on the past they are in fact accepting the decoding and encoding of others and have become complicit in a passive process.

As a contemporary artist is it possible for me to engage

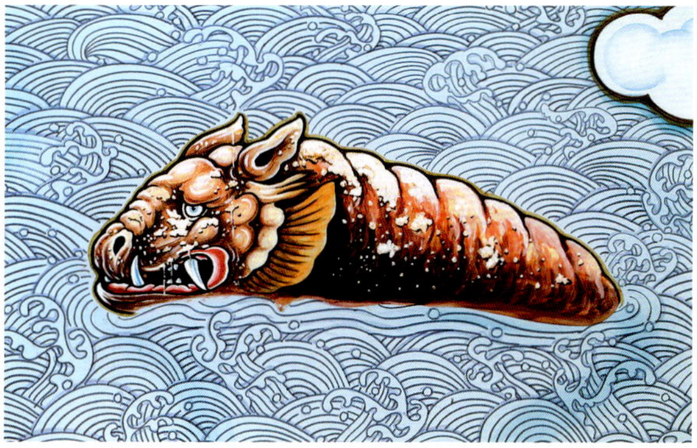

Detail of 'Treasure Hunt', mural painting.
Photograph: Jean-François Lanzarone, Powerhouse Museum, Sydney.

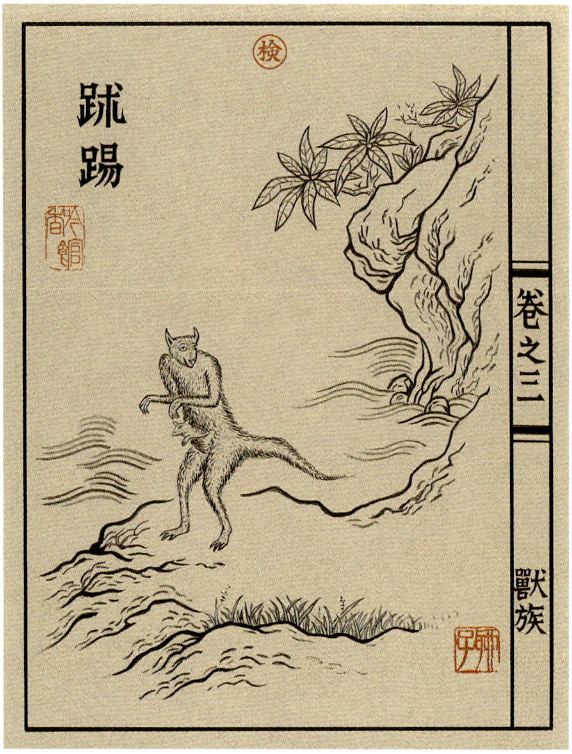

'Kangaroo', work on paper by Guan Wei.
Photograph: courtesy Powerhouse Museum, Sydney.

in an operation to challenge the accepted process of decoding and encoding objects? Can I fabricate cultural relics as art and create an artist's code that is presented as an exhibition in a museum so that the public can decode the artistic cultural relics? I believed that I could, by using artistically transformed cultural relics, provide visitors to the museum—this large body of non-experts—with an opportunity to actively participate in an exhibition and that together with them I could create an art-inflected version of history.

Zheng He's voyages took place long ago and there is little documentary material that can be cited and few artefacts that can be used as evidence. For historians this is cause for regret, but this lack provided me with a large canvas to give full reign to my imagination and greater freedom to construct Zheng He's heroic feats: it allowed for my recreation of Zheng He's fleet to land on Australian soil and to present a glorious 'other' history.

Chinese scholar-artists have a unique temperament when it comes to artistic practice. On the one hand, they approach the creation of artworks with great seriousness and care, and on the other hand with humour and light-heartedness. By mastering these two approaches they are able to achieve a feeling of aesthetic delight. In terms of the structure and production of the exhibition, I decided that the exhibition must be refined and pleasing to the eye as well as humorous and relaxed in mood. That is to say, it had to be carefully crafted but at the same time fun. I divided the exhibition into three sections that were both serious and lively: 'Emperor and Eunuch', 'In Search of Treasure and Navigational Charts' and 'The God of Longevity and the Southern Cross'.

The exhibition comprised nine large murals. The first few murals showed the early history of the Ming dynasty and the life of the Yongle Emperor as well as Zheng He, that is to say an orthodox history that was formulated long ago and accepted by most people. The following few murals were imbued with a strong imaginary element and related to the voyages, the search for treasure and arrival in Australia. They also collapsed time and space, because the paintings depicted Chinese people coming to Australia to pan for gold, which did not occur until some centuries later in the Qing dynasty. In addition to these nine large murals, I also painted on other available surfaces in the exhibition gallery, for example on the ceiling, plinths, bulkheads and other places where viewers would not expect to find any images. These additional motifs were not large but they were eye-catching and created a strong and integrated visual effect.

Over the past few years I have created many large-scale murals. In my experience, the characteristics of mural painting are, first of all, that there are no restrictions on space so that you can paint freely; secondly, because the works are site-specific they allow for greater spontaneity and flexibility compared to other media; and thirdly, that mural paintings are generally temporary and painted over at the end of an exhibition. If an artwork is not going to be permanent, it has a great bearing on one's mental attitude, so when painting you are more inclined to focus on the work as artistic expression and free yourself from the interference of commercial considerations. The mural paintings in this exhibition are large, were painted over a long period and can be regarded as a summation of my recent mural painting practice. They took one full month to complete, working with the assistance of my artist friends Frank Hope, Jin Sha, Yang Xifa and Zhao Baokang.

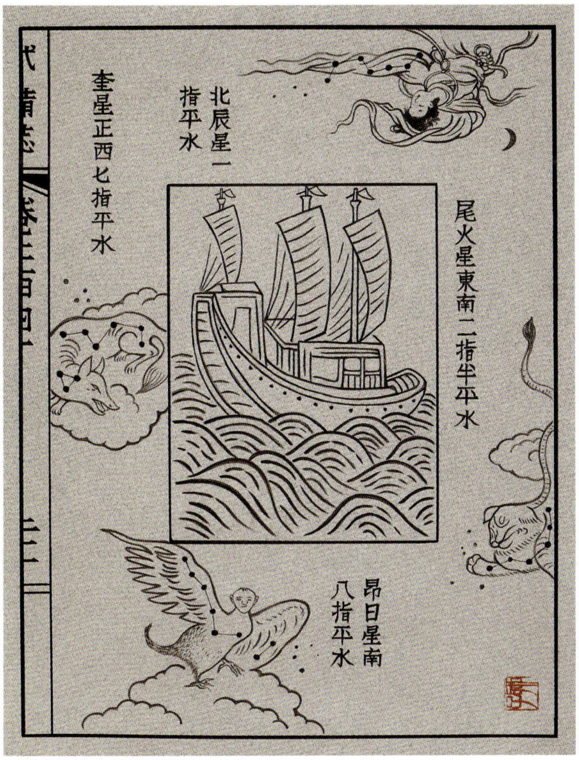

'Polaris', work on paper by Guan Wei.
Photograph: courtesy Powerhouse Museum, Sydney.

In addition to the mural paintings, I also incorporated into the exhibition many objects from the collection of the Powerhouse Museum, including ancient coins, ceramics, furniture and other objects. I gave the objects new names and arranged them differently, that is to say I bestowed on each of them a new status so that they could participate in the narration of other histories. For example, the God of Longevity and its story: the carved soapstone figure of the God of Longevity was acquired by the Powerhouse Museum in 1950. According to the Museum's records, it was found in 1879 wedged in the roots of an old banyan tree near Port Darwin. It is still a mystery how this artefact, which was obviously made in China, came to be in Australia. Was it brought to Australia hundreds of years ago by members of Zheng He's fleet or by others? Because the story of this object remains a mystery, I simply made use of it to tell a tale that had an ending. I deployed the God of Longevity to narrate a story. According to ancient Chinese books and records, the God of Longevity is known as the Old Man of the South Pole, the southern-most star in the night sky, so I conflated it with the Southern Cross that can be seen in the sky above Australia. In my version of the story, Zheng He and his fleet navigated in the northern hemisphere with Polaris as their coordinate, but, after crossing the equator, looked to the God of Longevity, the brightest star in the Southern Cross, as their coordinate and headed towards the land illuminated by the Old Man of the South Pole to Australia... And in the years that followed, guided here by the God of Longevity, generation after generation of Chinese migrants would follow the route opened up by Zheng He and set foot on this mysterious Great Southern Land to pan for gold in search of their fortune as in days gone by, or to study and seek employment as is the case today. The story of the God of Longevity was located in the third section of the exhibition. Two large murals, a vitrine in which the figure of the God of Longevity was displayed, and two large showcases containing the relics of Chinese migrants to Australia, conveyed the passage of Zheng He's fleet to Australia and the beginnings of trade and exchange between China and Australia.

To incorporate museum objects into a contemporary art exhibition is not only about expanding and making use of the resources of a museum, nor is it simply about adding to the interactivity of a museum. The placement of museum objects that have been given a new status in an installation relates to both art and reality, and within a contemporary art environment this was a new experiment.

The Arabic-speaking scholar Ma Huan (1371–1433) was the interpreter for Zheng He's fleet and his book *The Overall Survey of the Ocean's Shores* (1433) is based on what he saw and experienced on his voyages with Zheng He. The book records text and images relating to the customs, flora and fauna of places that include present-day Vietnam, Sri Lanka, Indonesia and countries in the Middle East. By referring to Ma Huan's text and various Ming and Qing dynasty illustrated editions of the *Classic of Mountains and Seas*, I painted some 30 works for 'Other Histories' that recreated ancient woodblock prints of people, plants and animals as well as maps and navigational and astrological charts. These works on paper were individually framed and hung within the exhibition. The paintings drew on disciplines such as archaeology, history, navigation and meteorology that all relate to the interactions of human beings with the natural world. In terms of imagery, they incorporated blueprints of Australian species and presented the great geographical discoveries of Zheng He's voyages. These reproductions of ancient woodblock prints greatly enriched the content of the exhibition, added a different element and increased the interest of its component parts, thereby expanding the scope of the exhibition within the context of the Museum.

The display of authentic artefacts alongside these woodblock reproductions that were to be regarded as real objects blurred the line of demarcation between conventional categories of objects within a museum. Visitors could view the exhibition as a display of archaeological and historical artefacts, decorative art or folk art, or a contemporary art exhibition combining two-dimensional painting and installation.

In the process of presenting 'Other Histories', I was conscious of Australia's natural and cultural resources. Through social history and human relationships with the natural world, I extended the content of the exhibition to include references to Indigenous culture, colonial culture and cultural diversity; and through the recreation of oceans, islands and the desert interior, I

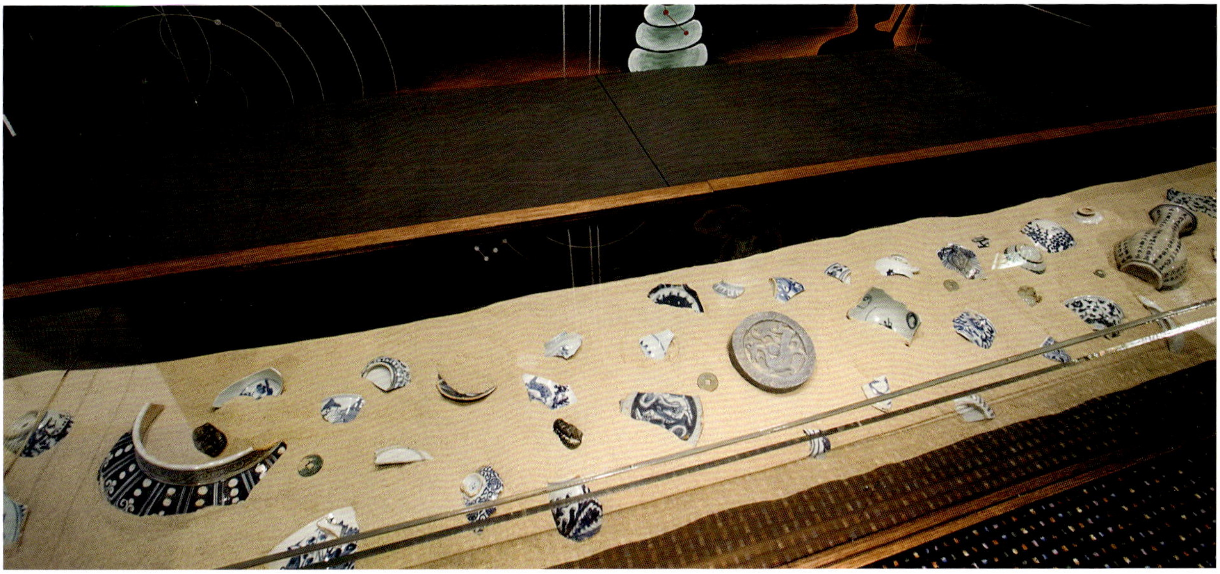

Installation of sand with ceramic shards, reproduction and found objects.
Photograph: Marinco Kojdanovski, Powerhouse Museum, Sydney.

made connections with subjects such as navigation, exploration, searching for treasure, migration and the influence of and response to globalisation. These subjects are all part of the rich artistic resource that has provided impetus for my own explorations into new forms of visual expression.

Both the history of Zheng He's voyages and their significance, transcend readings in terms of fact and of navigation. Readings are made by employing ideas drawn from people's generational backgrounds to achieve their own understanding of Zheng He, a Zheng He that is symbolic and imbued with new meanings. As a contemporary artist who was born in China and has lived for a long period in Australia, this artwork is informed by my own personal experience. From the beginning, I located my creative activity within Zheng He's voyages so that my artwork would become an integral part of its history. As my depiction of events and the storyline unfolded, the natural process of artistic creation impelled me to subvert orthodox history. According to my version of the story, Zheng He's fleet came to Australia and challenges the conventional understanding of history (that apart from Indigenous Australians, the British were the first people to 'discover' Australia), and thus creates an 'other' history with a distinct Guan Wei inflection.

'Other Histories' is not necessarily history. In presenting 'Other Histories' it has been my aim to subvert a singular ideological approach and encourage free-form imagining. Today we live in an environment full of nervous tension and anxiety. I sincerely hope that the 'other' history inherent in my own version of the story of Zheng He's fleet will encourage people from different racial and cultural backgrounds to connect with one another, seek friendships with one another and live together in harmony.

Translated by Claire Roberts

① Emperor and eunuch.

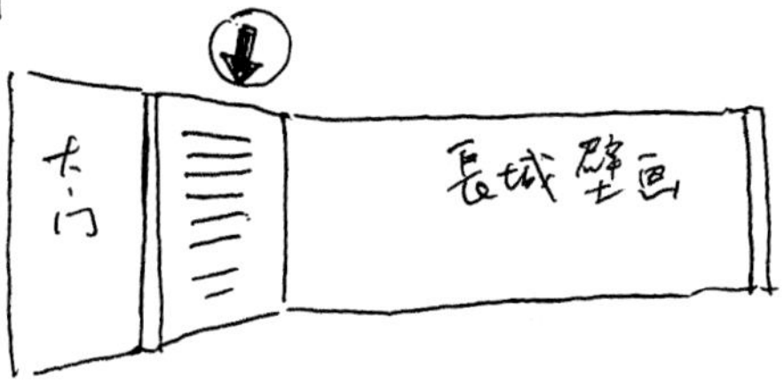

这段文字可放在进大门之左侧墙面上。

② Zheng He 以有了，③ Emperor Yongle 也有了图。

④ In search of treasure.

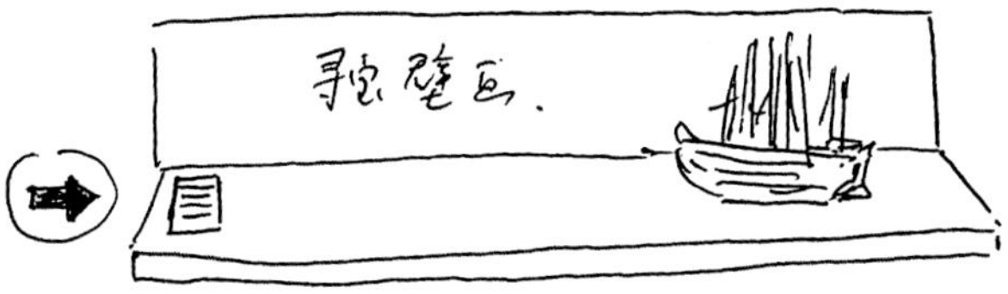

小牌子立在台子上，

⑤ Unfamiliar lands.

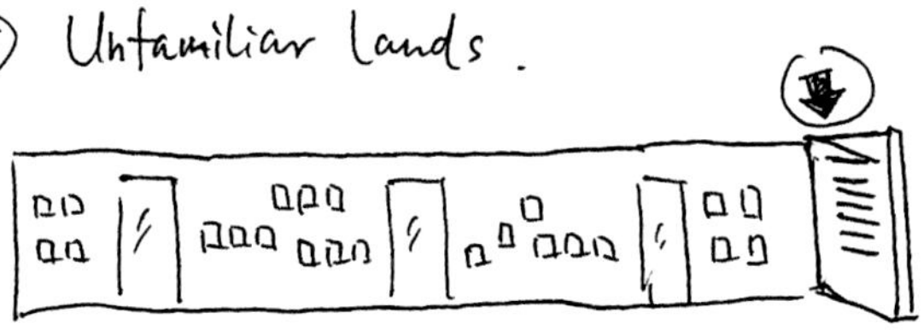

文字在侧面墙上。

⑥ Great southern land.

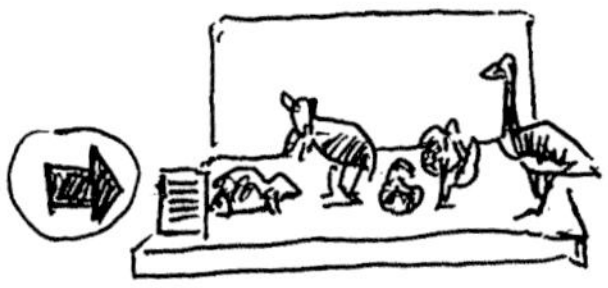

小牌子立在台子上，

⑧ The southern Cross
见附图

⑦ Great southern land.

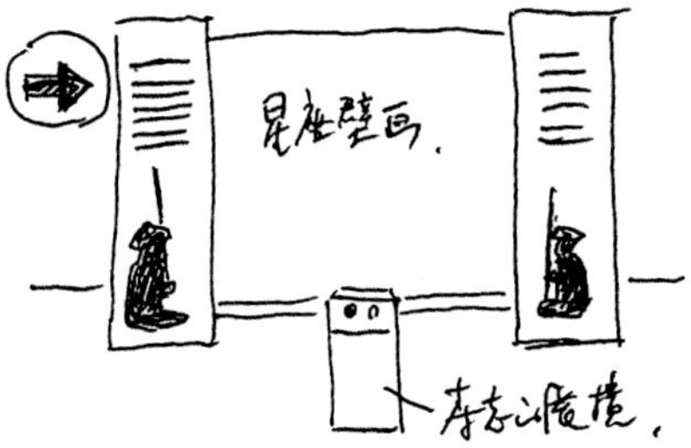

文字写在两面之柱子上，
下面是土著人之墙画，

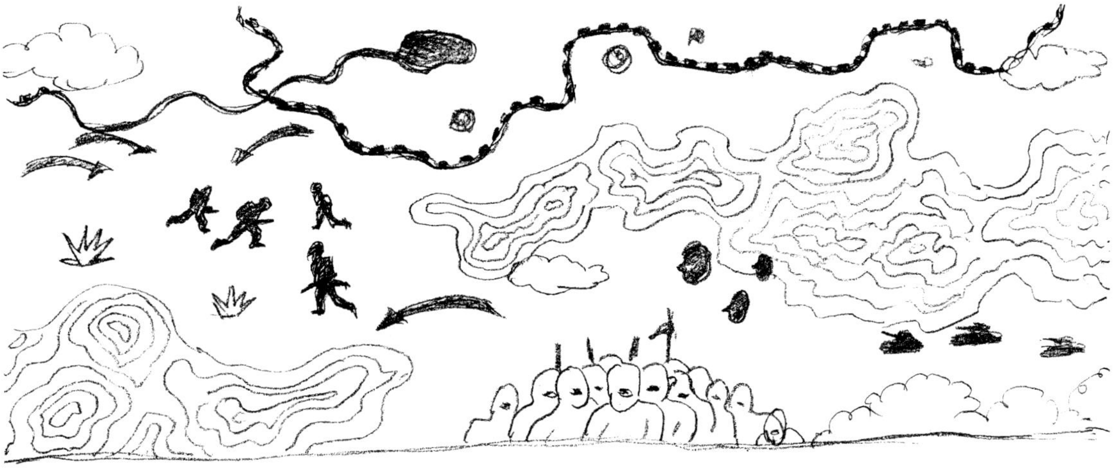

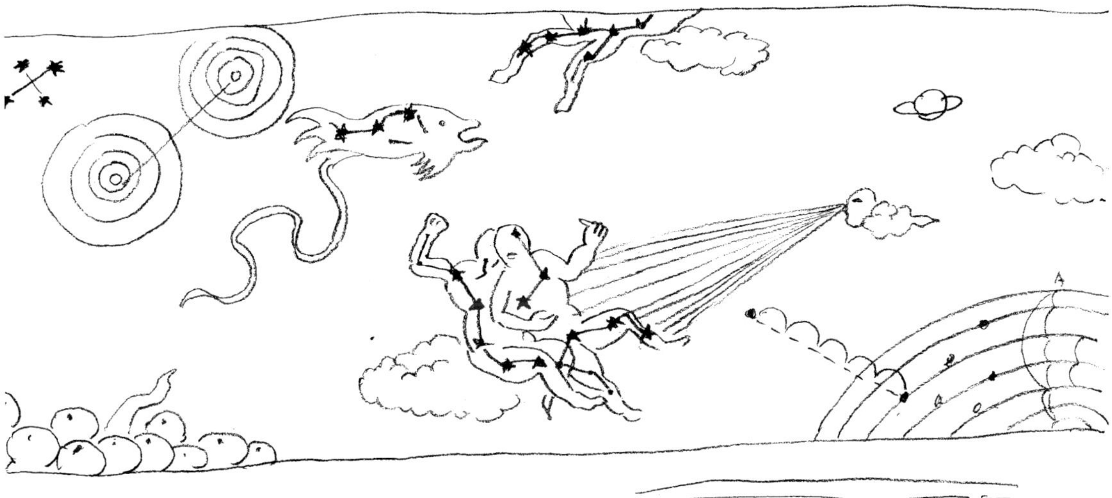

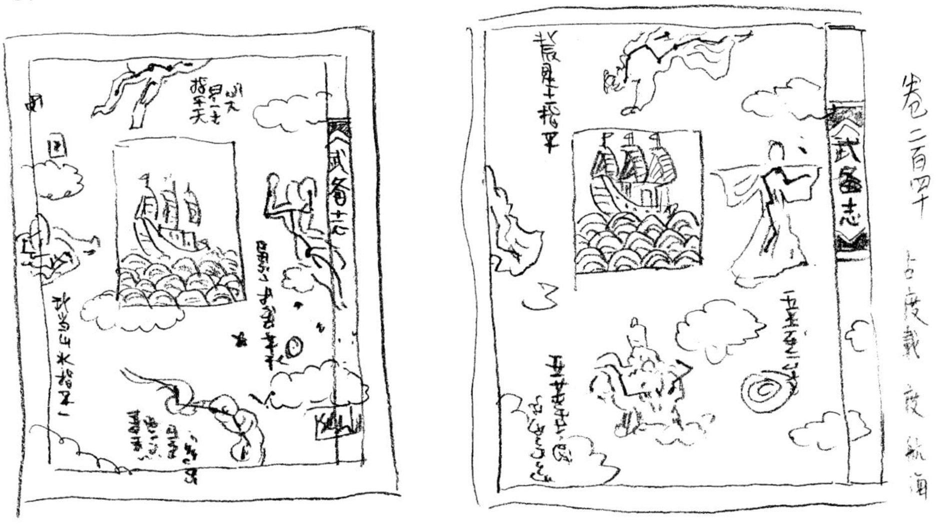

Working drawings by Guan Wei. Photograph: courtesy Guan Wei.

—SC 1.— (一)

A.4422-5. 不变.

A.4935. 〃

A.4669. 加一句. Ming Dynasty.

A.4721. 〃 Ming Dynasty.

A 4422-3 不变.

A.4719 不变.

A. 6558 〃〃

A. 2453. 〃〃.

—SC. 2. 和 3—

231A. 双佛像. gilt-bronze. 郑和船队访问苏门答腊(今印度尼西亚)时所送之纪念品.
Ming Dynasty. 私人收藏.
231A.

A 4512. 明砖. 不变. earthenware

A 2624. 仙人骑凤. 用在皇宫、屋檐 (庙宇) 顶端之装饰物. 有逢凶化吉之象征意义. 南京. Ming Dynasty. A2624.

A.2623. 天马. earthenware. 屋顶装饰物. 代表勇猛, 也作吉祥之化身. 南京. Ming Dynasty. A2623.

A. 2622. 狮子. earthenware. 屋顶装饰物. 有勇猛威严之象征. 南京. Ming Dynasty. ~~A2622~~.

A. 3290. Buddha, gilt bronze, mad in Tibet [1402—1424] Ming 永乐年间. powerhouse 收藏. A3290.

头面换了.

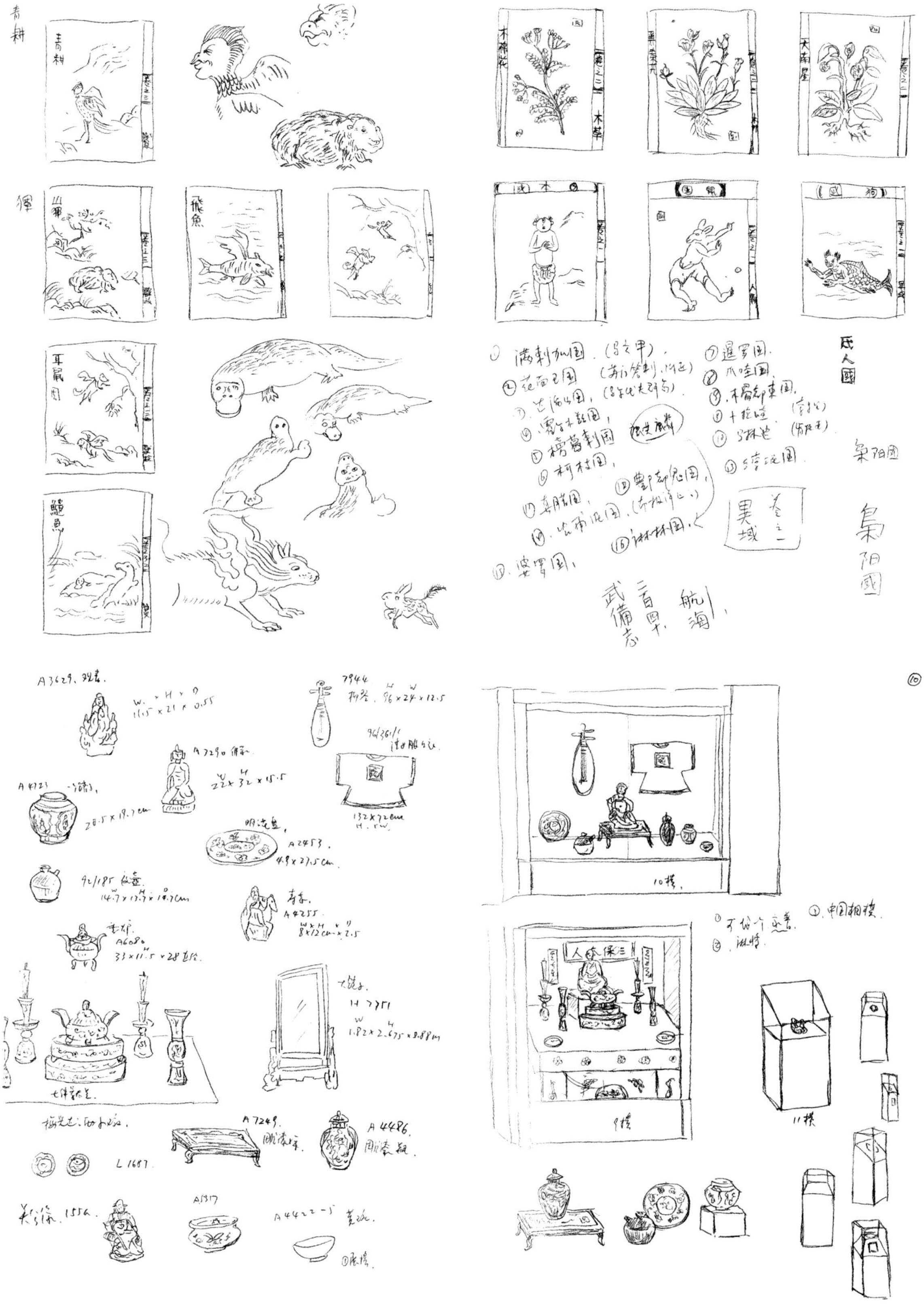

Working drawings by Guan Wei. Photograph: courtesy Guan Wei.

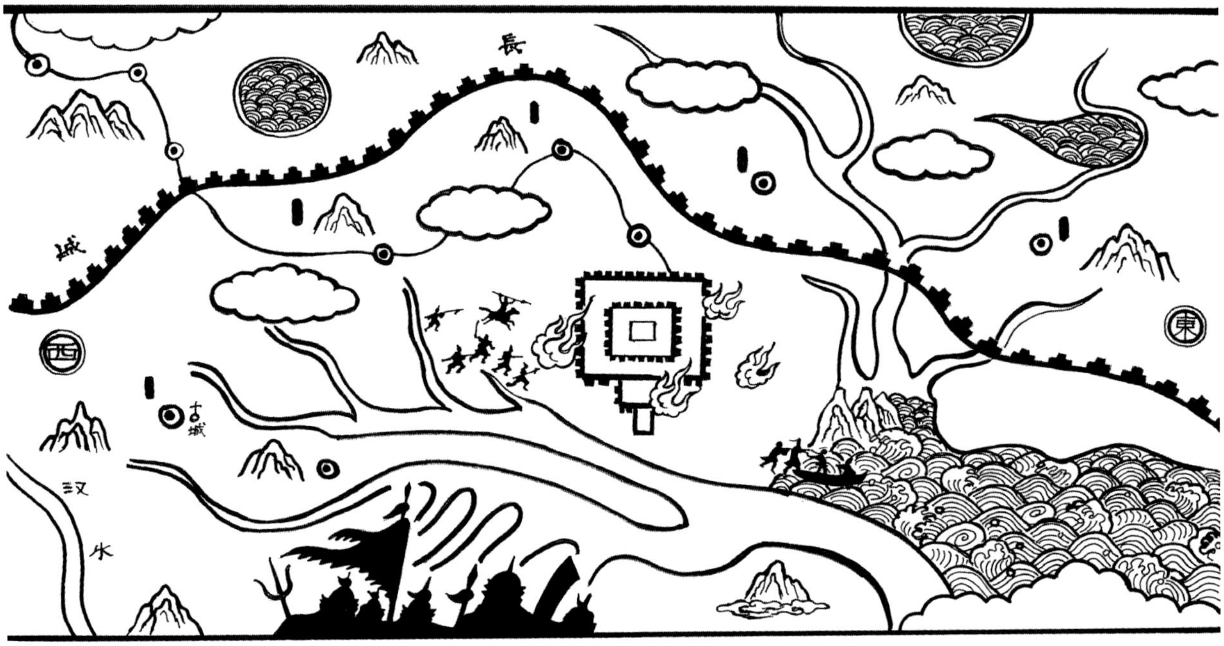

Guan Wei 06

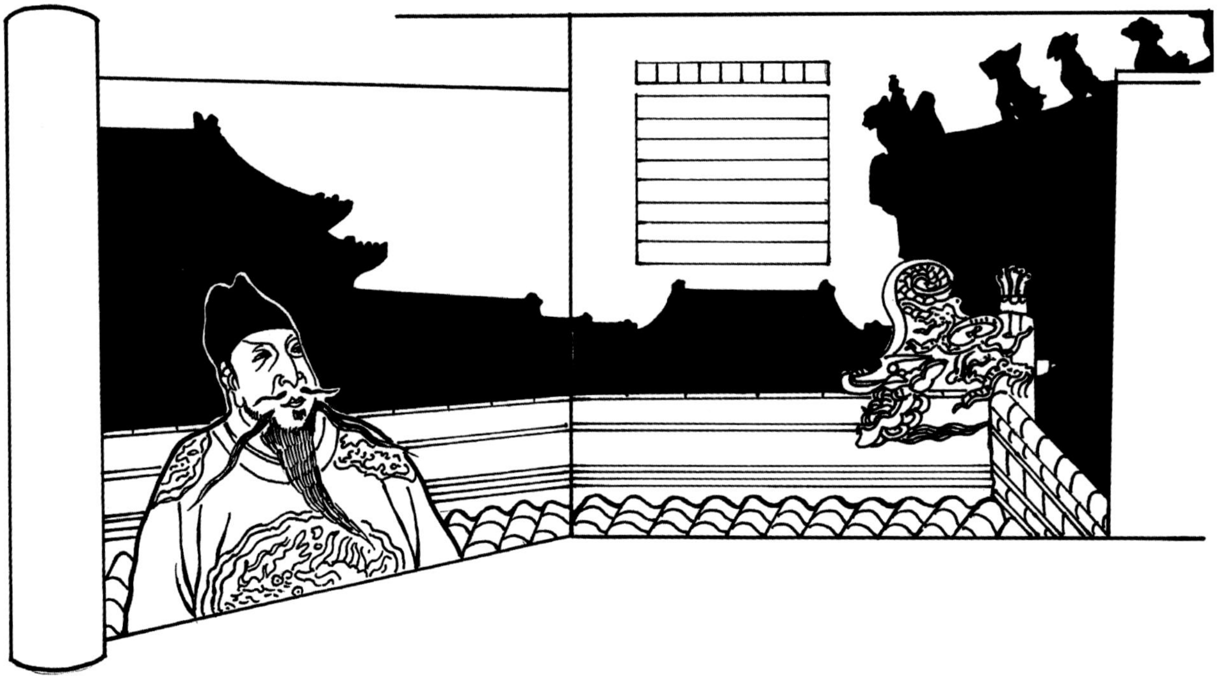

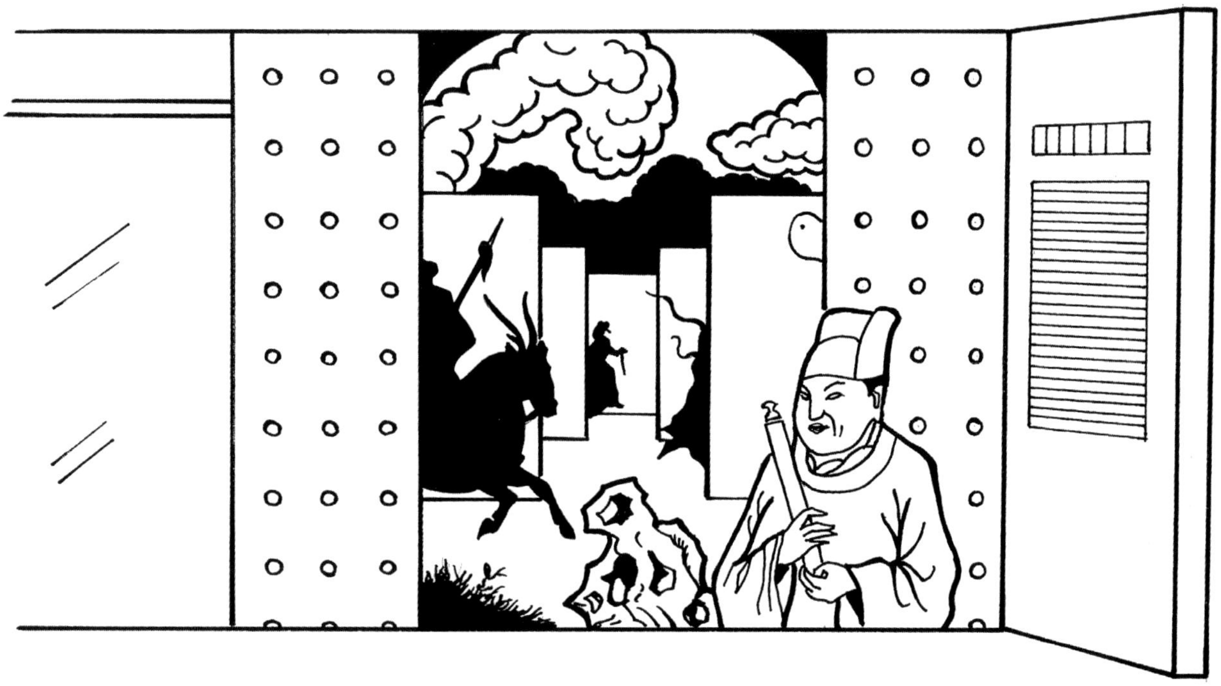

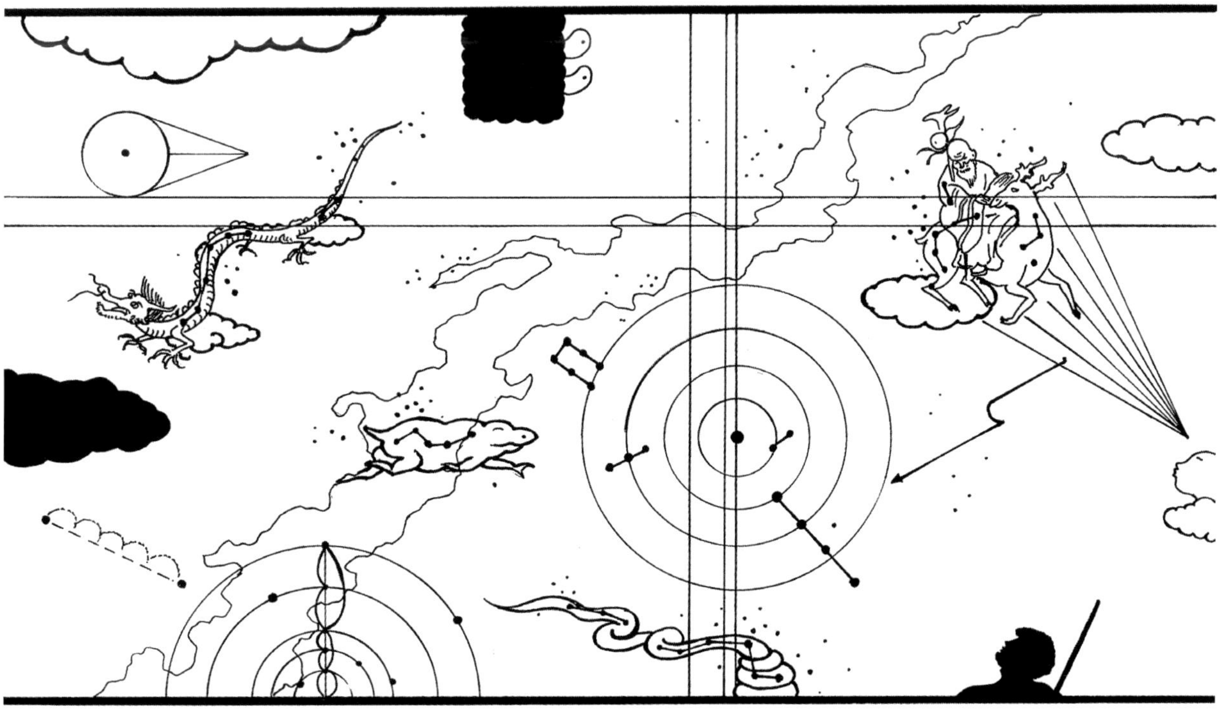

Guan Wei 06

Working drawings by Guan Wei. Photograph: courtesy Guan Wei.

SC.04 B

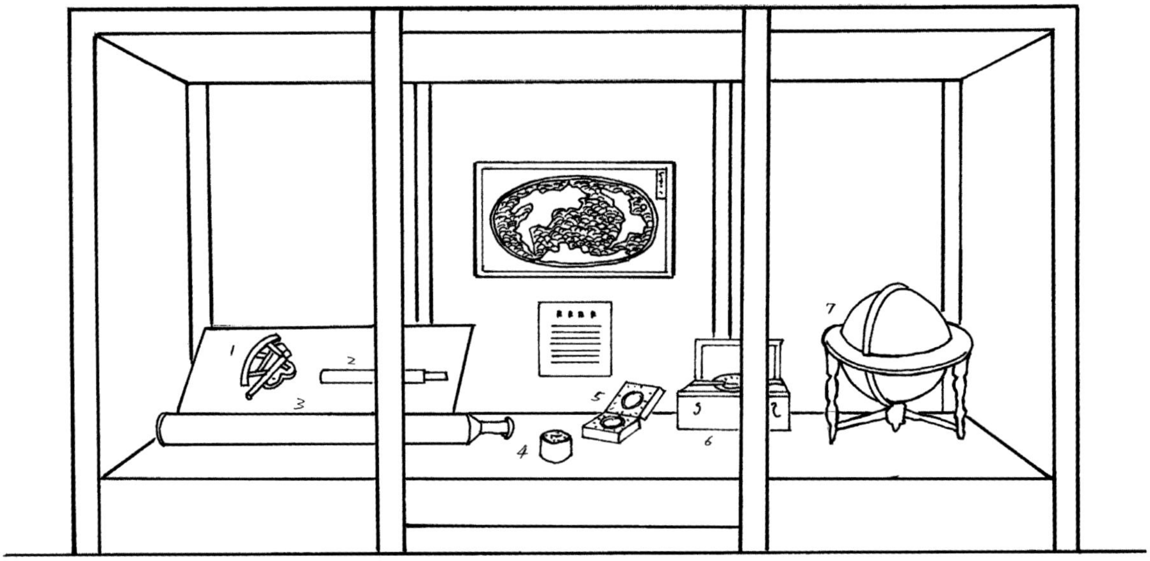

1. H 10399
▲ 2. ?
3. H 10257
4. H 3162
5. H 7728
6. B 747-1
7. H 7504

SC 05 B

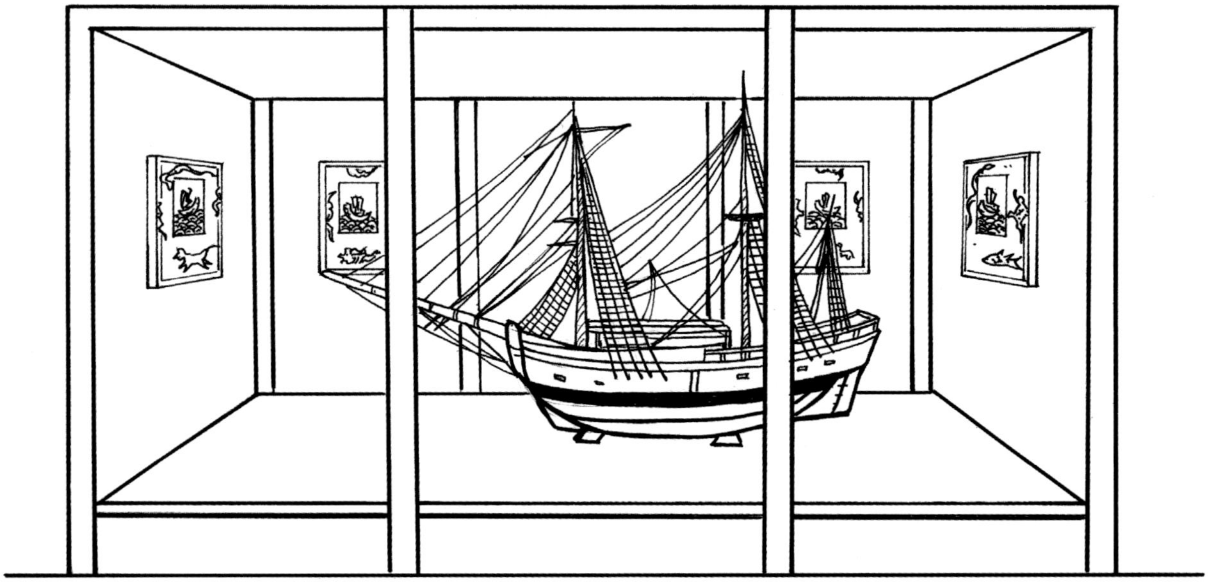

A 8855.

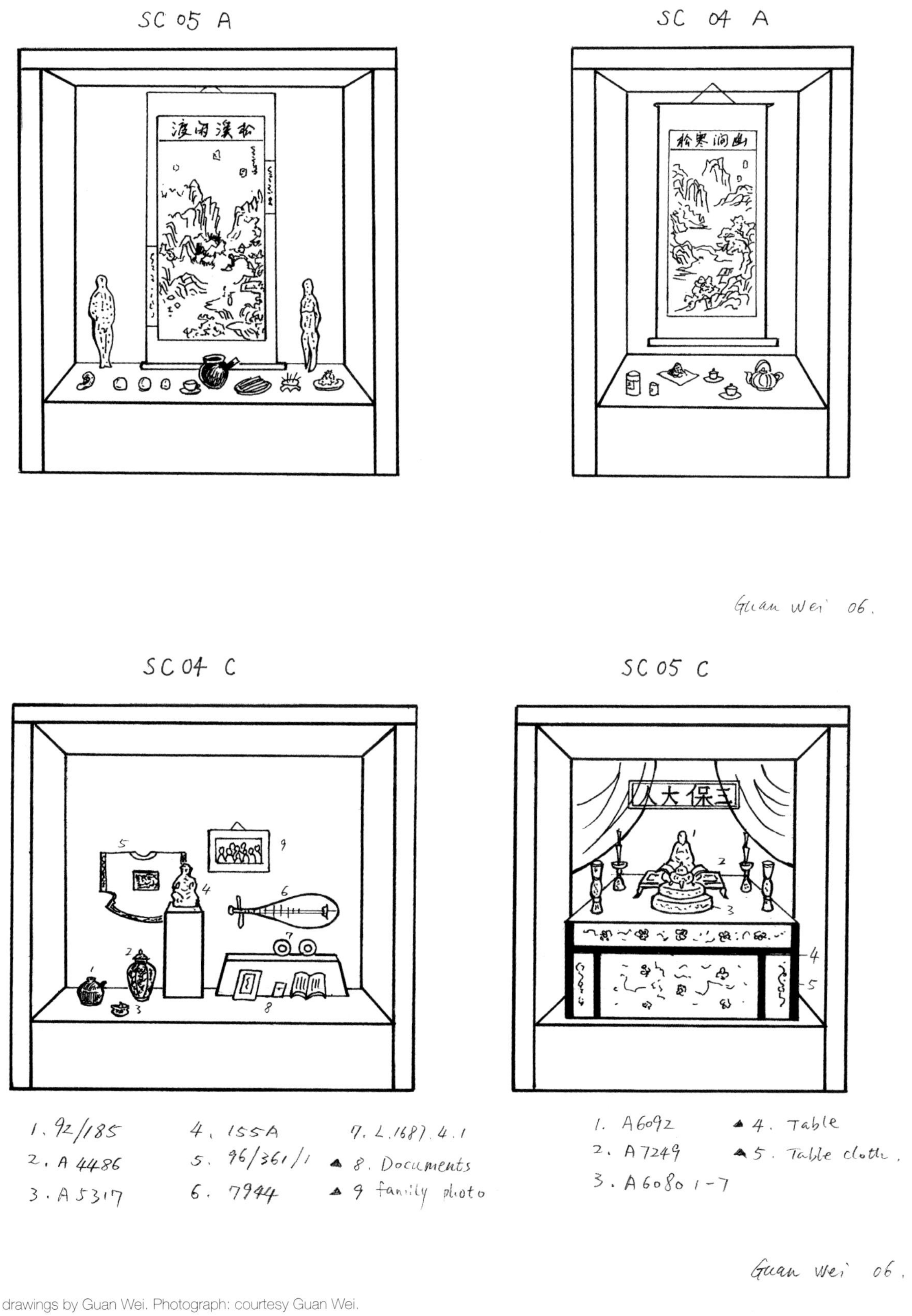

Working drawings by Guan Wei. Photograph: courtesy Guan Wei.

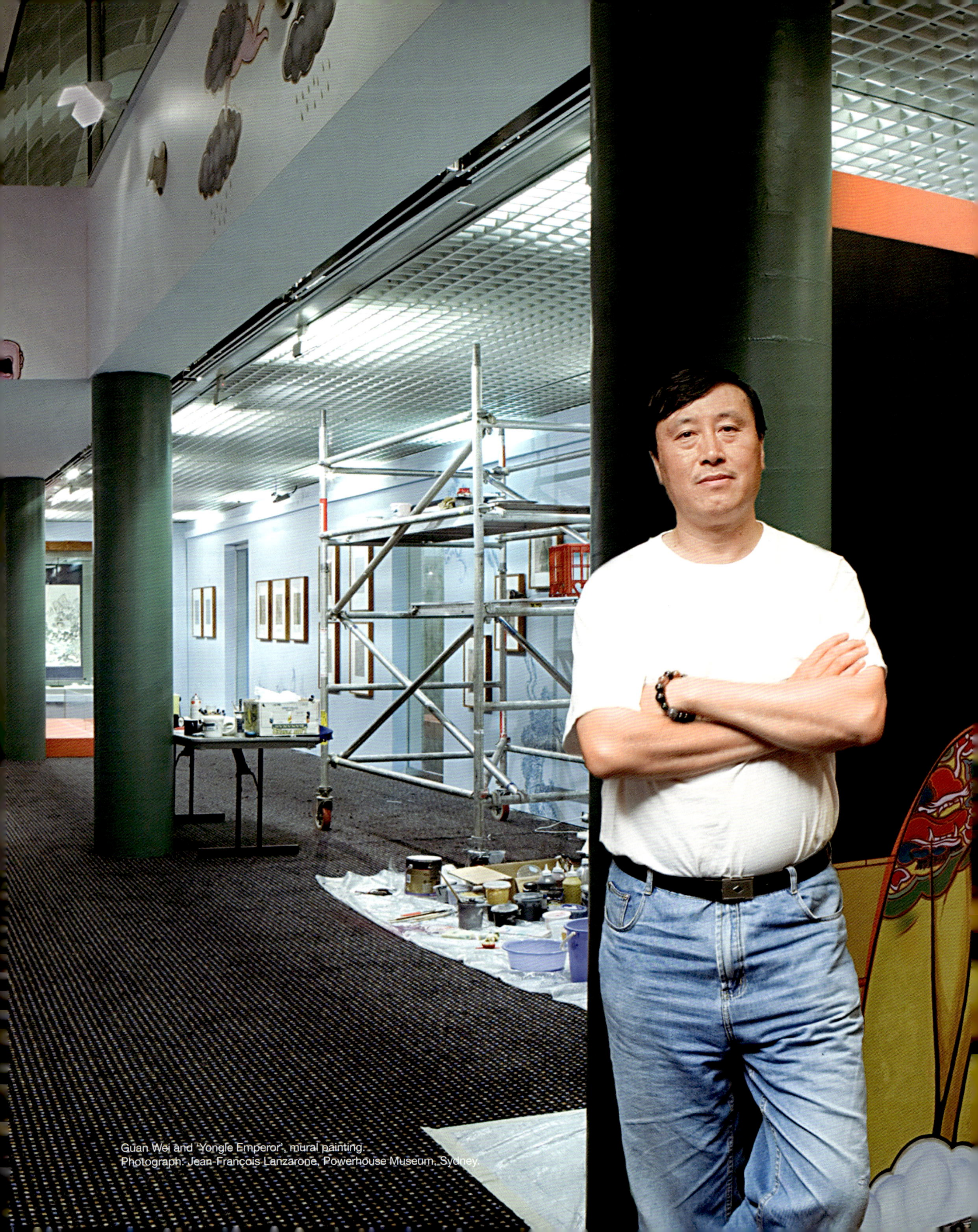

Guan Wei and 'Yongle Emperor', mural painting.
Photograph: Jean-François Lanzarone, Powerhouse Museum, Sydney.

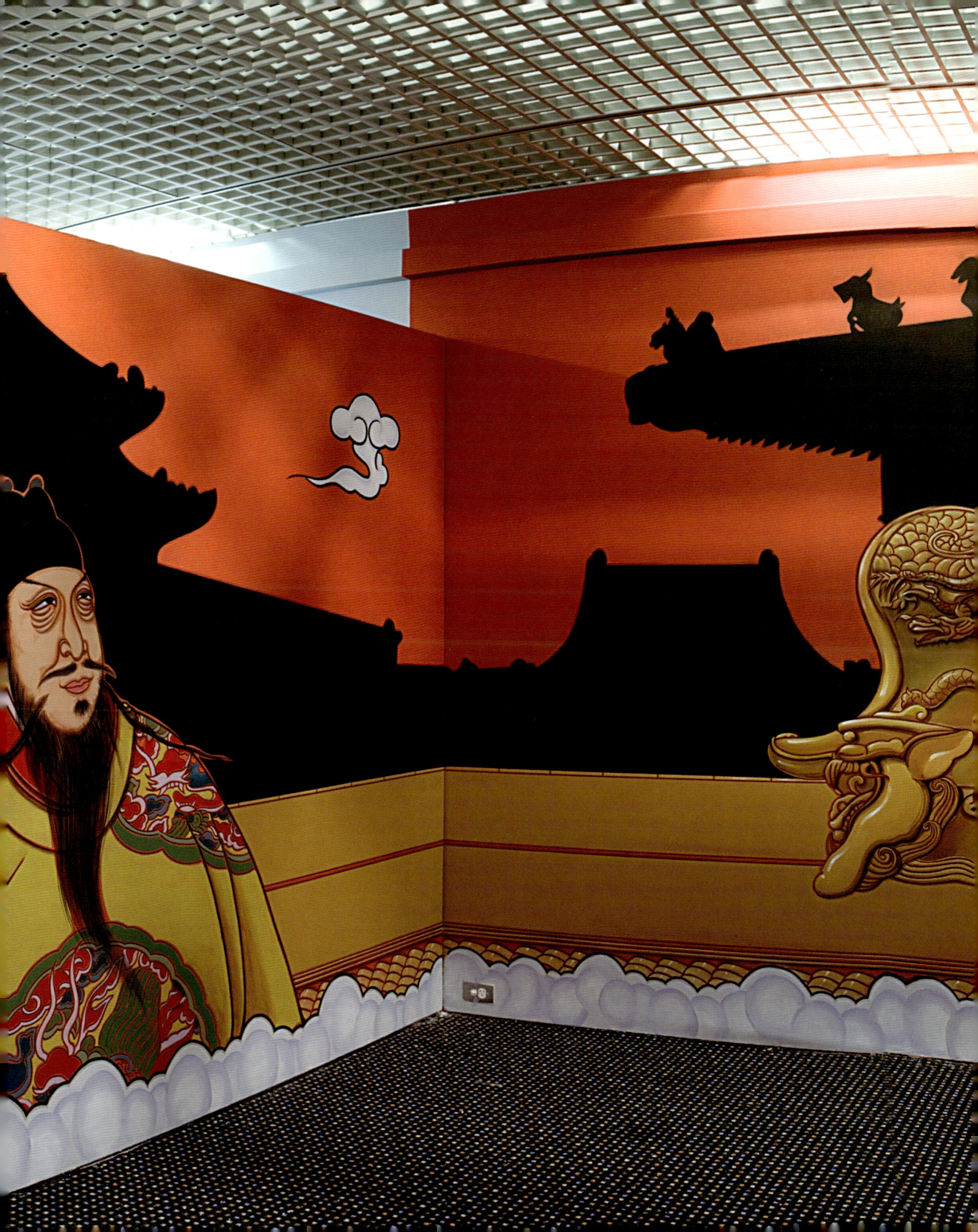

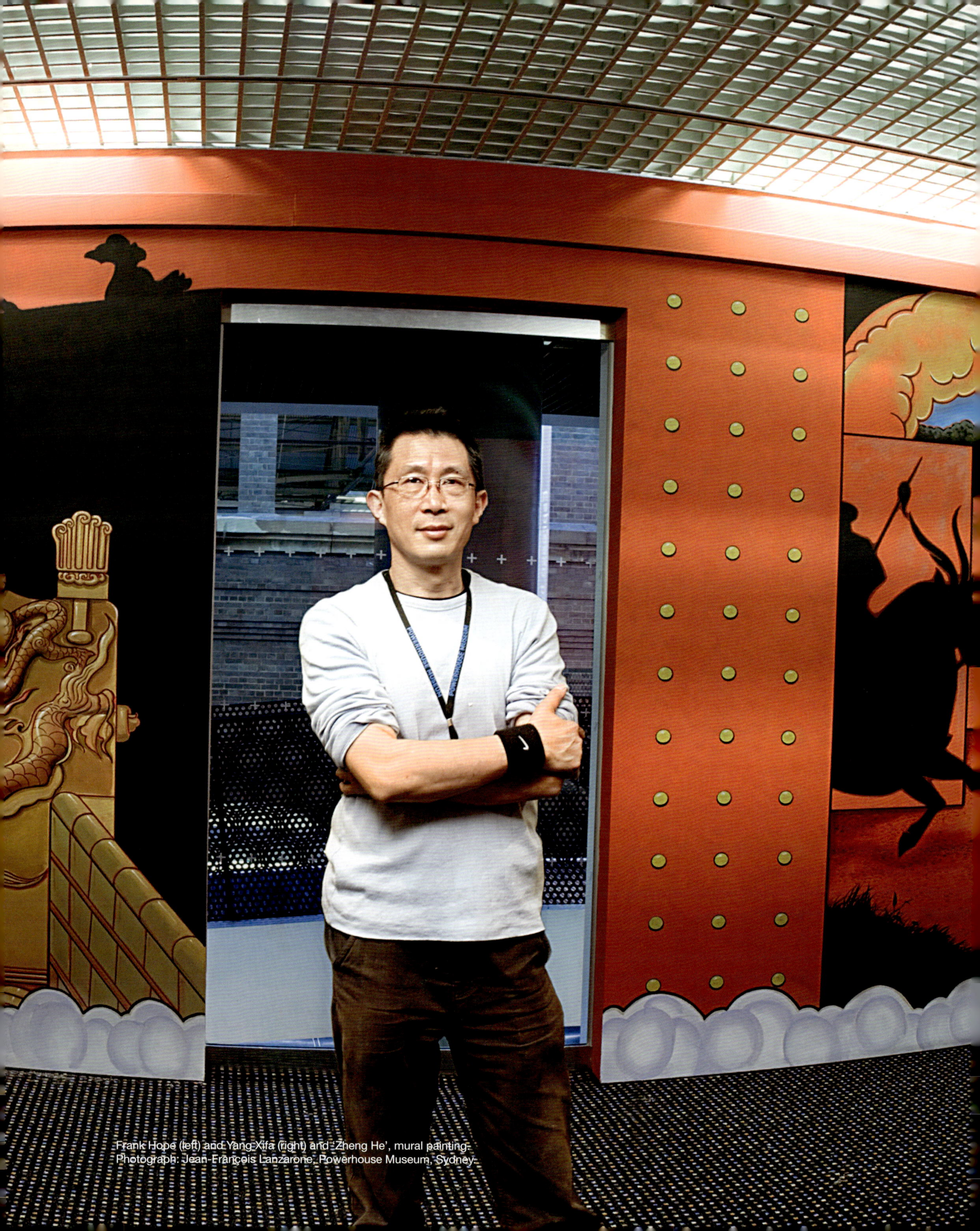

Frank Hope (left) and Yang Xifa (right) and 'Zheng He', mural painting.
Photograph: Jean-François Lanzarone, Powerhouse Museum, Sydney

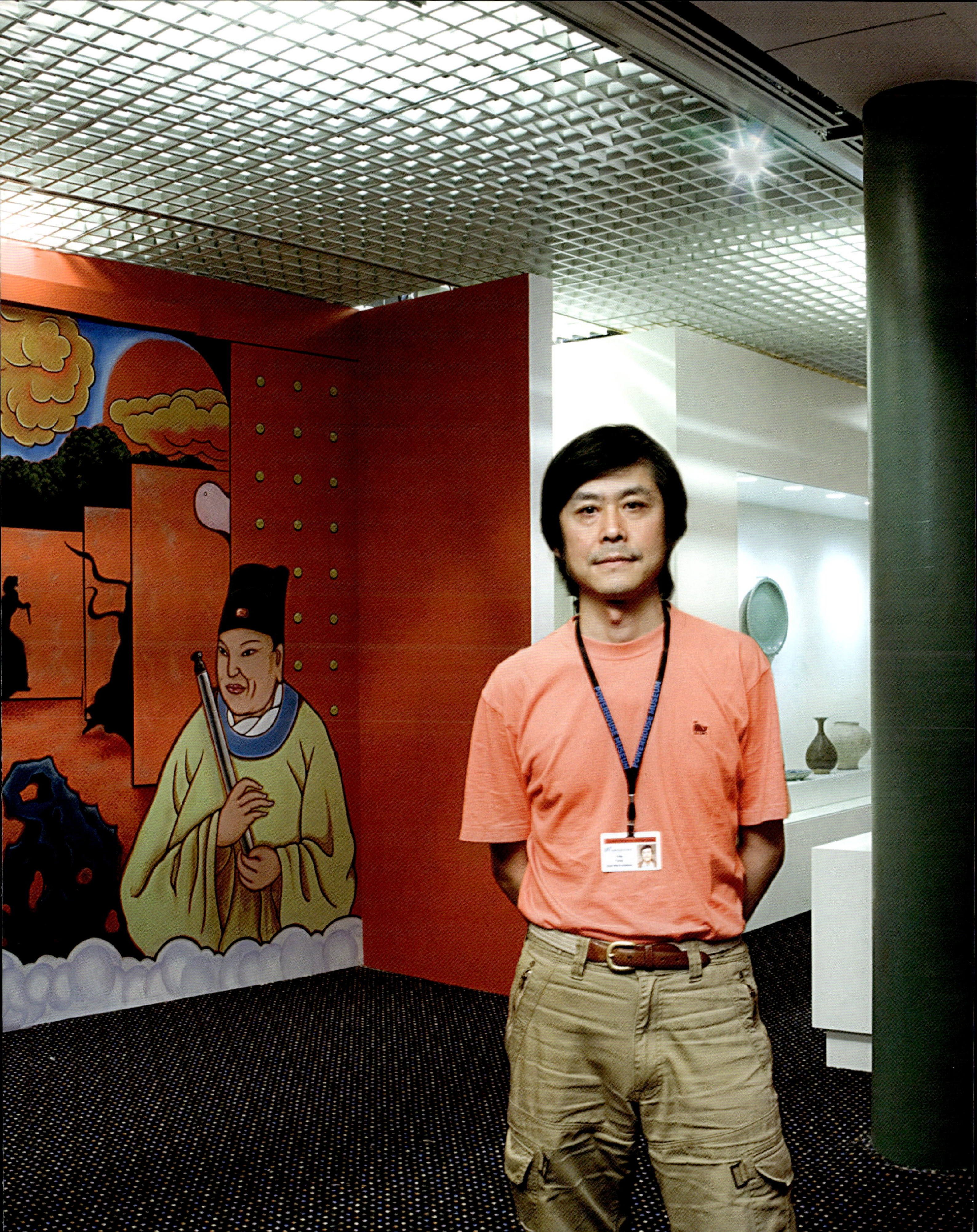
POWERHOUSE MUSEUM

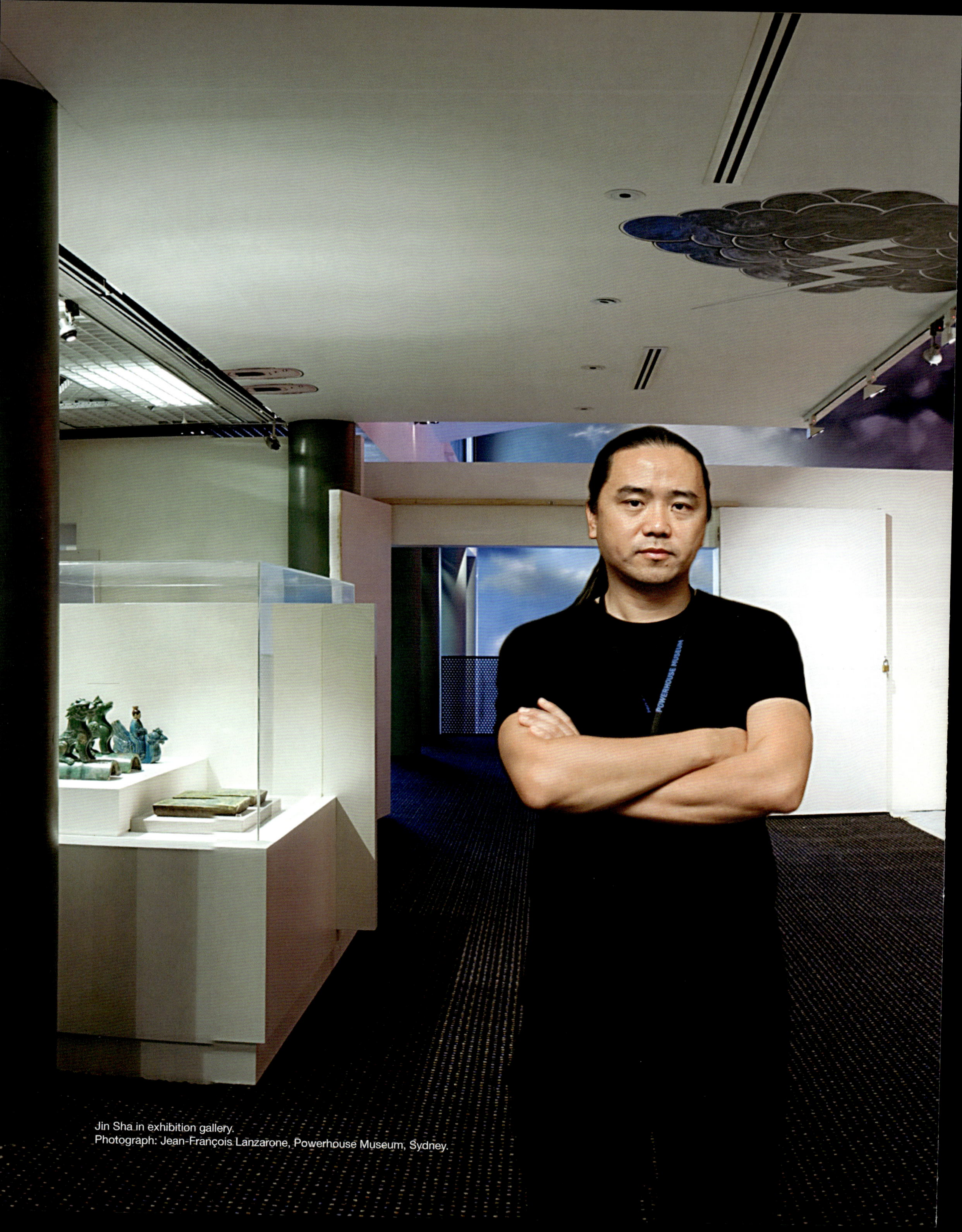

Jin Sha in exhibition gallery.
Photograph: Jean-François Lanzarone, Powerhouse Museum, Sydney.

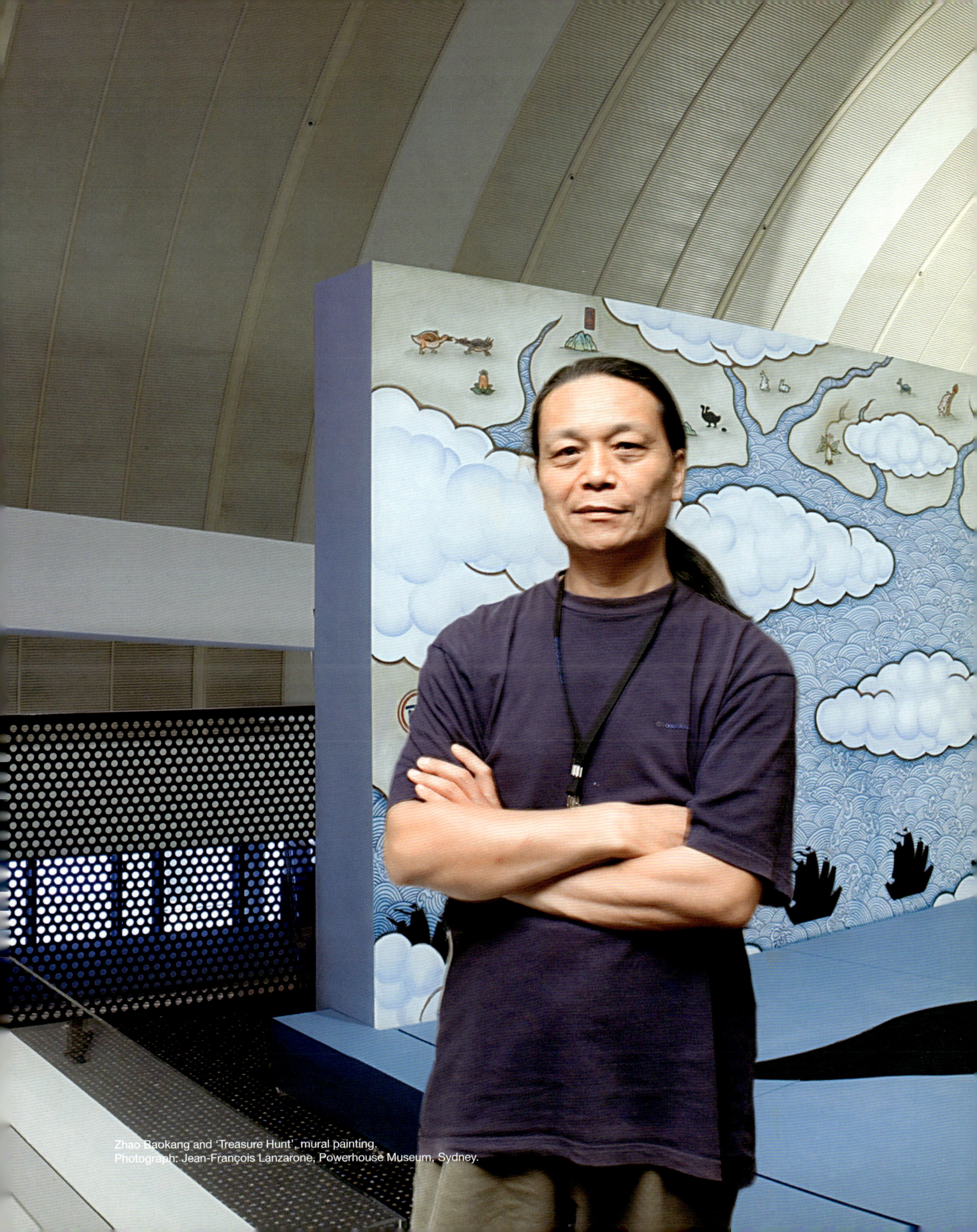

Zhao Baokang and 'Treasure Hunt', mural painting.
Photograph: Jean-François Lanzarone, Powerhouse Museum, Sydney.

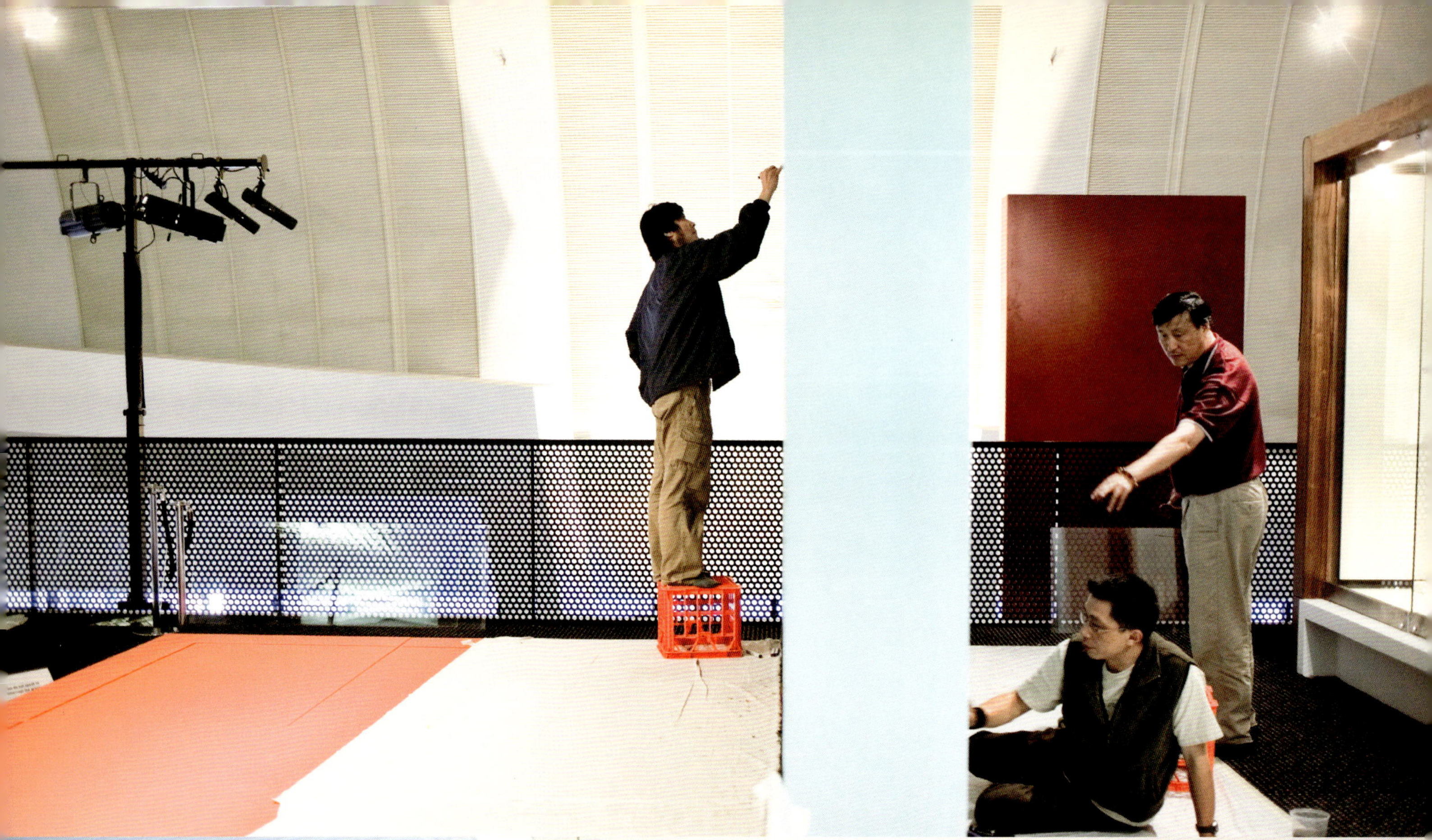

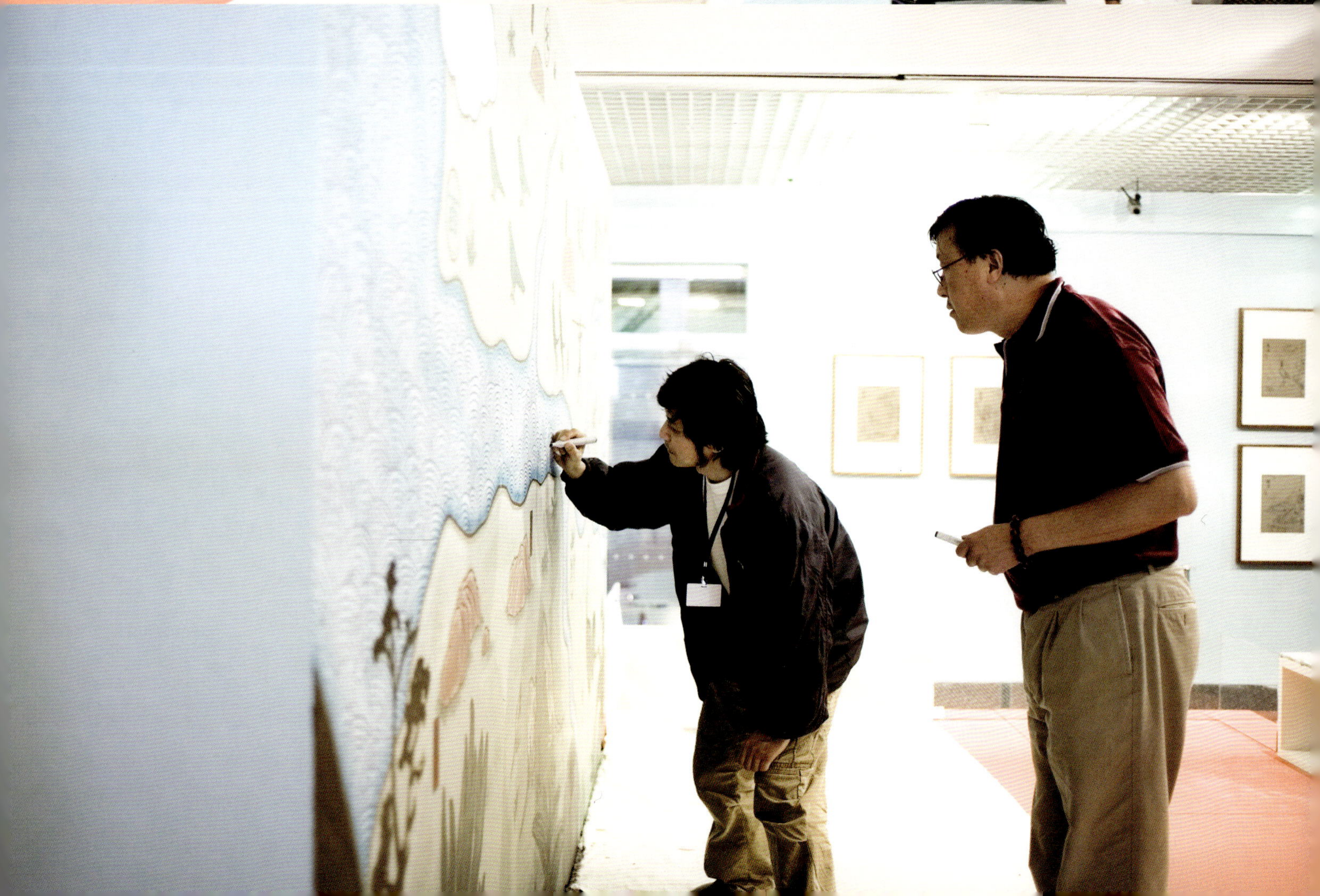

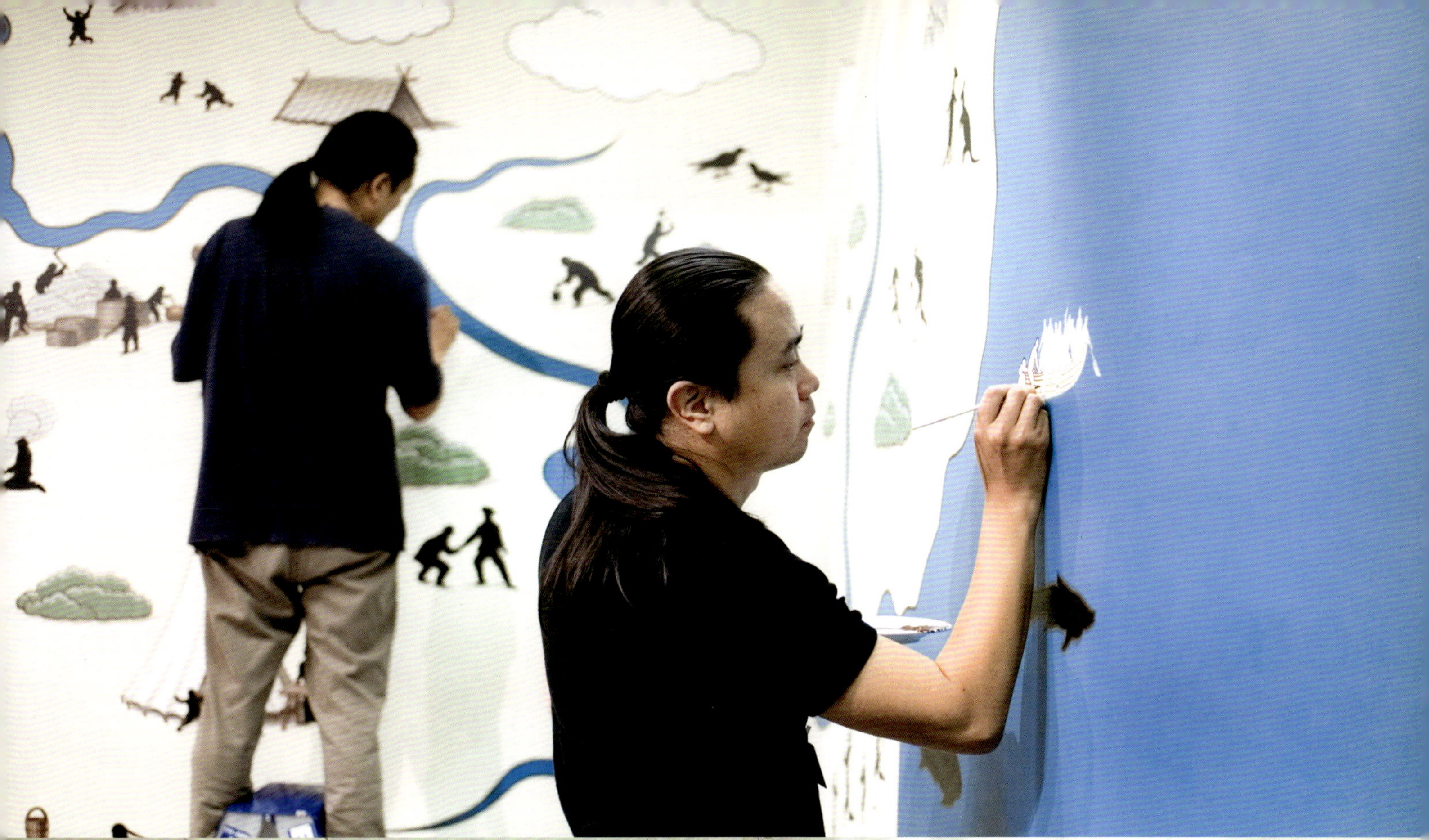

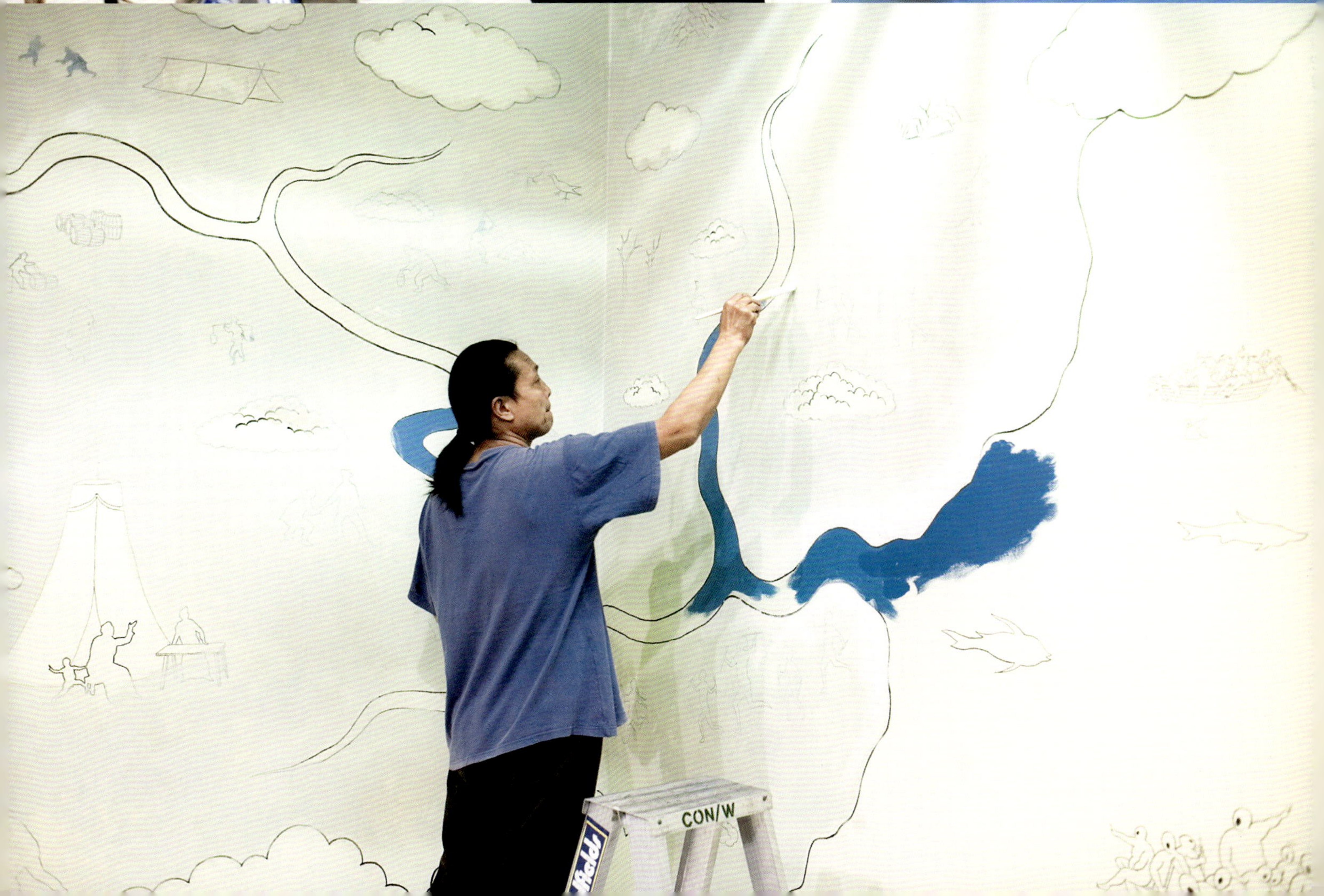
CON/W

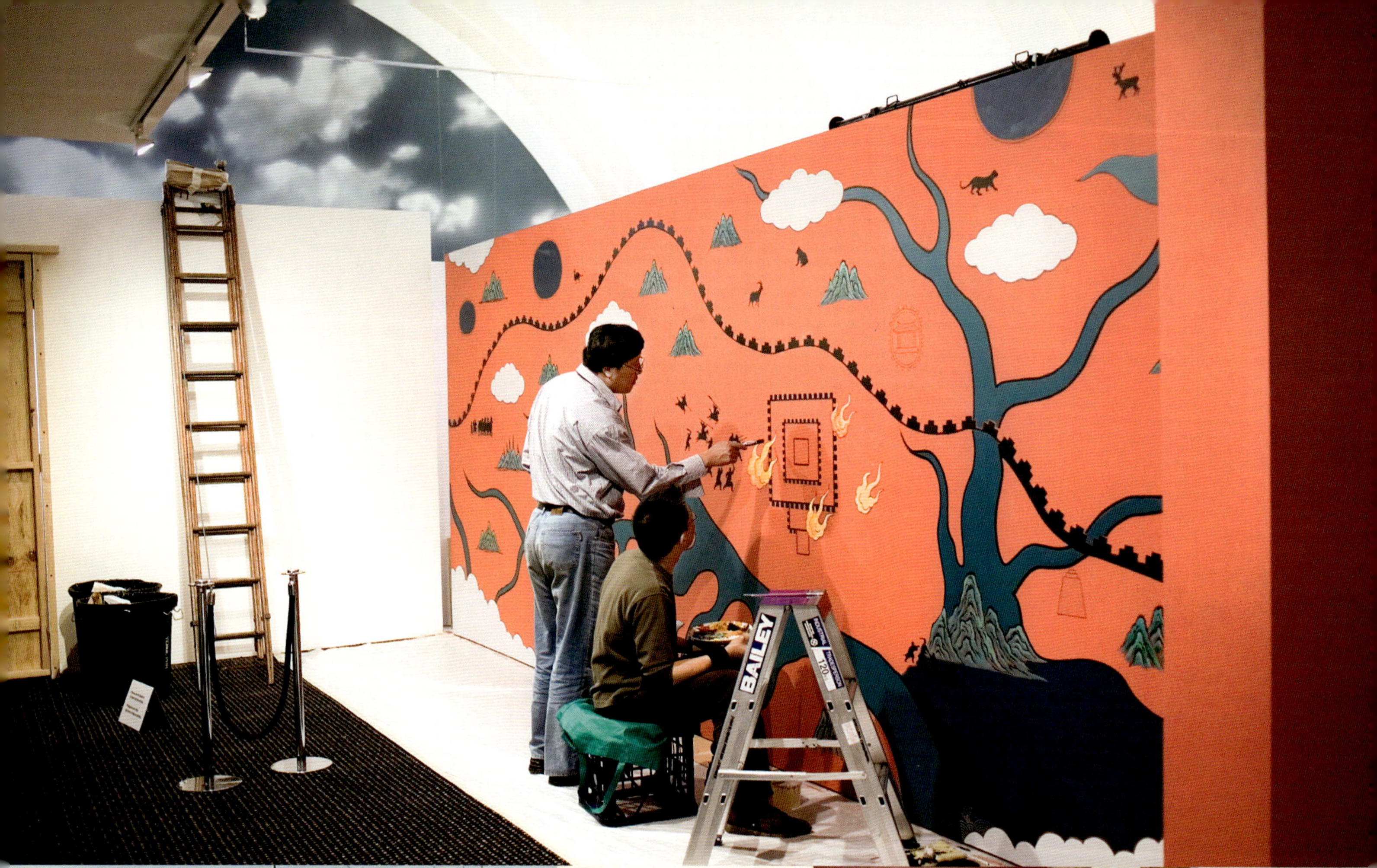
BAILEY

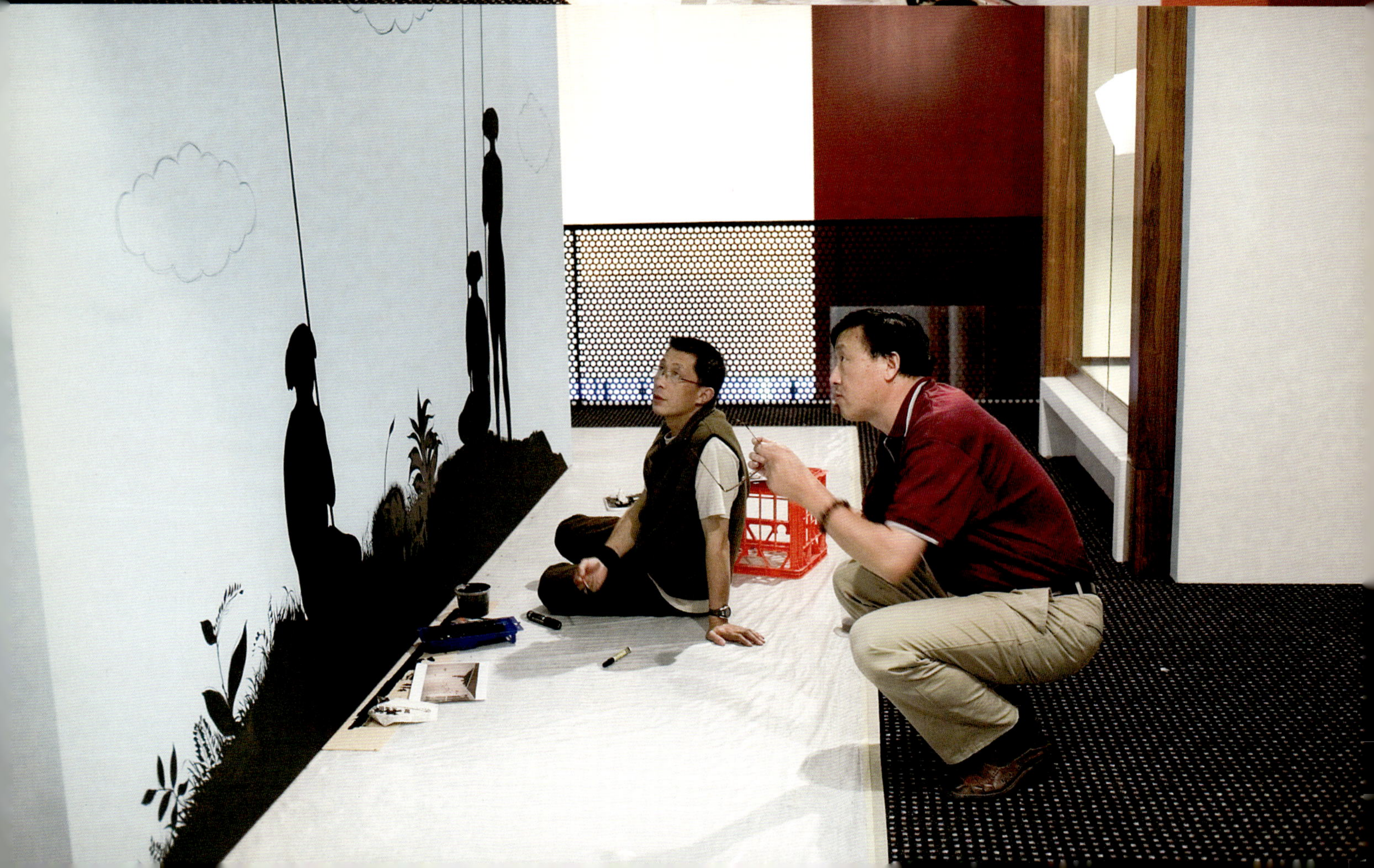

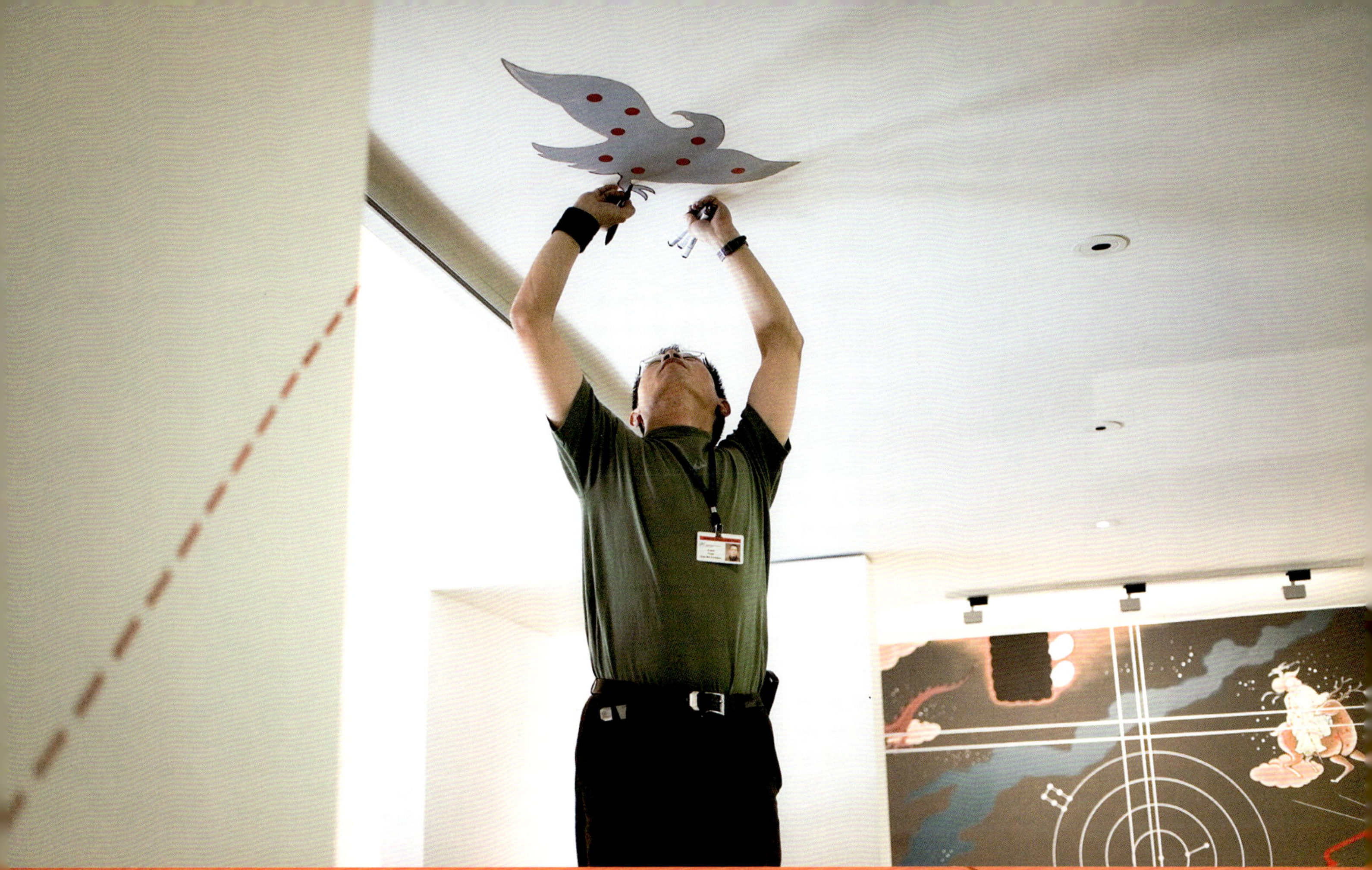

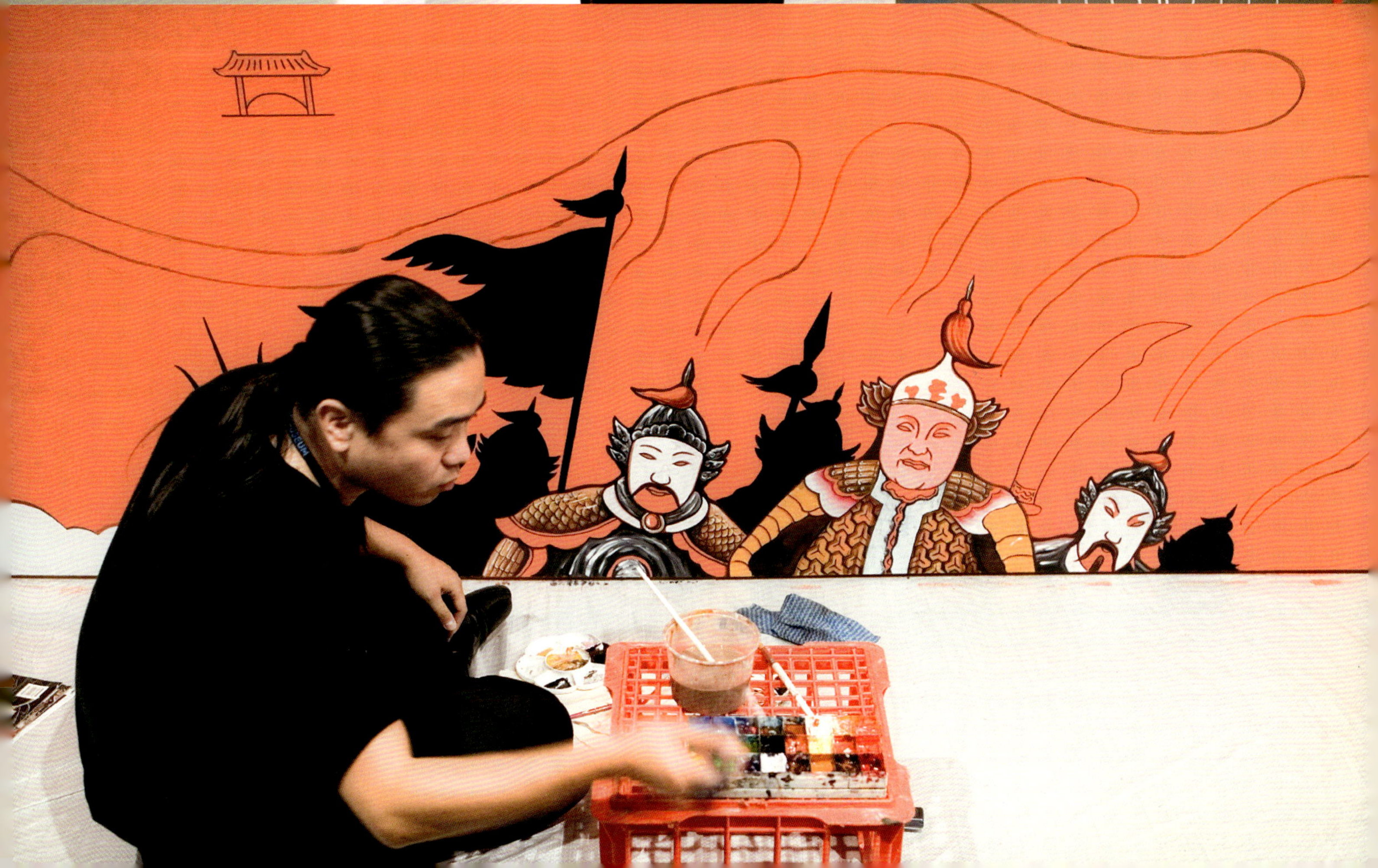

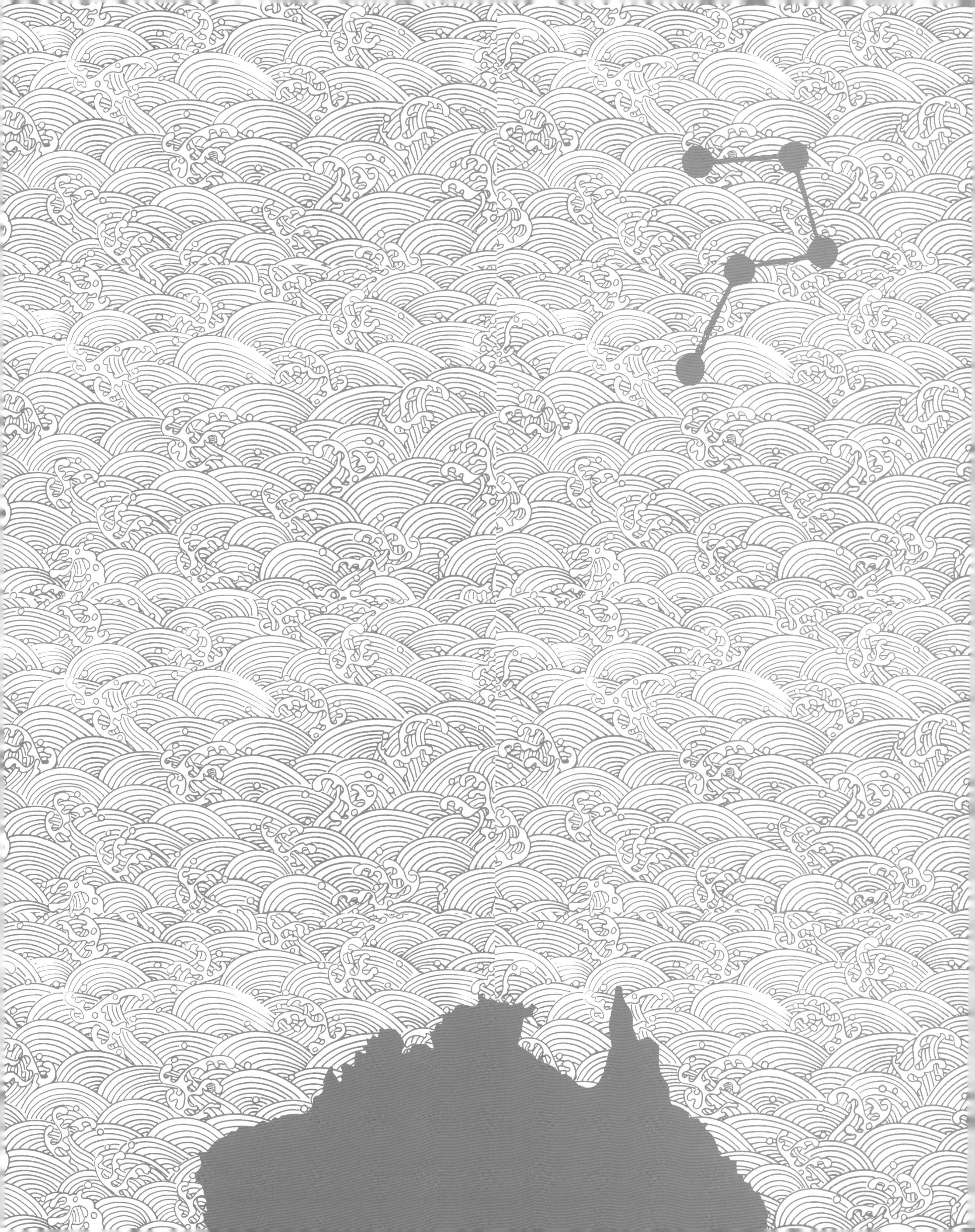

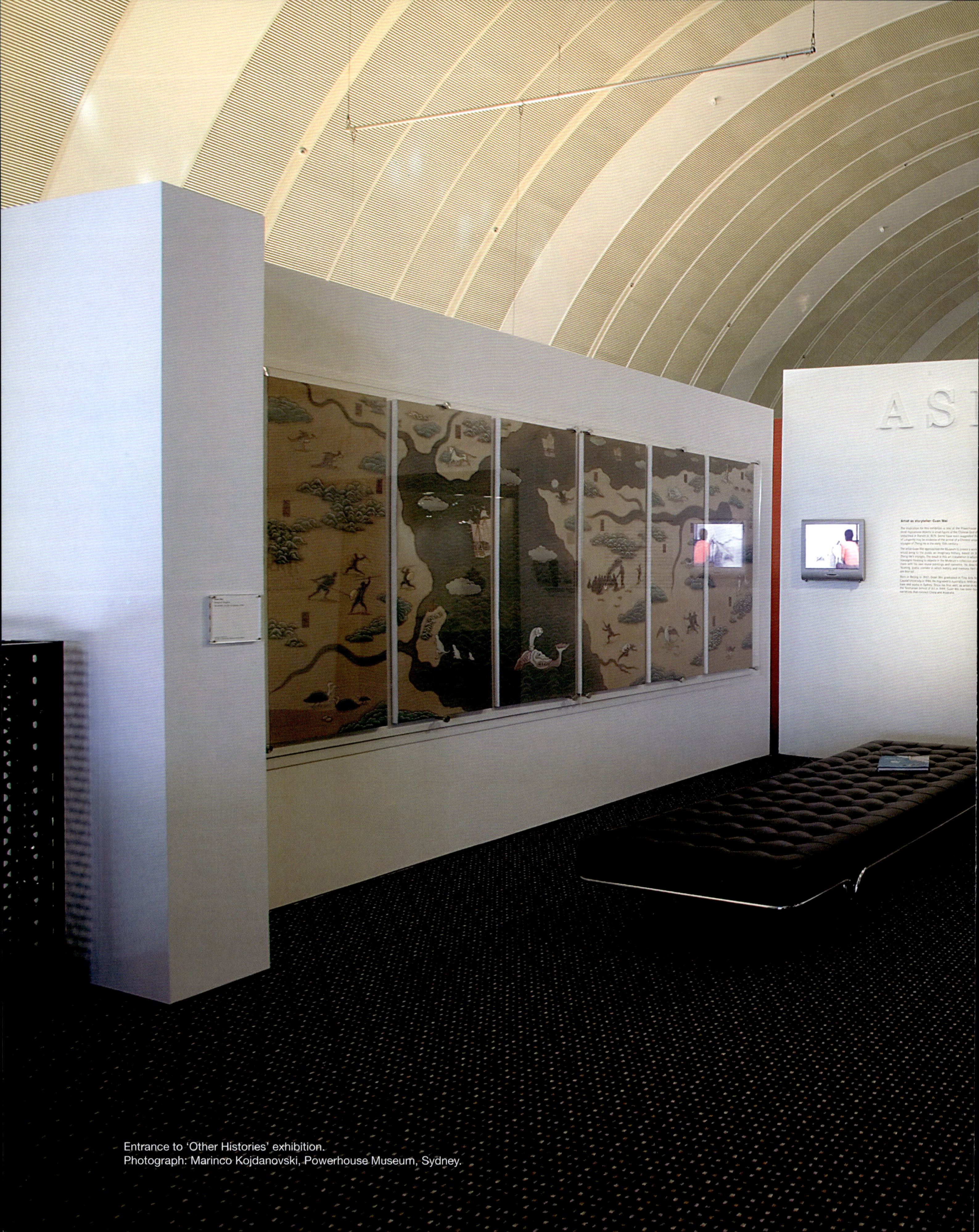

Entrance to ‘Other Histories’ exhibition.
Photograph: Marinco Kojdanovski, Powerhouse Museum, Sydney.

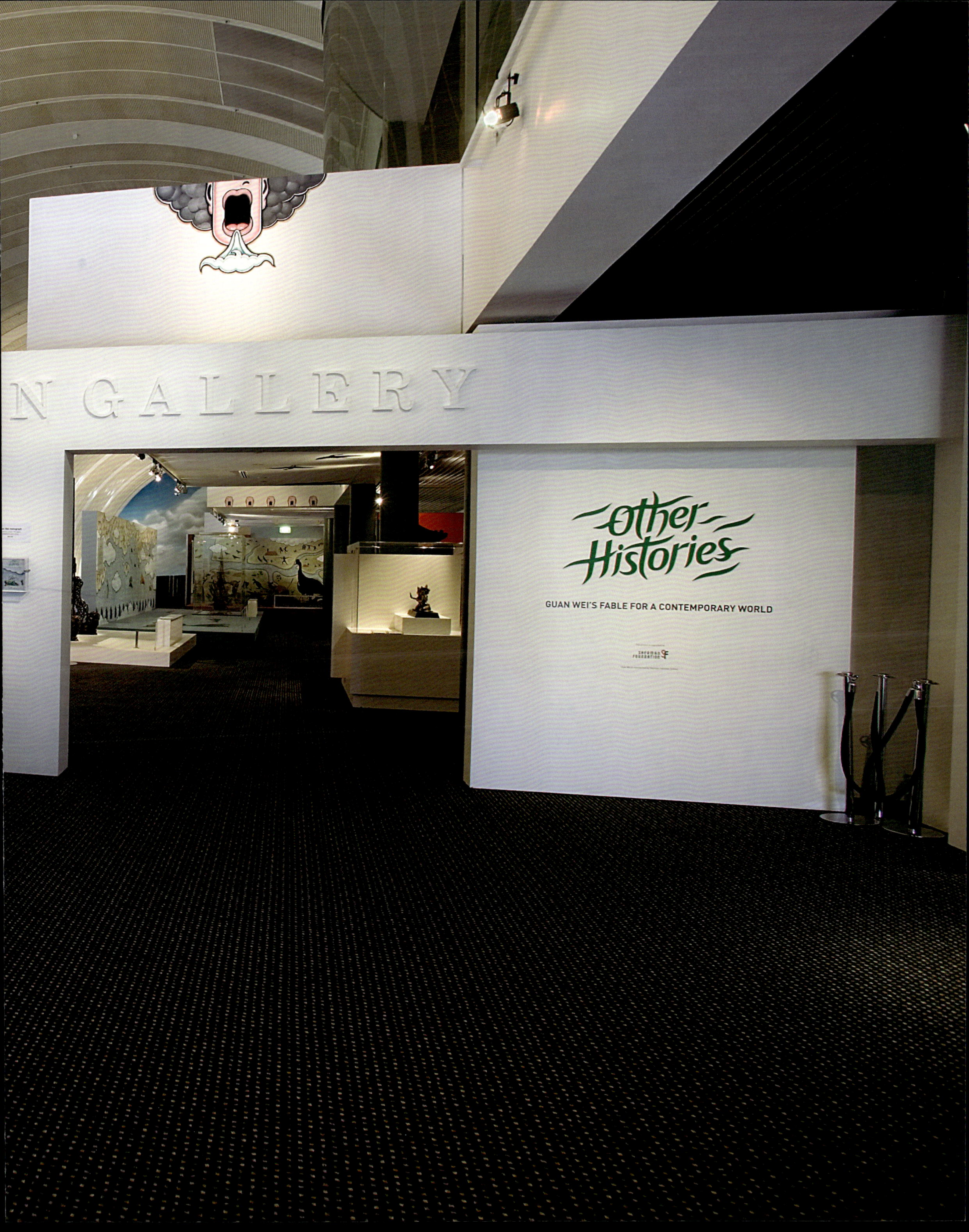
N GALLERY
Other Histories
GUAN WEI'S FABLE FOR A CONTEMPORARY WORLD

Guan Wei: Artist as Storyteller

Claire Roberts

Guan Wei is an artist of our times. Much of his work has been informed by the past and yet he is keenly attuned to the mood of the present. Themes that he has explored include migration, the plight of refugees, the 'War on Terror' and pollution. Guan Wei does not seek to educate in a didactic manner, but rather uses humour and an economy of painterly means to help us see more clearly the folly of our ways and the importance of appreciating our common humanity. In his recent work, 'Other Histories', described by the Australian art critic John McDonald as 'maybe Guan Wei's masterpiece',[1] he narrates his own version of Chinese history and Chinese-Australian history

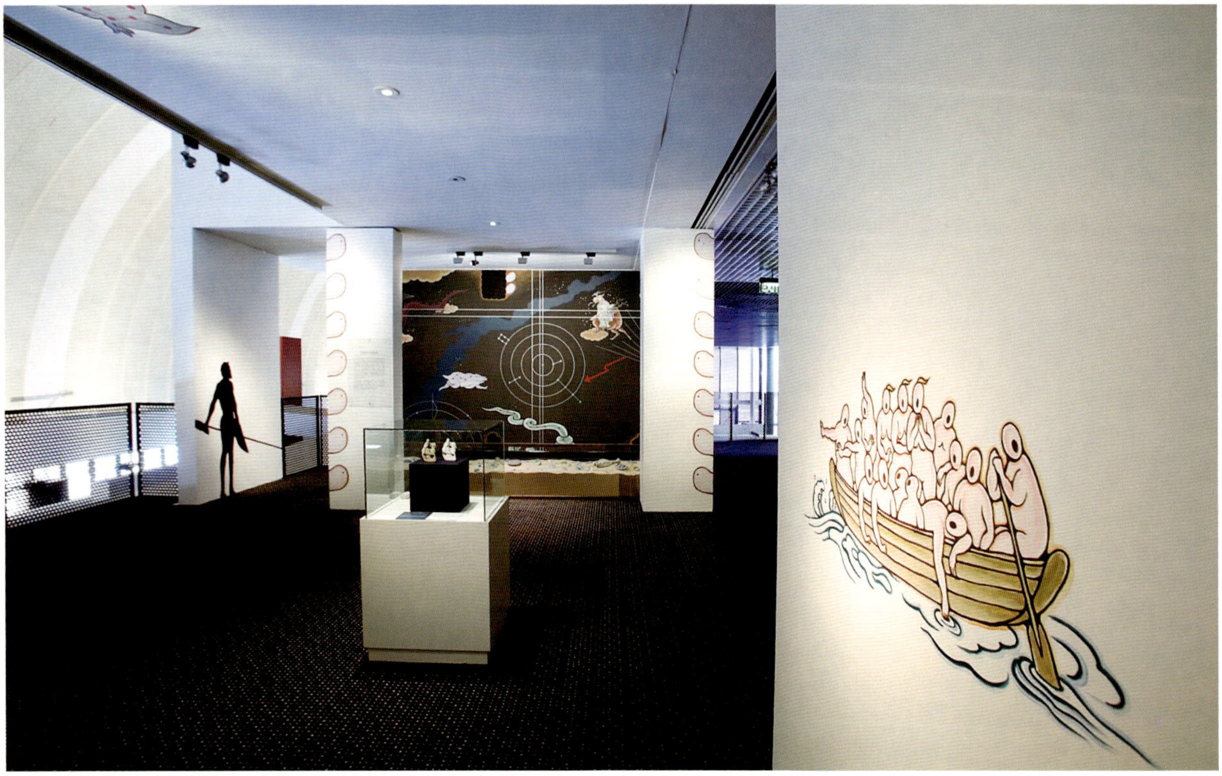

God of Longevity figure and mural paintings.
Photograph: Marinco Kojdanovski, Powerhouse Museum, Sydney.

through a large-scale installation that may be understood as a personal form of historical re-enactment. He co-opts history and high-concept themes as a form of retrospective travel that is fun and experimental. It is history from below; a gesture of utopianism that allows him to select his own past in reaction to a conflicted present.[2]

'Other Histories: Guan Wei's Fable for a Contemporary World' was held at Sydney's Powerhouse Museum from 11 October 2006 to 22 April 2007. The exhibition was based on an imaginary history and the idea of a Ming dynasty admiral's epic voyages in the early fifteenth century. Guan Wei, who was born in Beijing and migrated to Australia in 1990, cast himself in the role of artist as storyteller and created an art installation that combined museum objects together with his own wall paintings, narrative and artistic recreations in order to substantiate an assumed history. Members of the public were taken on a journey with the Muslim eunuch admiral Zheng He and his men from the Ming Empire, to unfamiliar lands, and ultimately to Australia. The exhibition would, Guan Wei hoped, function as a 'floating poetic corridor in which history and memory, fact and fiction are blurred'.[3]

Responding to queries about the conceptual veracity of his portrayal of the historical events and mythology surrounding the voyages of Zheng He—said to have involved an armada of 'treasure ships' and some 27,000 men who travelled a distance of 70,000 nautical miles, over 28 years—and the idea that they might have reached Australia more than 350 years before Captain Cook, Guan Wei is reported to have said: 'It doesn't matter, I am an artist.'[4] He is free to create his own version of history.

'Other Histories' had a long gestation and Guan Wei's original idea evolved significantly in the course of its development. The first draft of his proposal, written in 2002, was titled 'Re-creation of Relics: The Pioneering Discovery of Australia by the Chinese'. It was in part stimulated by Gavin Menzies' controversial bestseller *1421: The Year China Discovered the World*, first published in 2002. Guan Wei was intrigued by the way Menzies was able to conjure an array of historic relics as evidence that Zheng He had 'discovered' Australia. In the proposal Guan Wei noted that Menzies brought some intriguing questions to light, but he queried whether the evidence of such antiquities could substantiate scholarly demands. Was there an element of hidden history embedded in those ancient items and how should they be interpreted? In a later communication with me Guan Wei reiterated what was for him a key question: How does one understand and interpret history?[5] Central to his proposal were his own recreations of historical objects, maps and specimens. The project, he said, 'is designed as an archaeological discovery show, to be displayed in a museum-like style, with the walls painted dark red and spot-lights shone on the items, thus creating a mysterious and secret air.'[6] Guan Wei was fascinated by the idea of fabricating history through an assemblage of 'evidence' and employing a museum-like installation to legitimise his own version of history.

Guan Wei contacted the Powerhouse Museum in 2004 hoping that an exhibition could be staged the following year to coincide with official celebrations in China to mark the 600th anniversary of the voyages of Zheng He. In a revised version of his proposal Guan Wei stated that his objectives were to: 're-examine the function of a museum; break down the barriers of museum exhibitions; re-interpret the museum's collection; and question mainstream theory about the history of Australia.'[7] The prospect of exhibiting in a museum environment sharpened his focus and provided an opportunity to work collaboratively with professional staff in a large public institution.

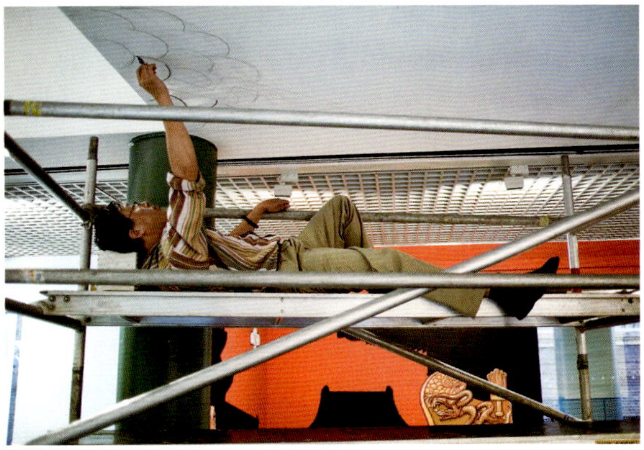

Guan Wei at work.
Photograph: Jean-François Lanzarone, Powerhouse Museum, Sydney.

Around the same time Guan Wei had begun to experiment with painting on walls, marking a move away from his signature multi-panel works. His first wall paintings were featured in group exhibitions held in Berlin, Melbourne and Sydney in late 2003 and 2004.[8] Guan Wei was attracted by the scale and immediacy of wall painting, and the idea of travelling light—not having to worry about the freight and handling of stretched canvases, or the sale of the works.

Wall painting is site-specific, monumental in scale and not for the faint-hearted. Guan Wei cites the ancient Buddhist frescoes of the Mogao Caves in Dunhuang as a source of inspiration.[9] Contained within caves carved from sandstone mountains, the murals depict Buddha and his attendants and stories associated with his life and afterlife, as well as portraits of donors making offerings. The caves are located in the Gobi desert on the ancient Silk Road trade route in far northwestern China. For exhausted pilgrims who had crossed the desert and arrived at the oasis town of Dunhuang, seeing the brilliantly coloured mural paintings must have been a revelation. Many of the frescoes remain, and today Dunhuang is a major site for tourist pilgrimage, although Guan Wei has never seen the paintings other than in reproductions.

In twentieth-century China the ancient and enduring art of wall painting was modified to suit the times. During the Cultural Revolution, when Guan Wei was growing

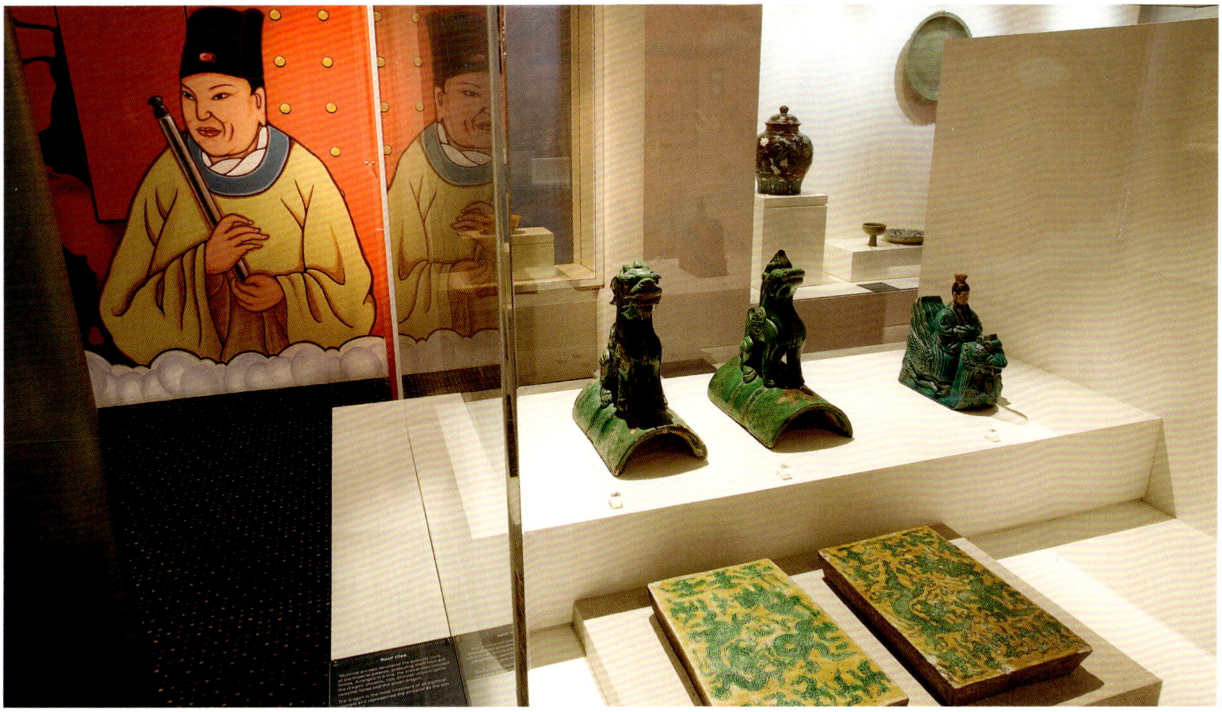

Chinese ceramics from the collection of the Powerhouse Museum.
Photograph: Jean-François Lanzarone, Powerhouse Museum, Sydney.

up, images and texts were painted directly onto outside walls to communicate political dogma and were visible to all passers-by. Today, it is difficult to see remains of the once all-pervasive slogans, except in some out-of-the-way towns where ghost-like vestiges can still be seen on old buildings through the layers of whitewash. These politically motivated markings were also a source of inspiration for Guan Wei.[10]

Beginning in the late 1970s wall paintings could also function as interior decoration. But as the famous case of the 1979 Beijing International Airport murals demonstrates, the medium is not hazard-free. One of the murals, painted by the avant-garde artist Yuan Yunsheng (b. 1937), was inspired by the Water Festival of Xishuangbana, Yunnan province, and contained images of three naked women, reflecting the cultural practices of the Dai people during that festival. In 1980, after the mural had been completed, the presence of naked women sparked a controversy and officials claimed the painting was offensive to the Dai people. It was covered with a curtain and then boarded over during a 'socialist morality' campaign in 1981.

In the context of contemporary installation art where the artist is in complete control of the space, if not the reception of the work, wall painting is generally ephemeral. Like a play or an opera, it is made for a particular time and place. It is theatrical and transitory, releasing the artist from the physical limitations of formats and formulas of their usual artistic practice. At the conclusion of the exhibition the walls are painted over and returned to a state of nothingness.

As wall painting had become an important part of Guan Wei's practice it was logical that it became the primary narrative force of 'Other Histories'. The shift of emphasis away from freestanding painted screens and works on paper highlighted the experimental nature of the project and a willingness to embrace new possibilities offered by the context of a museum environment.

Collaboration: Artist and Museum

For Museum staff involved in the project, 'Other Histories' presented a unique chance to reflect on the roles that we play, as custodians and interpreters of historical relics. Working with Guan Wei, we could step away from the seriousness and didacticism of a conventional exhibition and actively challenge what is possible or accepted in a museum environment. Everyone involved in the project, including myself as the curator, the exhibition designer, graphic designer, exhibition co-ordinator, as well as the registration, conservation and education staff, was united by Guan Wei's vision and took delight in their role as a knowing accomplice in the construction of Guan Wei's story.

From the outset, Guan Wei envisaged an installation in which painting, objects and text were integrated. In the final proposal Guan Wei outlined the kinds of objects that he hoped to include in his installation—ceramics, Buddhist figures, coins, navigational equipment, objects connected with trade such as tea, Chinese medicine and objects that related to Chinese Australian history. These objects were to be drawn from the Museum's collection and Guan Wei would provide whatever could not be sourced.

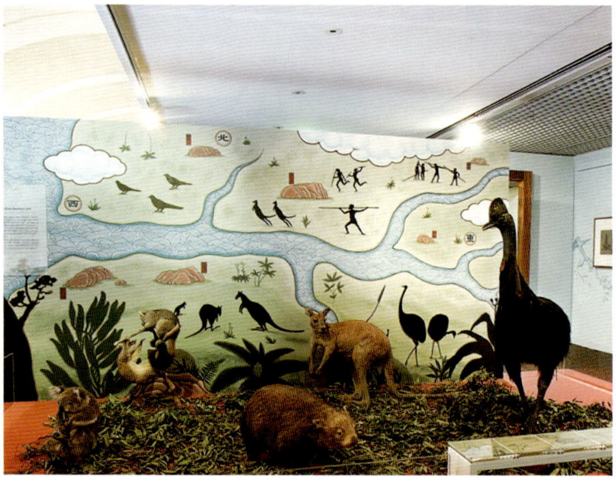

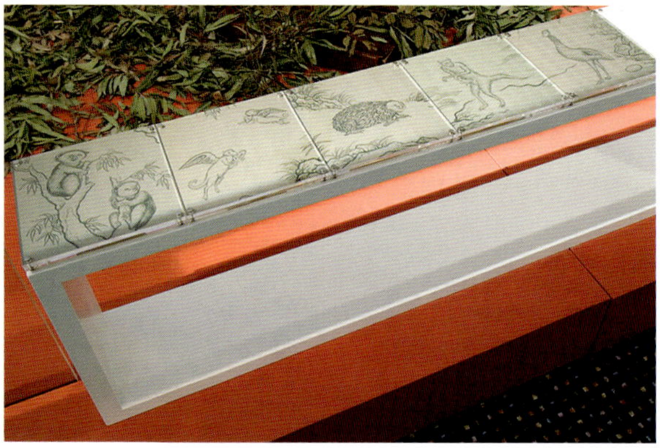

↑ 'The Great Southern Land', mural painting, and animal specimens from the collection of the Australian Museum.
Photograph: Marinco Kojdanovski, Powerhouse Museum, Sydney.

↓ Reproduced details of works on paper by Guan Wei.
Photograph: Marinco Kojdanovski, Powerhouse Museum, Sydney.

A list of potential objects held by the Museum was prepared for Guan Wei's consideration and together we examined them in storage. While in the end we agreed on what would be displayed, we were motivated by different considerations. Guan Wei was concerned about the type of objects he wanted represented, whereas I was conscious of the history and provenance of particular objects. As we refined the list it became clear that there were fascinating areas of 'play' to be explored in relation to actual or hoped-for connections between individual objects and Guan Wei's narrative.

The centrepiece of the exhibition was a small object from the Museum's collection—an enigmatic figure of the Chinese God of Longevity that was unearthed in Darwin in 1879—found buried deep among the roots of an old banyan tree. From the time of its discovery, the figure has been the subject of considerable speculative and scholarly enquiry.[11] Writers and historians have suggested that it may be evidence of the arrival of a Chinese vessel from the voyages of Zheng He in the early fifteenth century, more than 350 years before James Cook landed at Kurnell on the eastern seaboard of Australia, and it is illustrated in Gavin Menzies' book. In the Museum's view the figure is a folk carving that most likely dates from the 1800s and relates to Chinese contact and the early settlement of Darwin. In 'Other Histories', Guan Wei determined that the God of Longevity was an object belonging to one of Zheng He's men and was, in his view, the embodiment of the Southern Cross star constellation that led Zheng He's fleet, and many later Chinese migrants, to Australia, the Great Southern Land.

At an early stage of our discussions Guan Wei expressed a strong desire to include animal and bird specimens to allude to the strange and exotic fauna that Zheng He and his men would have encountered in Australia. The Powerhouse Museum has few such objects, so we borrowed specimens of a kangaroo, a koala, two possums and a cassowary from the Australian Museum, the repository for Sydney's collection of natural history objects. Guan Wei also added historic, fake and contemporary commercially available items to the list of objects, further blurring the boundaries between fact and fiction.

The Mural Painting Process

Owing to the size of the exhibition space and the scale of the murals Guan Wei carried out the work with the help of four assisting artists: Frank Hope, Jin Sha, Yang Xifa and Zhao Baokang. Guan Wei had worked with them on different projects in the past and they were all highly skilled artists in their own right. Each of them had migrated to Australia from China and felt an affinity with Guan Wei's narrative. The process of painting the murals took one month.

As artistic director, Guan Wei managed the involvement of the assisting artists. He prepared small studies on paper, which provided the compositional and colour detail for the artists to follow. Guan Wei directed each artist to work on a different mural, and selected subjects that would maximize their skill and interests. For example, Jin Sha excelled at sea creatures, and Yang Xifa at water, waves, and freehand bird and flower painting, Frank Hope at silhouettes and Zhao Baokang at landscapes. Compositions were drawn up using charcoal and were then given form through the application of layers of flat and graded acrylic colour. The gallery space became a large studio dotted with pots of acrylic paint and brushes. Stencils were used to block in recurring motifs such as the fleet of Zheng He's 'treasure ships', and Yang Xifa patiently created a vast expanse of ocean waves with thick black texta pens, line by line.

Many of the historic motifs that appear in Guan Wei's paintings are copied and adapted from history books, books of sailing ships, folios of paintings by Chinese court artists, Australian colonial artists, as well as

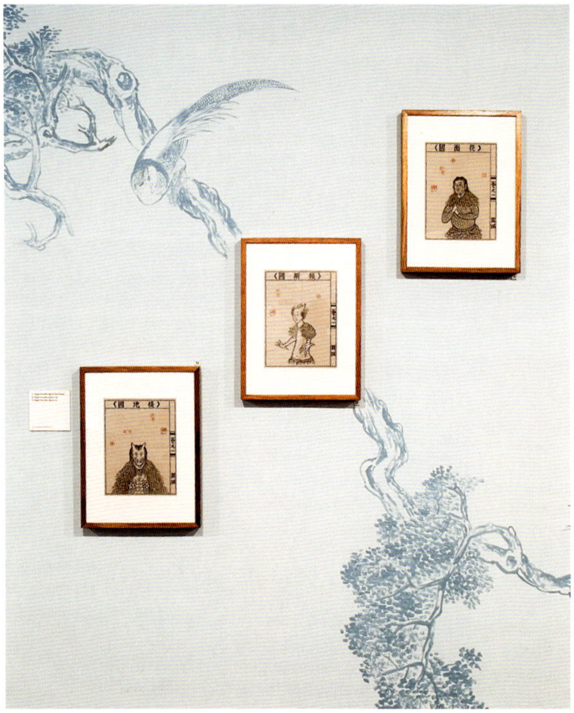

'People From Other Regions', works on paper by Guan Wei.
Photograph: Jean-François Lanzarone, Powerhouse Museum, Sydney.

woodblock printed images from ancient Chinese texts. In the studio-gallery space there were piles of books and magazines offering visual references that the artists would pick up, refer to and copy from as required. Guan Wei consciously appropriates motifs and delights in their historical resonance, but the borrowed imagery quickly succumbs to his distinctive painting style to become detail in a large and coherent new schema.

The Museum's and other objects were installed progressively, so each day there was something new to see on the walls and in the showcases. The process of creating the exhibition and the wonder that it evoked thus became a key element of the unfolding, revelatory nature of the project. During the final three weeks of wall painting members of the public were invited to view Guan Wei and the artists at work. Viewing occurred in the afternoons from behind barriers. One visitor expressed her delight and wrote: 'Seeing the artist Guan Wei and his assistants painting... was a rare privilege. His work was (and is) inspiring and thought-provoking. It was also great to talk to him.'

In the last few days of wall painting new figures and strange markings appeared in unexpected places, on columns and skirting areas, and on ceilings and bulkheads, motifs that were never part of the original proposal. Wherever you looked there was something new and unexpected—silhouettes of Indigenous Australians, British and European explorers, early Anglo-Saxon settlers, and boatloads of refugees, as well as humorous touches including naked chubby Guan Wei figures, laughing heads, gremlins, snakes, lightning, rain clouds and Chinese seals. One of the most charming last-minute additions was a free-hand painting of a flowering bough and birds executed by Yang Xifa. It was painted in blue on a pale blue wall and provided a decorative and naturalistic backdrop for a series of framed works on paper by Guan Wei that were inspired by an ancient Chinese illustrated text of the *Classic of Mountains and Seas*, depicting plants, animals and people from unfamiliar lands. These playful, last-minute additions further integrated the various components into a single whole and heightened the mysterious and secret atmosphere that Guan Wei sought to evoke.

Before people entered the exhibition space an introductory text panel advised that once they crossed the threshold of the gallery they were entering Guan Wei's world and would become active participants in his journey of discovery. Within the exhibition an interpretive text panel accompanied each of Guan Wei's murals. The text was presented in English and in quotation marks in order to highlight the fact that it represented Guan Wei's voice and not the Museum's. Each object label carried two layers of information. Guan Wei's interpretation of what he wanted the object to be for the purpose of his narrative came first in bold type and enclosed in quotation marks. This was followed by the Museum's catalogue information containing details of what the object actually was. This textual solution was aimed at making it plain to viewers that the exhibition was not a conventional museum exhibition but an art installation that was a playful dialogue between history and fantasy. In this way visitors became actively engaged with the objects and the role they were called upon to play in Guan Wei's fantasy narrative.

In the booklet accompanying 'Other Histories' Guan Wei expressed the hope that visitors would be encouraged to reflect on our common humanity. He wrote: 'I hope that this exhibition will inspire visitors to remember all that is wondrous about life and encourage them to reflect on shared experiences. The world is full of beauty and things that hold a strange fascination. We, who come from different cultural backgrounds, need to better understand one another, connect with one another and seek friendship with one another. It is imperative that we find a shared set of values to ensure our survival.'

Guan Wei is an artist who is conscious of his role as a living link to an intriguing past. He employs personal experience and a fertile imagination to reflect on history and re-think the present with a view to improving our prospects for the future. Guan Wei works like a detective sifting through 'evidence' and approaches fabulous historical characters and events as raw material as an open rather than closed body of knowledge to take apart, re-assemble and improve upon. Guan Wei's attempts to re-write history are imbued with a utopian optimism. We are not presented with history as it was, but how it might have been. In 'Other Histories' Guan Wei has cast himself in the lead roles of both artist and storyteller.

---

1. John McDonald, 'The Barrier That United a Culture', *Sydney Morning Herald* (14-15 October 2006), Arts and Entertainment, p. 17.
2. Vanessa Agnew, 'What is Reenactment?', *Criticism*, 46. 3 (Summer 2004): 327-335.
3. Guan Wei, quoted in Claire Roberts, 'The Artist as Storyteller', in the exhibition booklet *Other Histories: Guan Wei's Fable for a Contemporary World* (Sydney: Powerhouse Publishing, 2006), p. 3.
4. Sunanda Creagh, 'You Can See the Political Situation in My Work: These Bodies With No Eyes', *Sydney Morning Herald* (9-10 September 2006), Arts & Entertainment, p. 5.
5. Fax dated 10 August 2004.
6. Guan Wei's exhibition proposal titled 'Re-creation of Relics: The Pioneering Discovery of Australia by the Chinese', 2002.
7. Guan Wei's revised exhibition proposal, '"Zheng He" Exhibition at the Powerhouse Museum. Post-production: Cultural Relic Exhibition', 24 August 2004.
8. 'Face Up: Contemporary Art from Australia', Hamburger Banhof Museum, Berlin, 2 October 2003-4 January 2004; 'Cycle Tracks Will Abound in Utopia', Australian Centre for Contemporary Art, Melbourne, 7 August-28 October 2004, and 'Terra Alterius: Land of Another', Ivan Dougherty Gallery, Sydney, 20 August-25 September 2004.
9. Natalie King, 'Chinese Whispers: The Work of Guan Wei', in Dinah Dysart, Natalie King and Hou Hanru, *Guan Wei* (Sydney: Craftsman House, 2006), p. 84.
10. Ibid.
11. Collection of the Powerhouse Museum, Sydney, A4255. The God of Longevity figure, carved from pinite, is said to have been found wedged in the roots of a banyan tree in 1879 in Doctor's Gully, near Port Darwin, Northern Territory. A plaster cast of the object was donated to the Museum in 1889 and the actual object was purchased in 1950. See John Wade, 'Shou Lao: A Chinese Figurine Excavated at Darwin in 1879', *Australian Society for Historical Archaeology Newsletter*, 7. 2 (June 1977): 13-16.

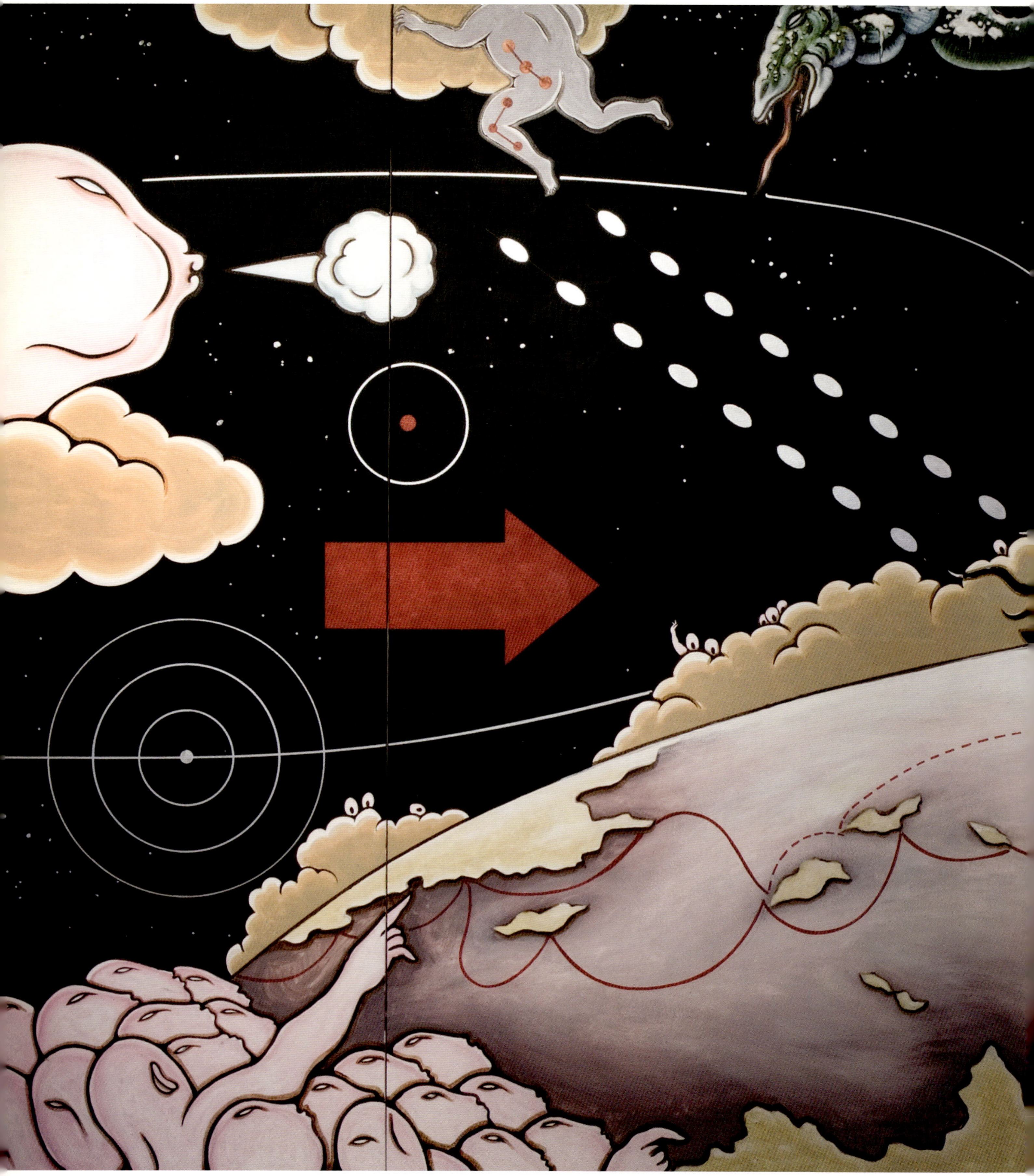

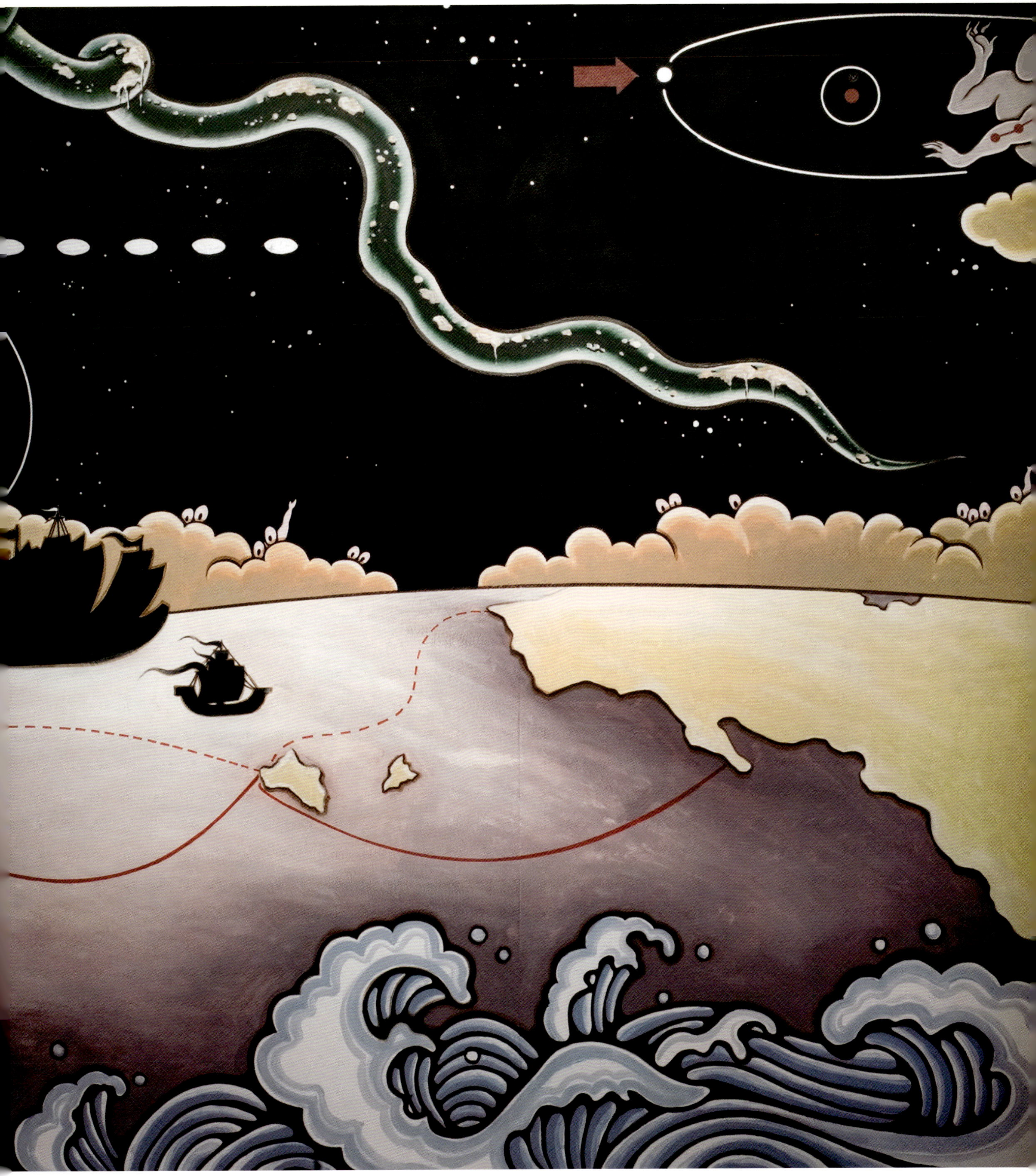

'Zheng He and Columbus', mural painting. Collection: Powerhouse Museum. Gift of Guan Wei, 2008.
Photograph: Jean-François Lanzarone, Powerhouse Museum, Sydney.

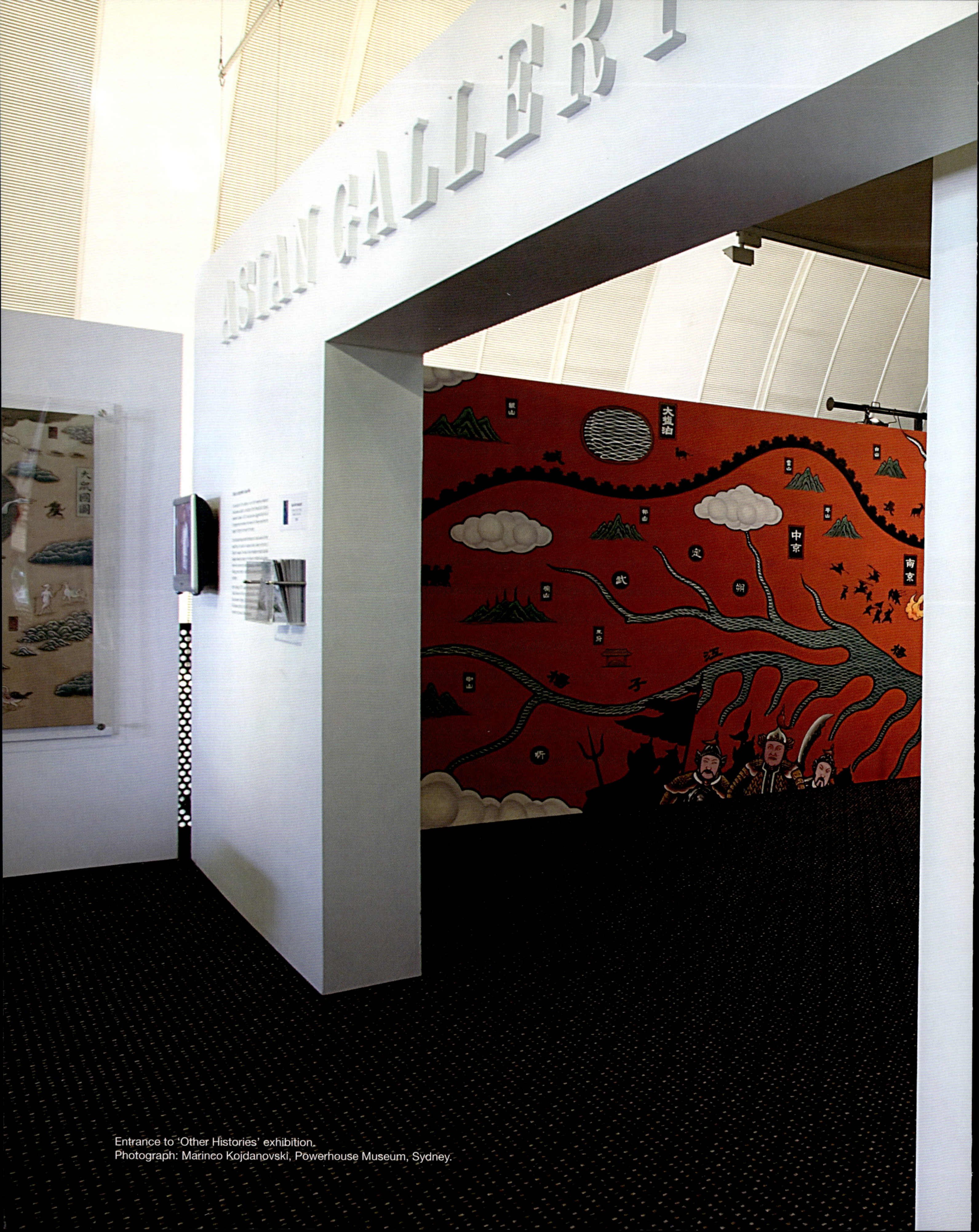

Entrance to 'Other Histories' exhibition.
Photograph: Marinco Kojdanovski, Powerhouse Museum, Sydney.

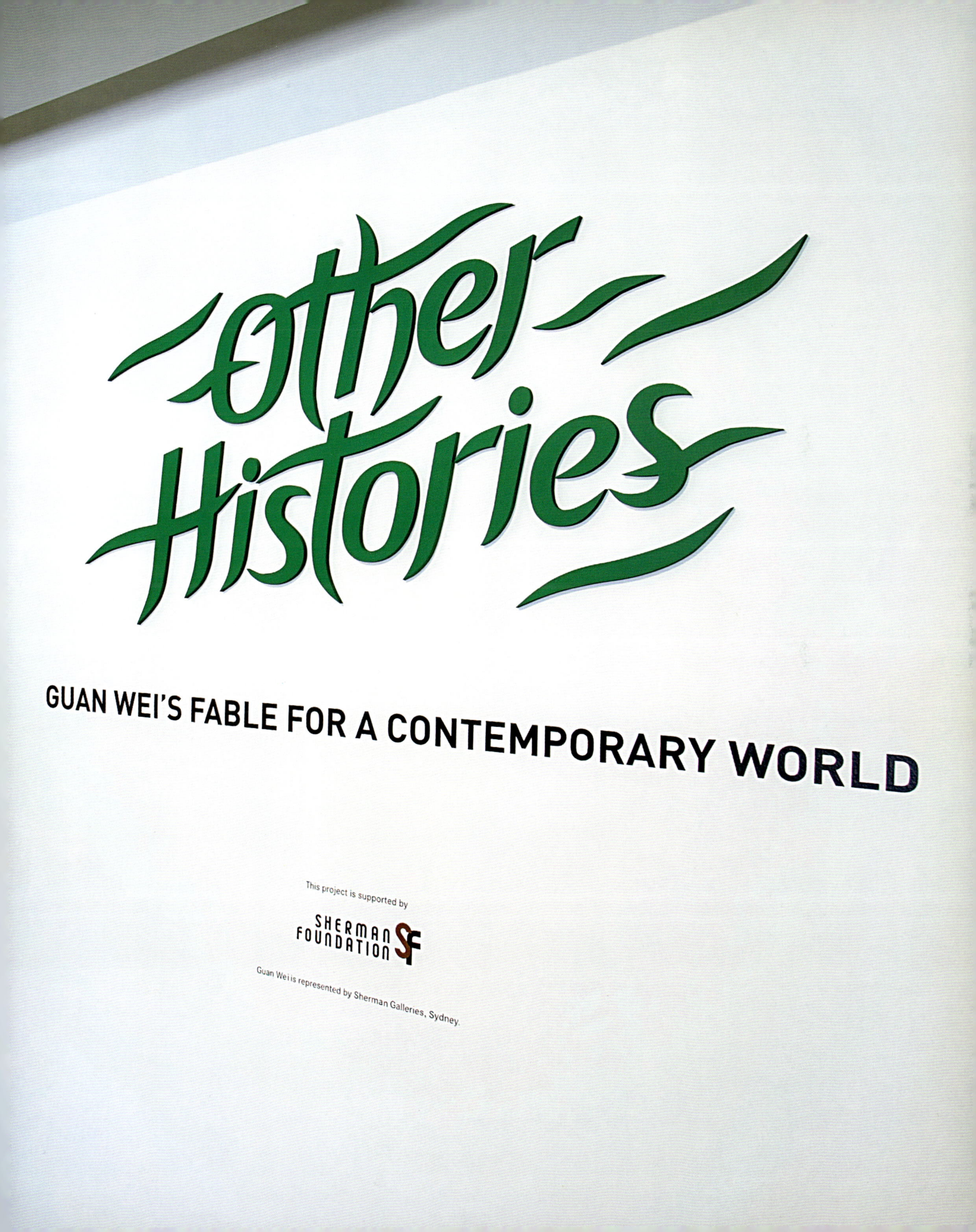
Other Histories
GUAN WEI'S FABLE FOR A CONTEMPORARY WORLD
This project is supported by
SHERMAN FOUNDATION
Guan Wei is represented by Sherman Galleries, Sydney.

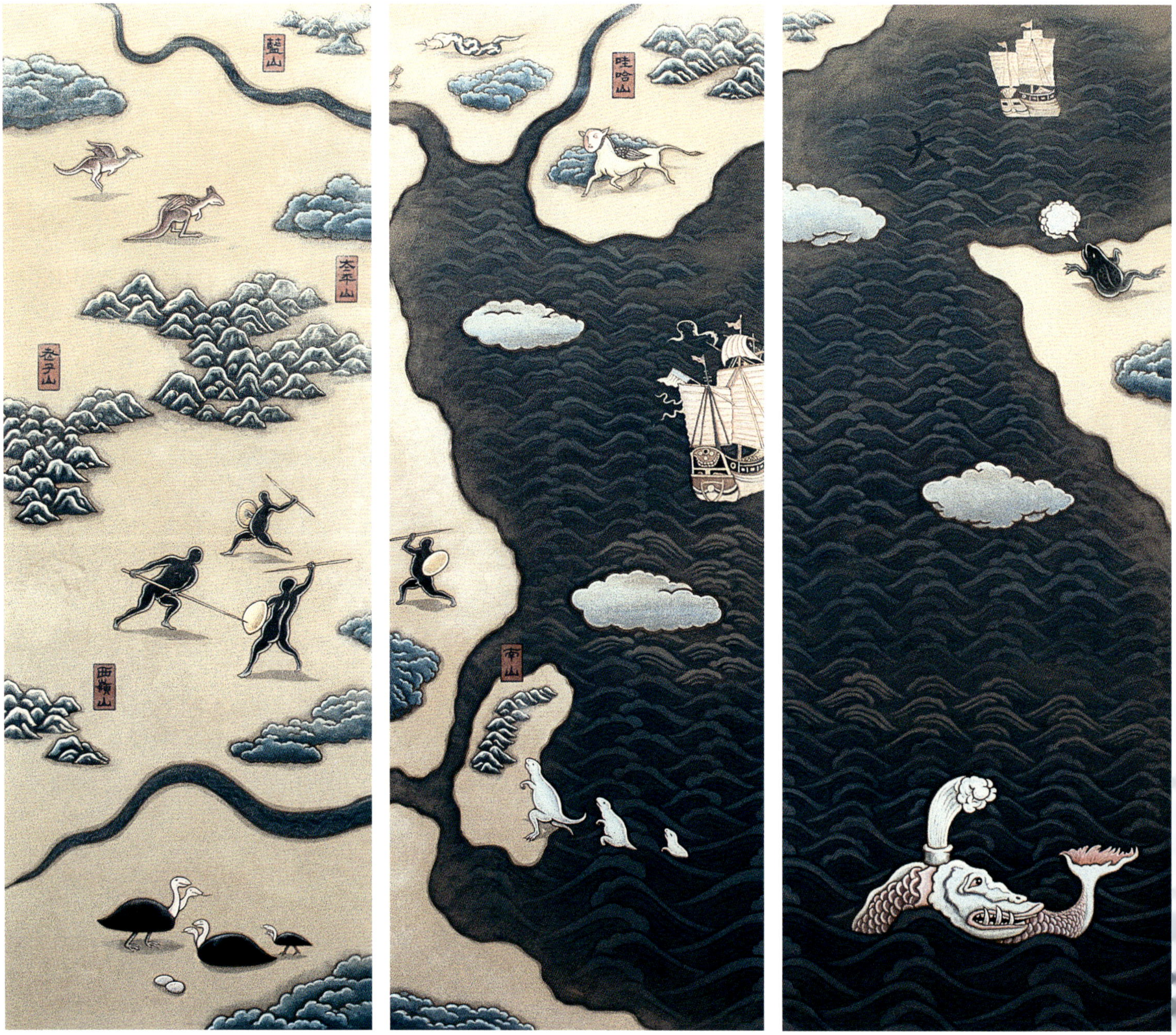
藍山
太平山
老子山
哇哈山
南山
大

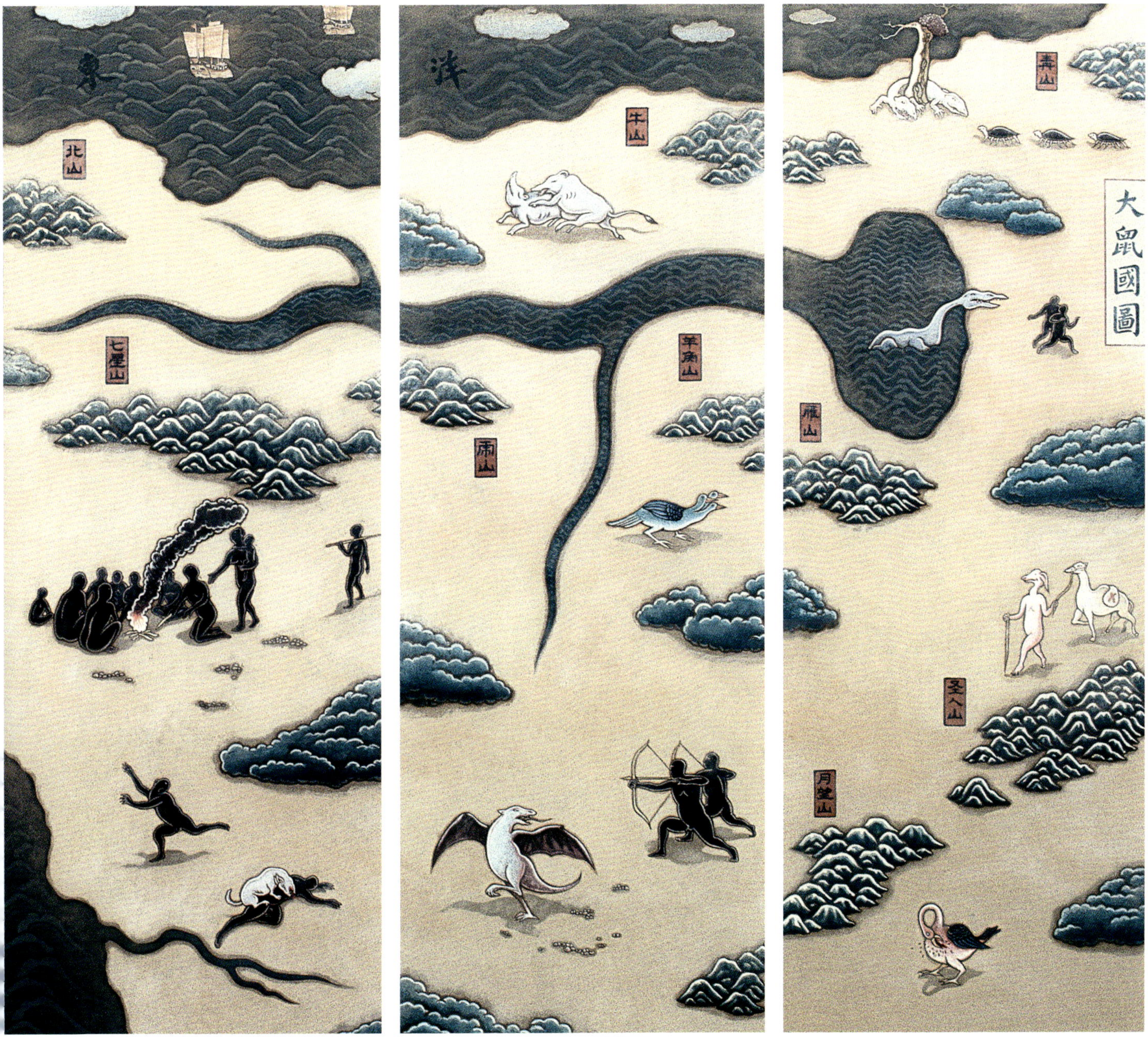

'Kangaroo Kingdom', 2005, acrylic on canvas, 6 panels, 137 x 300 cm. Collection: Dr Gene and Brian Sherman.
Photograph: Sue Blackburn.

The Ming Dynasty: A Battle for Power

'The first emperor of the Ming dynasty, Zhu Yuanzhang (r.1368–1398), founded the capital in Nanjing, in the south of China. After the emperor's death, his eldest grandson Zhu Yunwen (1377– ?) took the throne. The new emperor's uncle, Zhu Di, was in command of the northern city of Yandu, capital of the state of Yan (Beijing). From there he guarded the Great Wall and defended the Ming Empire against invaders.

'This powerful uncle in the north eventually took the throne for himself, occupying Nanjing under force of arms. His nephew, the dethroned emperor Zhu Yunwen, disappeared. According to legend, a monk told the new ruler, who reigned as the Yongle Emperor, that the defeated nephew had fled the land via the seaport of Quanzhou (Zayton) in Fujian province.'

大明王朝：权力之争

"明代的第一个皇帝朱元璋（1368 年 –1398 年在位）夺取全国政权后奠都南京，当他去世之后，长孙朱允炆（1377 年 – ？）继承了皇位，号建文帝。这位新皇帝的叔父燕王朱棣当时镇守在北方的燕都北平（现今的北京地区），在那里他守卫着古老的长城，防范着来自北方的王朝颠覆者。

"这位拥有强大实力的叔父于 1399 年发动靖难之役，三年后攻占南京，以武力夺得了皇位，成为永乐皇帝。但是，当他进入南京的时候，被废黜的皇帝朱允炆失踪了。依照传说，他出家当了云游四方的和尚，但是也有人告诉新的统治者永乐皇帝说，那个被击败的小外甥经福建泉州的海港逃离了大陆。"

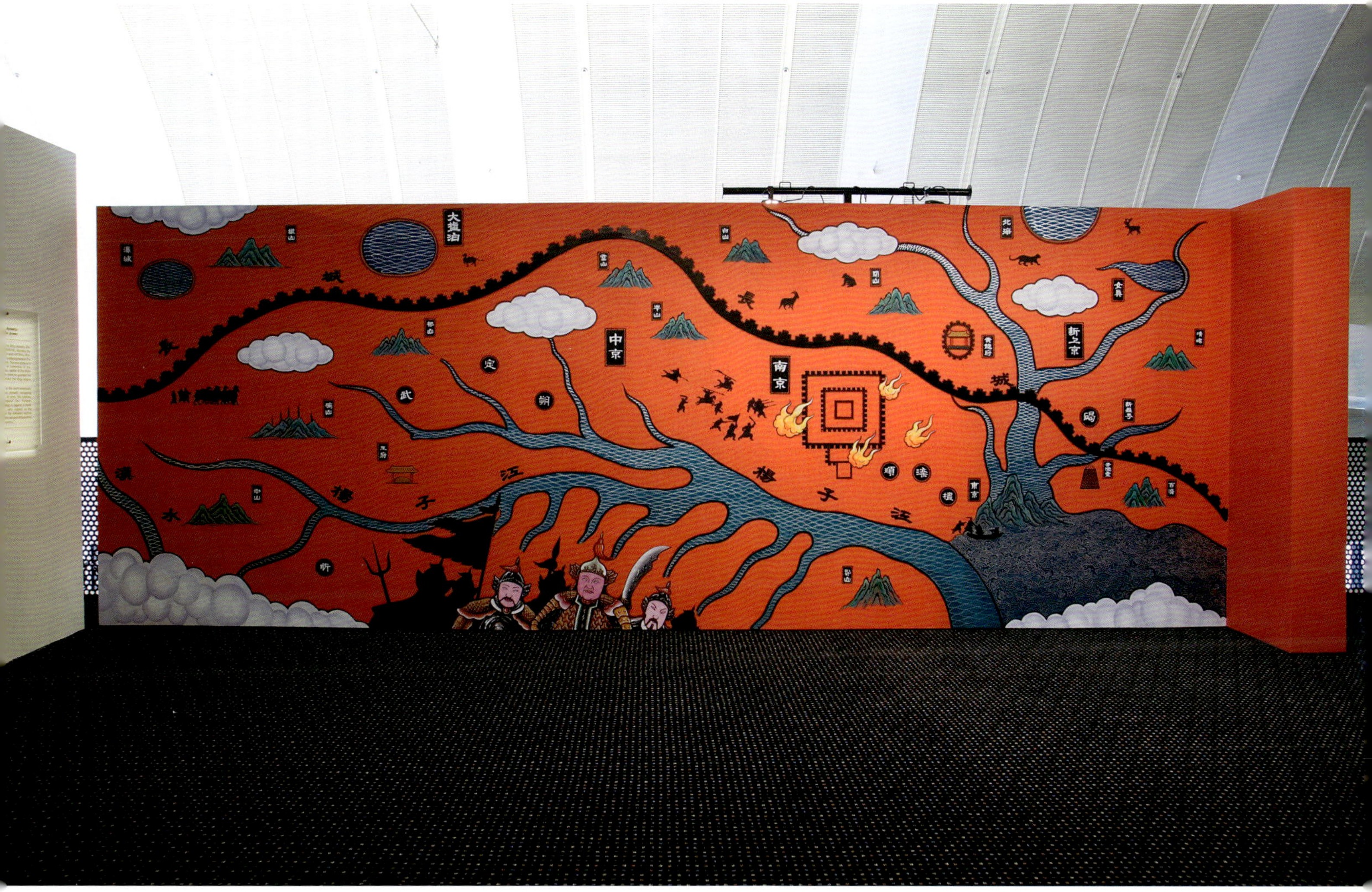

'The Ming Dynasty: A Battle for Power', mural painting.
Photograph: Marinco Kojdanovski, Powerhouse Museum, Sydney.

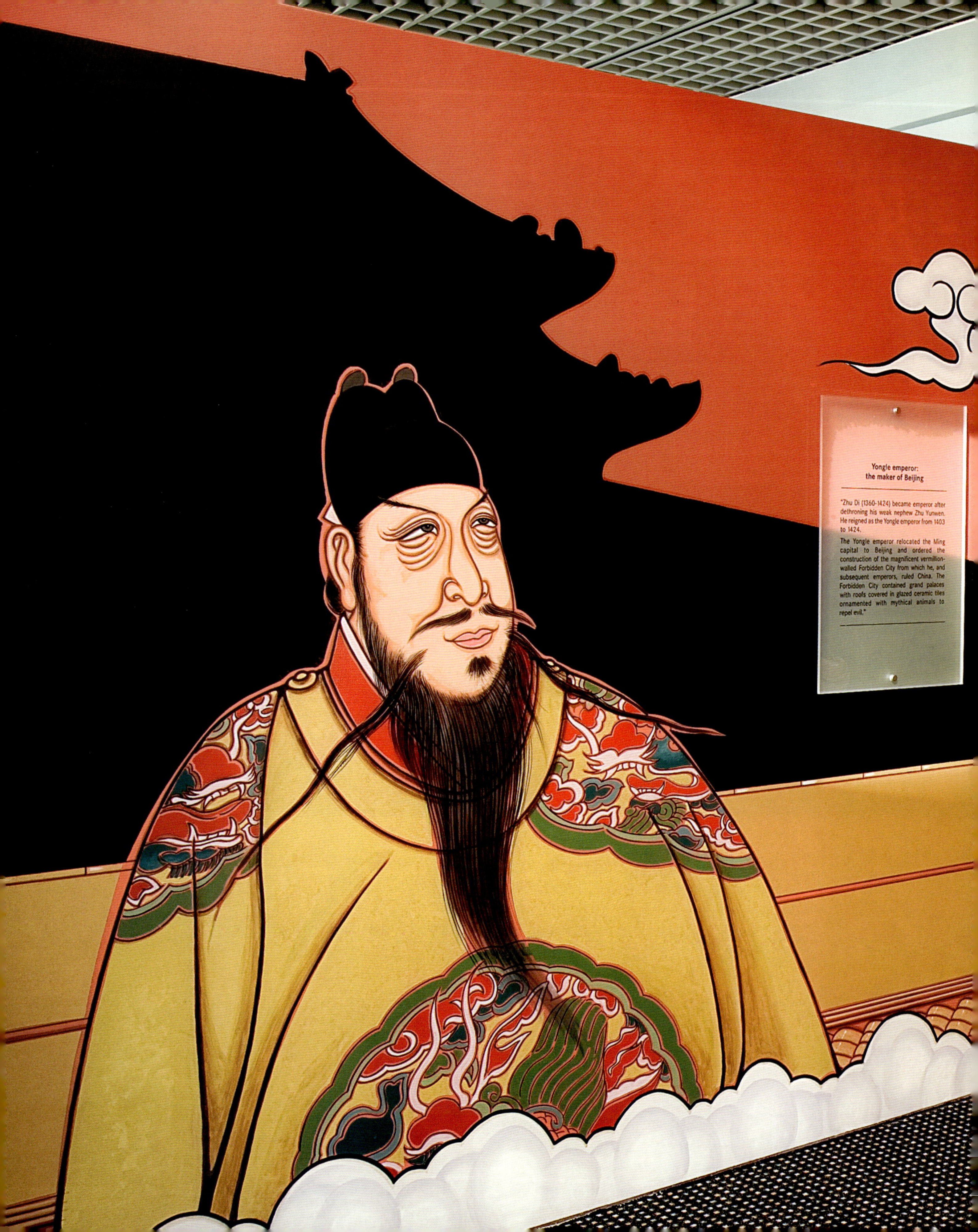
Yongle emperor:
the maker of Beijing
"Zhu Di (1360-1424) became emperor after dethroning his weak nephew Zhu Yunwen. He reigned as the Yongle emperor from 1403 to 1424.
The Yongle emperor relocated the Ming capital to Beijing and ordered the construction of the magnificent vermillion-walled Forbidden City from which he, and subsequent emperors, ruled China. The Forbidden City contained grand palaces with roofs covered in glazed ceramic tiles ornamented with mythical animals to repel evil."

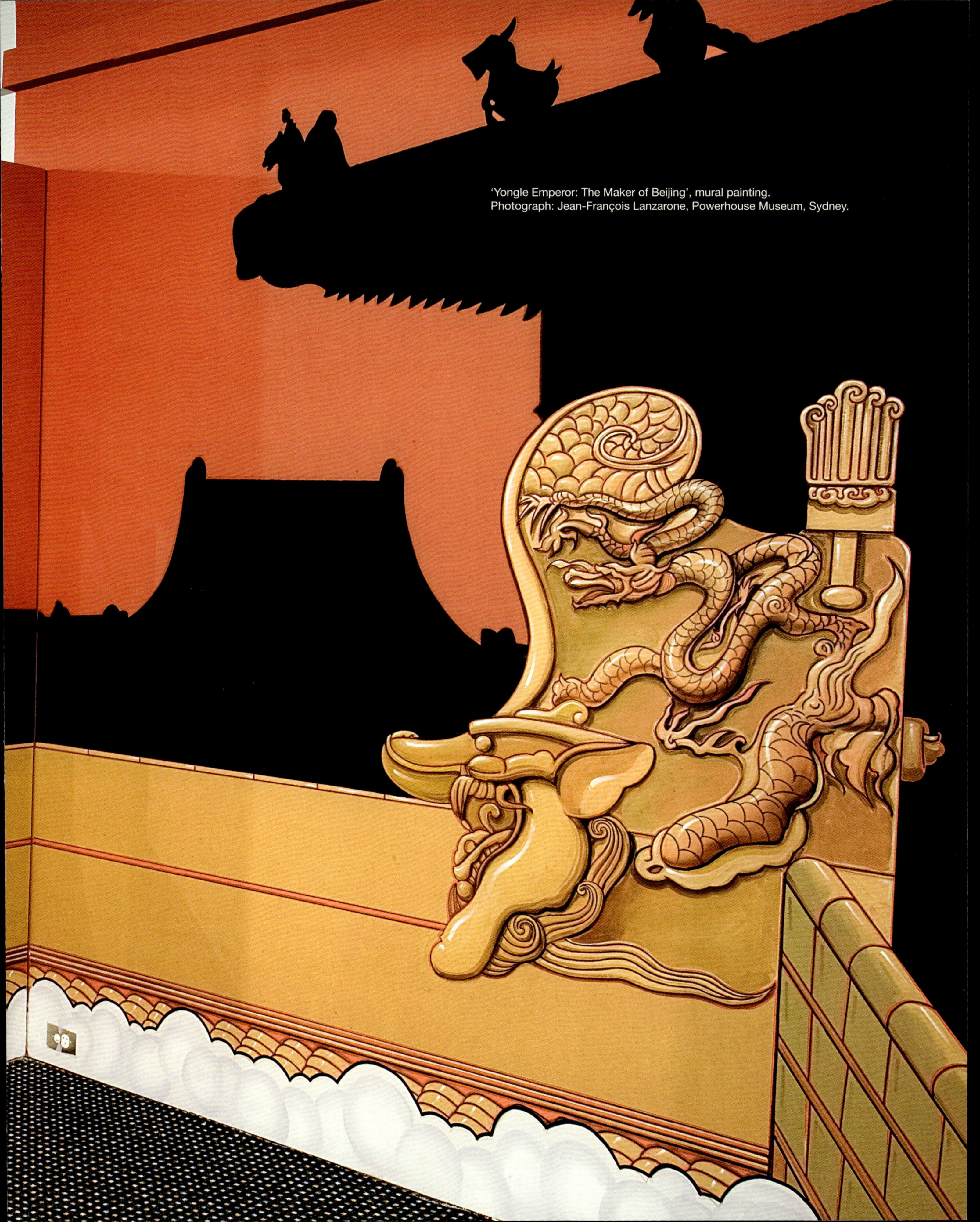

'Yongle Emperor: The Maker of Beijing', mural painting.
Photograph: Jean-François Lanzarone, Powerhouse Museum, Sydney.

Yongle Emperor: The Maker of Beijing

'Zhu Di (1360–1424) became the emperor after dethroning his weak nephew Zhu Yunwen. He reigned as the Yongle Emperor from 1403 to 1424.

'The Yongle Emperor relocated the Ming capital to Beijing and ordered the construction of the magnificent vermillion-walled Forbidden City from which he, and subsequent emperors, ruled China. The Forbidden City contained grand palaces with roofs covered in glazed ceramic tiles ornamented with mythical animals to repel evil.'

永乐皇帝：北京城的建造者

"朱棣（1360 年 –1424 年）废黜他软弱的外甥朱允炆后成为永乐皇帝，自 1403 年登基至 1424 年去世，统治中国二十余年。

"永乐皇帝将大明的首都迁移到了北京，建造了庄严恢宏的紫禁城和北京城，从此开始，明清两代的二十多个皇帝在这里统治中国长达数百年。紫禁城的壮丽宫殿上铺着黄色的琉璃瓦，屋脊装饰着琉璃瓦的吻兽、垂兽、蹲兽等脊兽和仙人，据说它们有着神奇的避邪能力。"

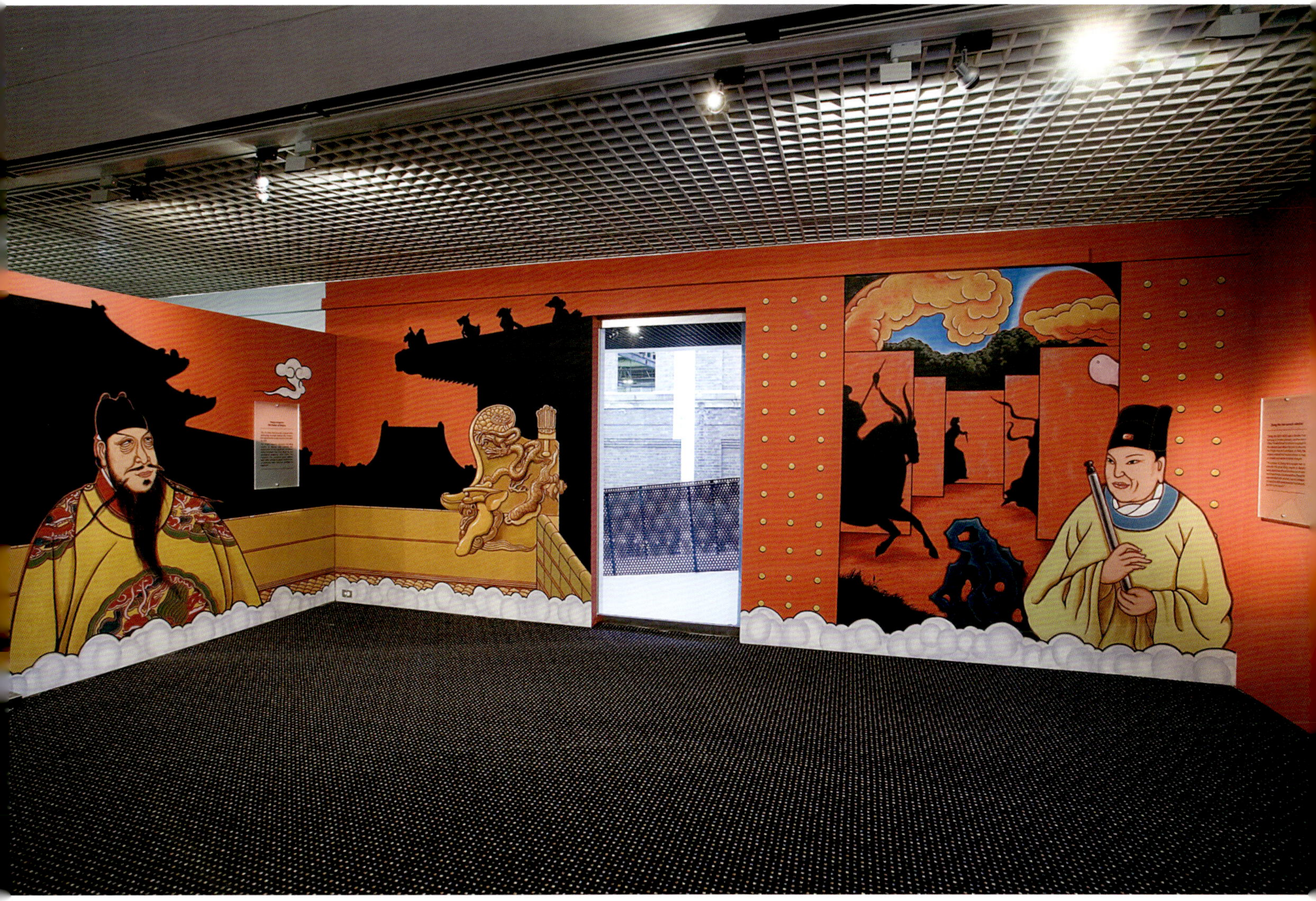

'Yongle Emperor: The Maker of Beijing' and 'Zheng He: The Eunuch Admiral', mural paintings.
Photograph: Marinco Kojdanovski, Powerhouse Museum, Sydney.

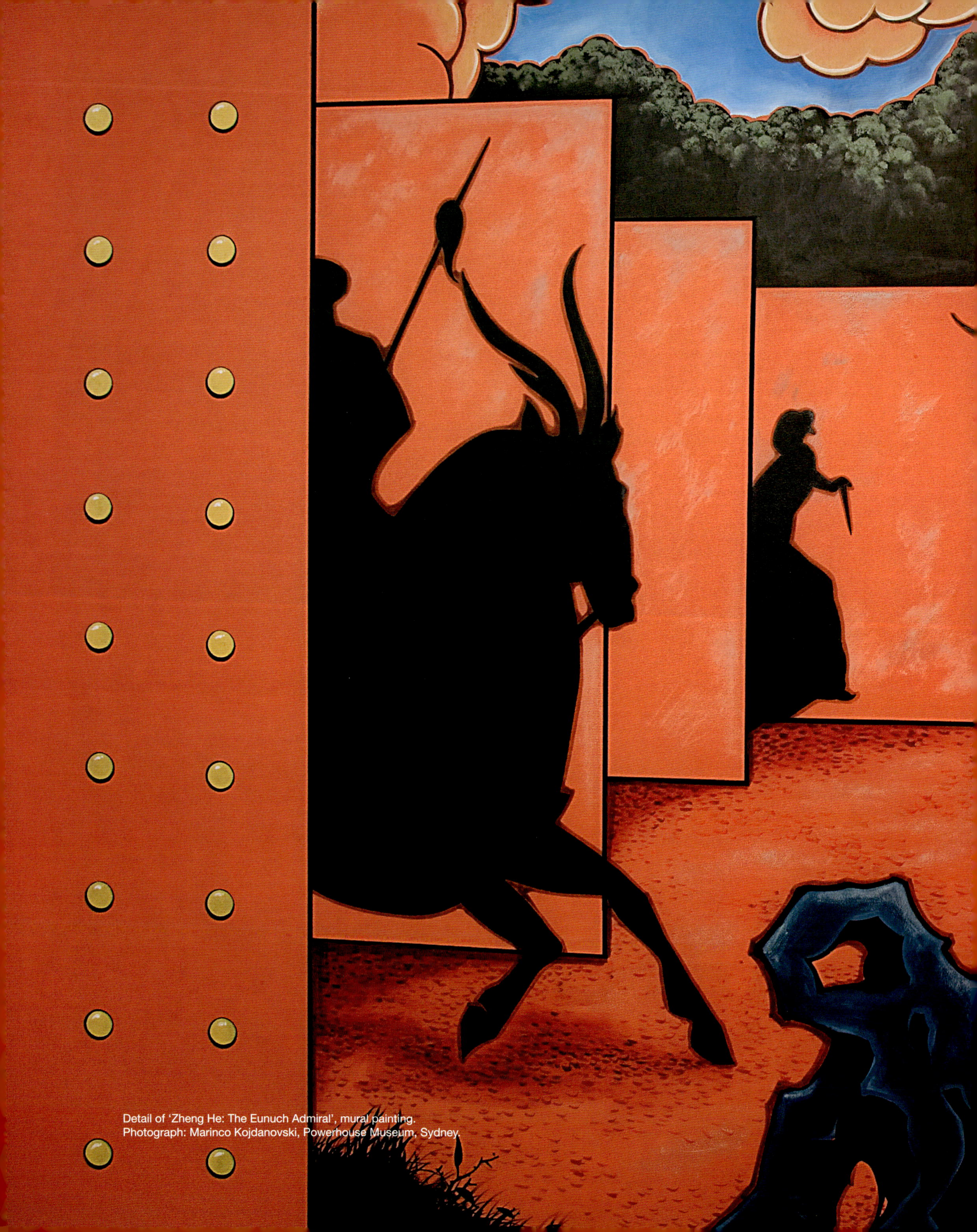

Detail of 'Zheng He: The Eunuch Admiral', mural painting.
Photograph: Marinco Kojdanovski, Powerhouse Museum, Sydney.

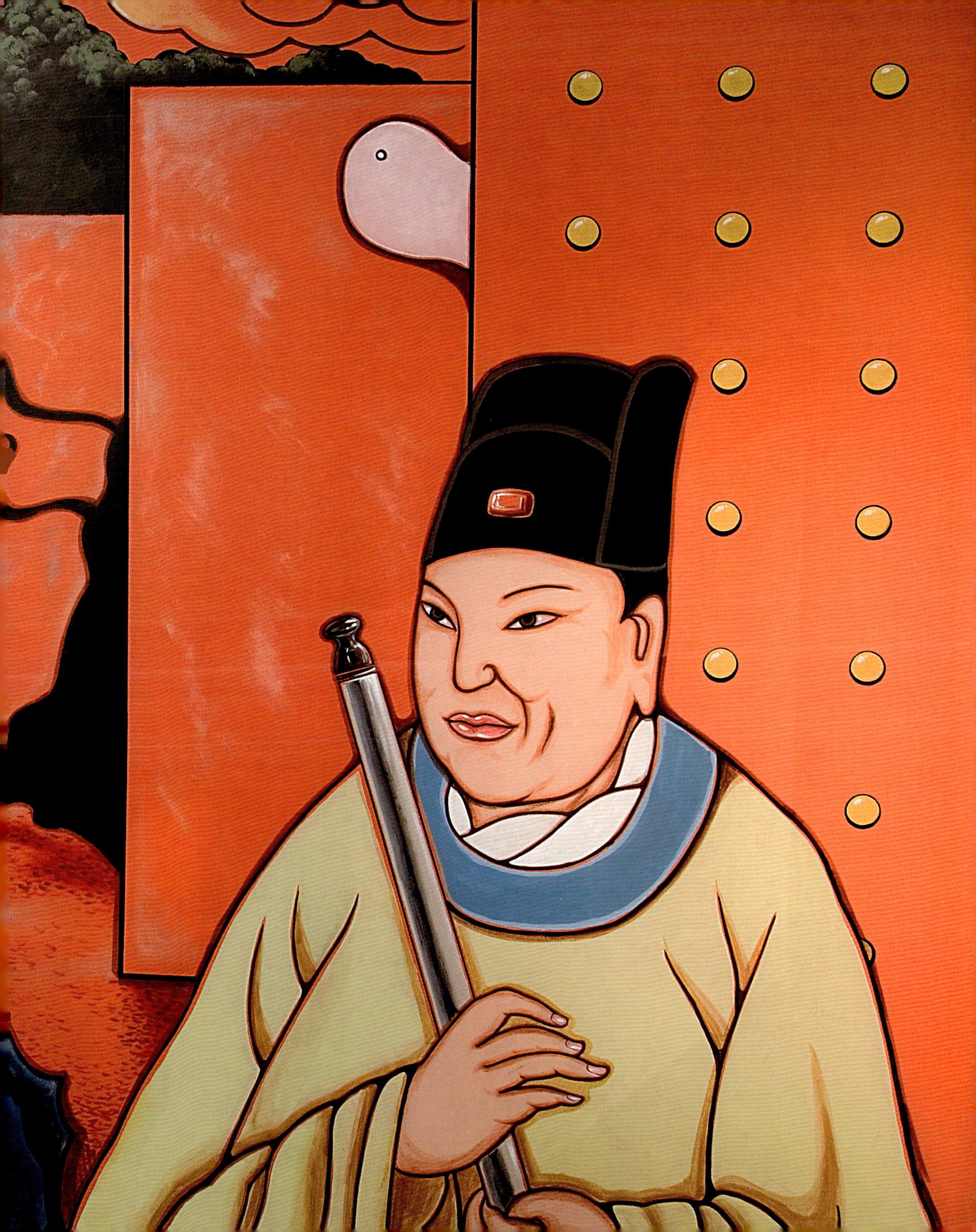

Zheng He: The Eunuch Admiral

'Zheng He (1371–1432) was a Muslim from Kunyang in Yunnan province, southwestern China. He was forced to become a eunuch in the imperial court where he rose to become the Yongle Emperor's confidant. In 1405, the emperor ordered his trusted adviser to lead an armada on a series of ocean voyages.

'The purpose of Zheng He's voyages was to promote the great Ming Empire in distant lands, and to search out precious goods and exotic specimens. It is said that Zheng He was also entrusted with a secret mission: to locate the dethroned imperial nephew and to put him to the sword.'

郑和：航海家与太监

"郑和（1371 年 –1432 年）是来自云南省晋宁县的穆斯林，幼年被阉割为太监。他后来在靖难之役立下了战功，在皇宫里升迁到永乐皇帝知己的地位。自 1405 年起，皇帝命他率领庞大的船队进行了多次远航。

"郑和航海的目的是向遥远的异域宣示大明帝国的权威，以及寻找奇珍异宝。但是根据《明史 · 郑和传》的记载，郑和的航海还负有秘密使命，那就是搜寻并且斩除被废黜的建文帝朱允炆。"

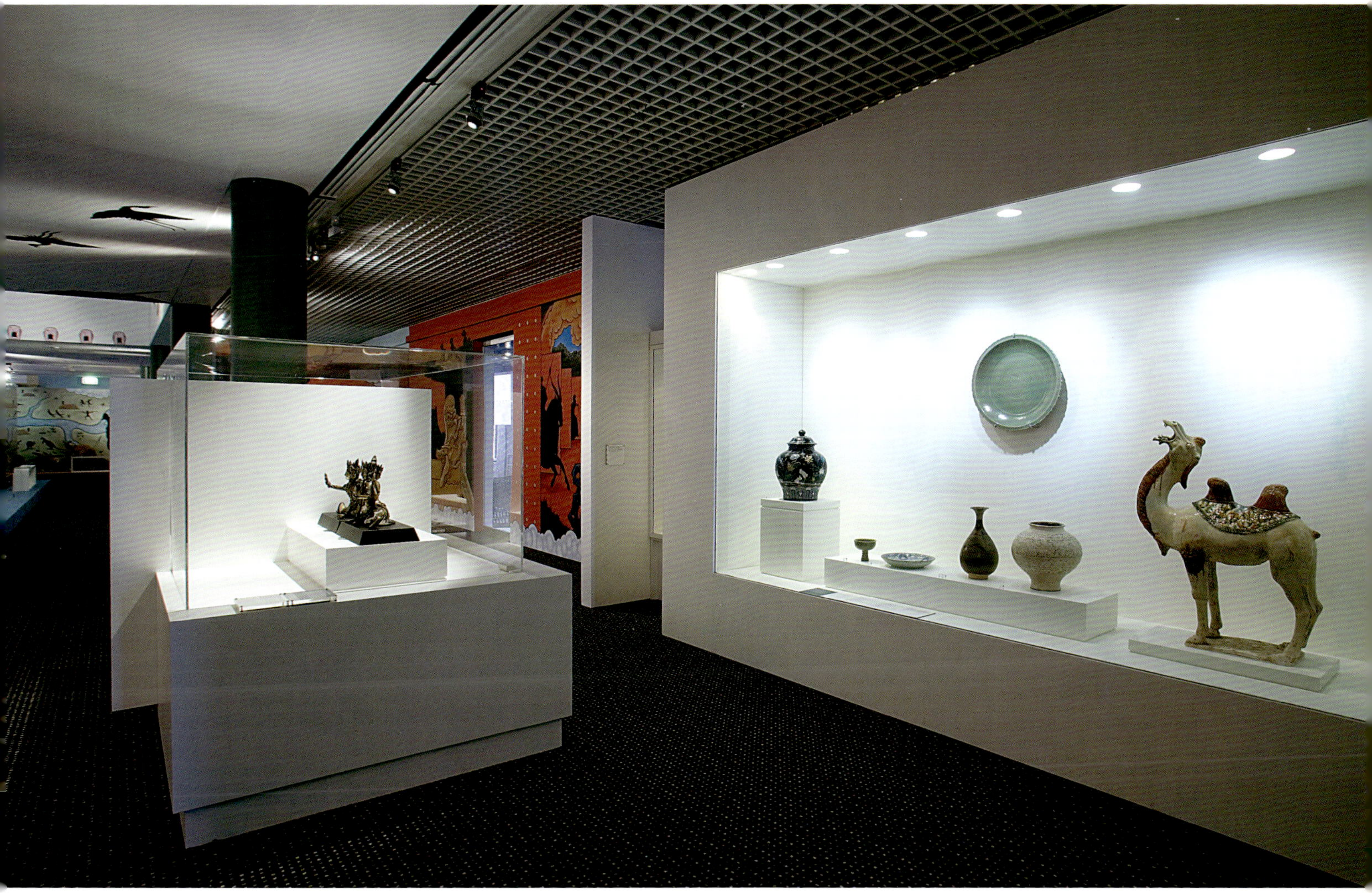

Chinese ceramic and Buddhist objects from the collection of the Powerhouse Museum.
Photograph: Marinco Kojdanovski, Powerhouse Museum, Sydney.

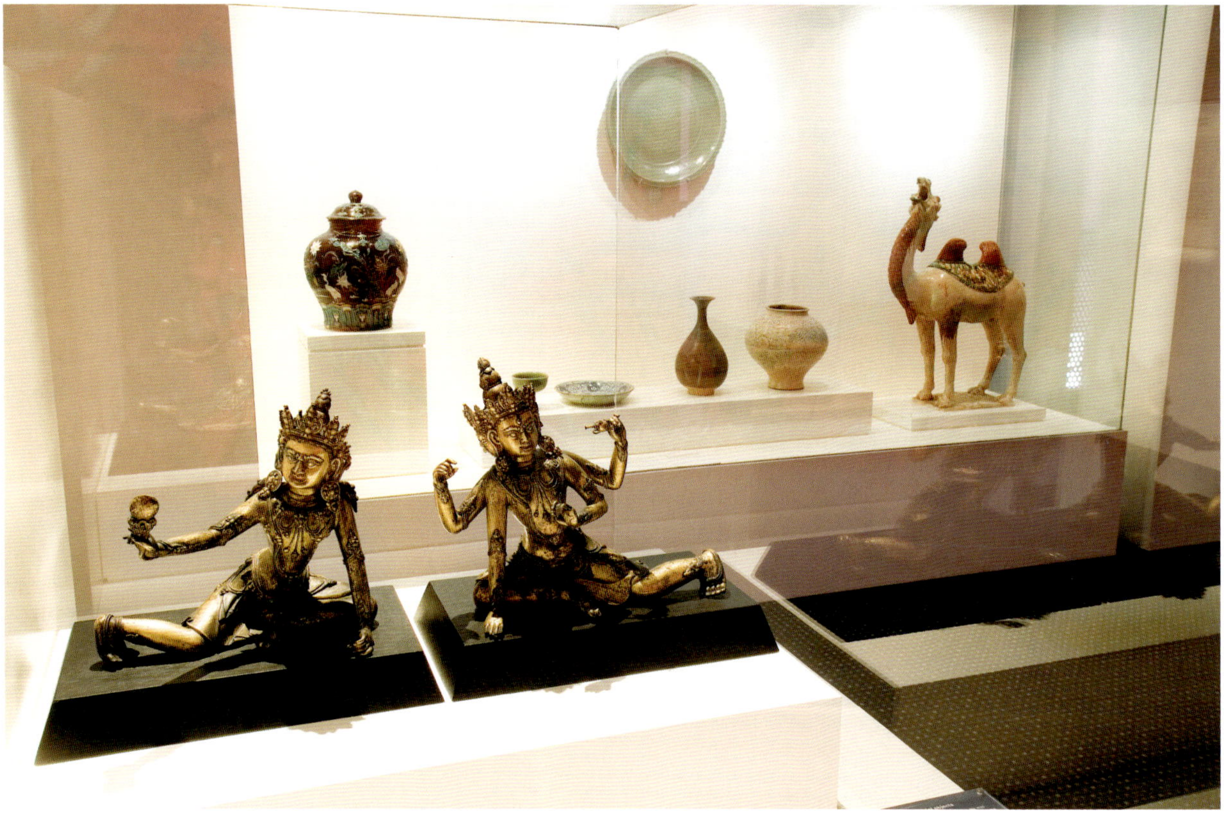

Buddhist and ceramic objects from the collection of the Powerhouse Museum.
Photograph: Marinco Kojdanovski, Powerhouse Museum, Sydney.

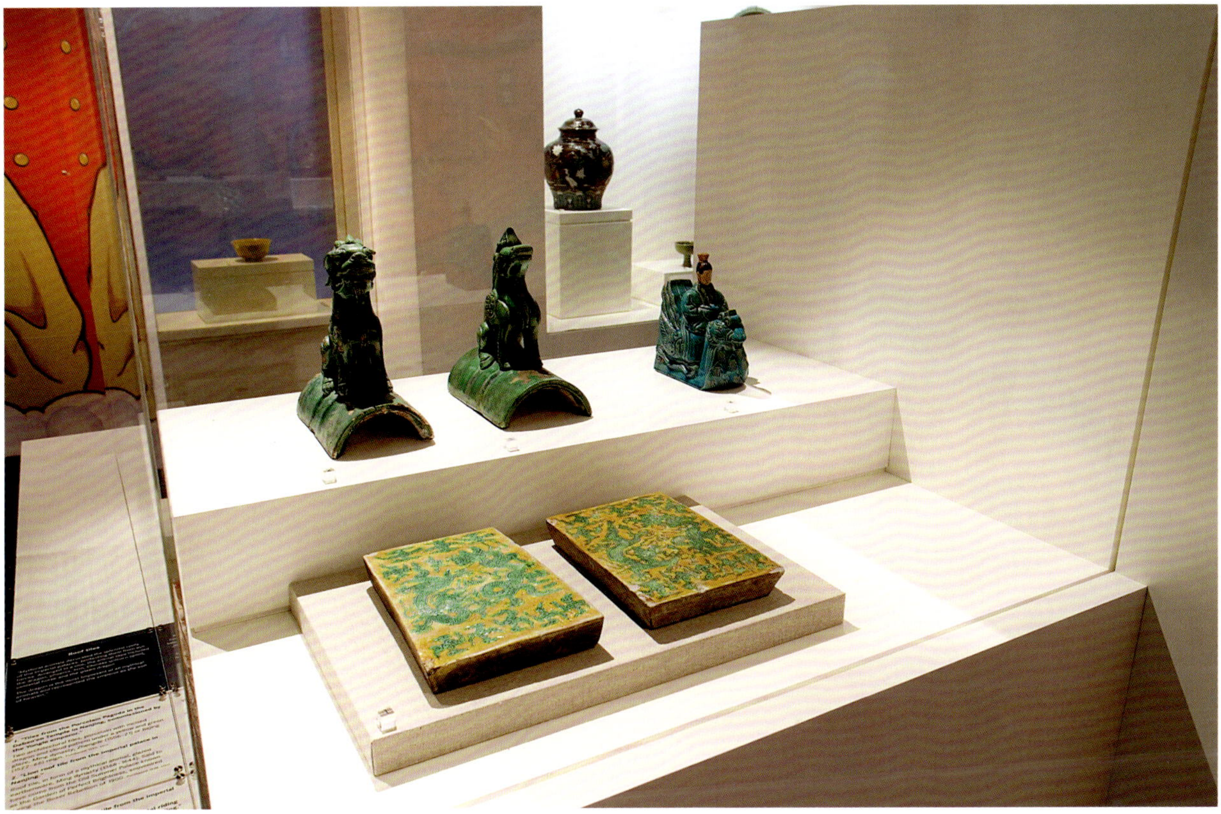

Chinese ceramics from the collection of the Powerhouse Museum.
Photograph: Marinco Kojdanovski, Powerhouse Museum, Sydney.

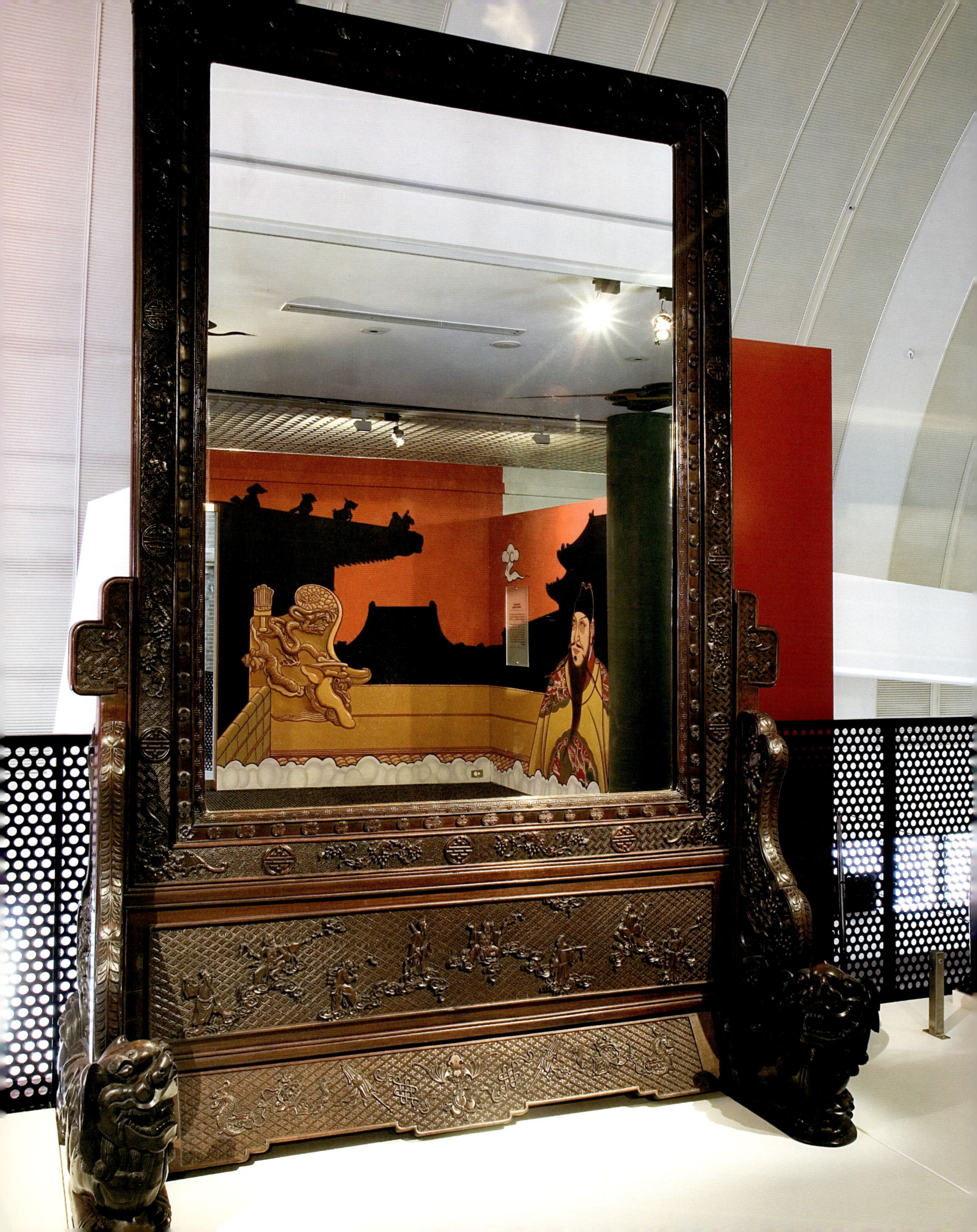

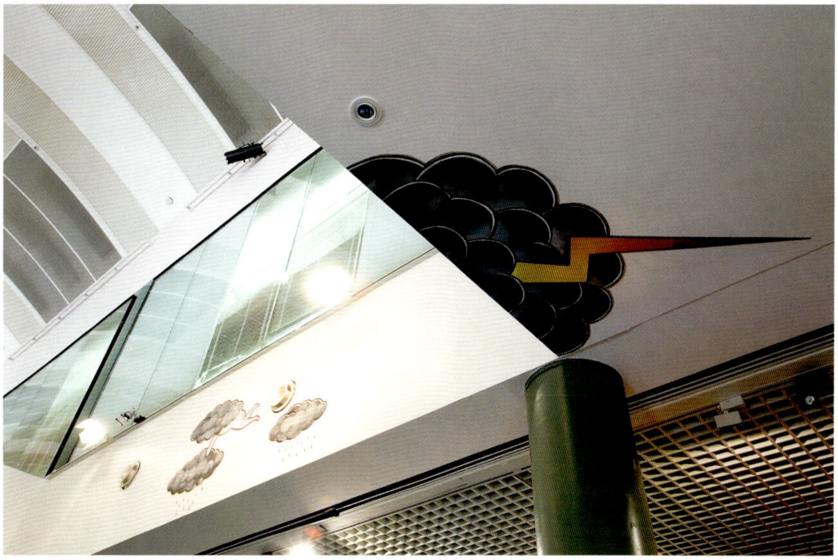

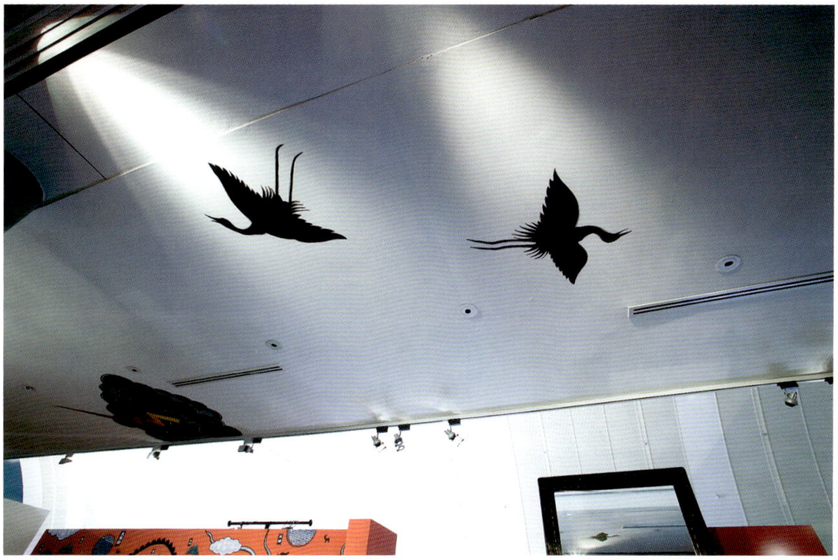

← Chinese mirror from the collection of the Powerhouse Museum.
Photograph: Jean-François Lanzarone, Powerhouse Museum, Sydney.
↑ Motifs painted on ceiling and other gallery surfaces.
Photograph: Marinco Kojdanovski, Powerhouse Museum, Sydney.

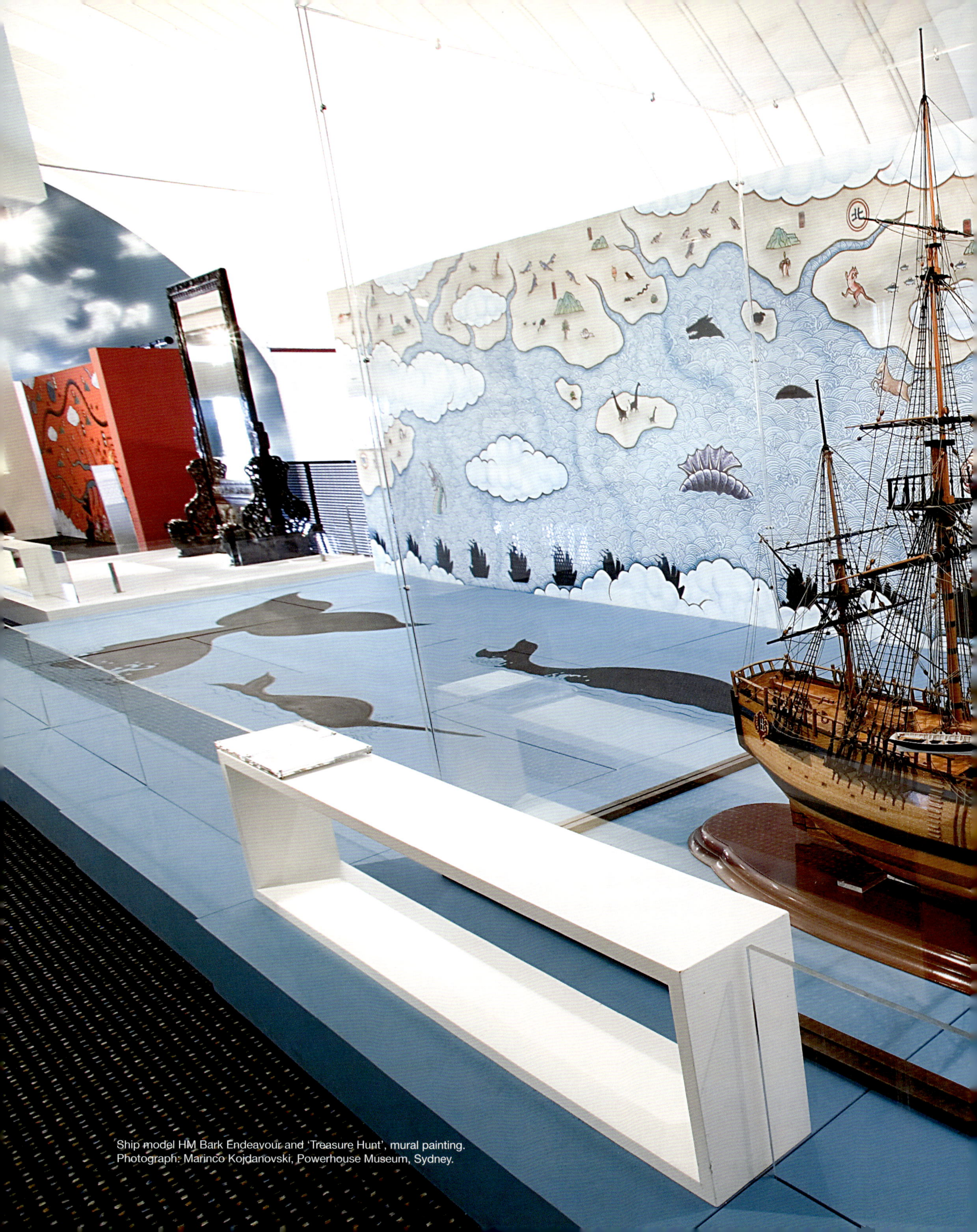

Ship model HM Bark Endeavour and 'Treasure Hunt', mural painting.
Photograph: Marinco Kojdanovski, Powerhouse Museum, Sydney.

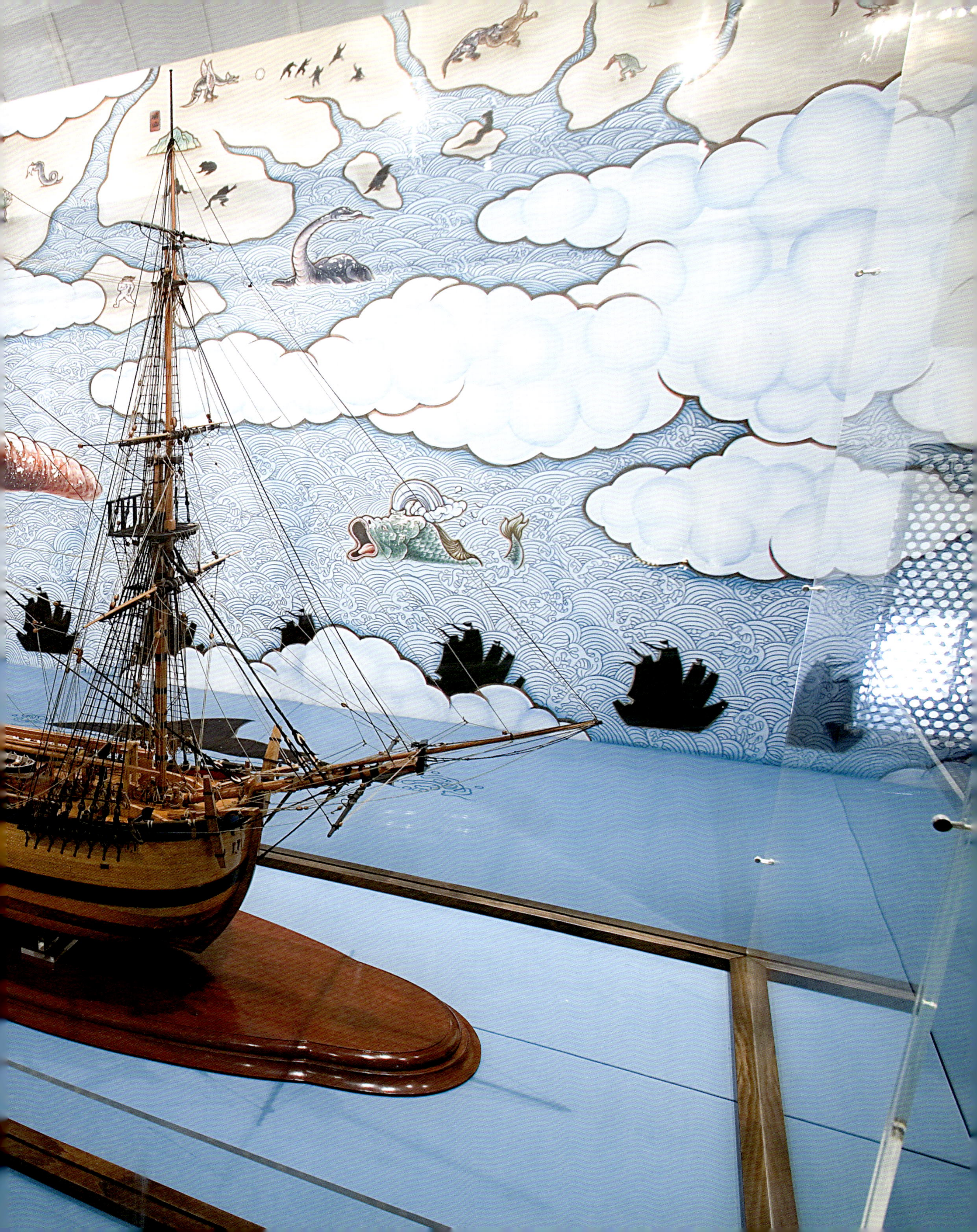

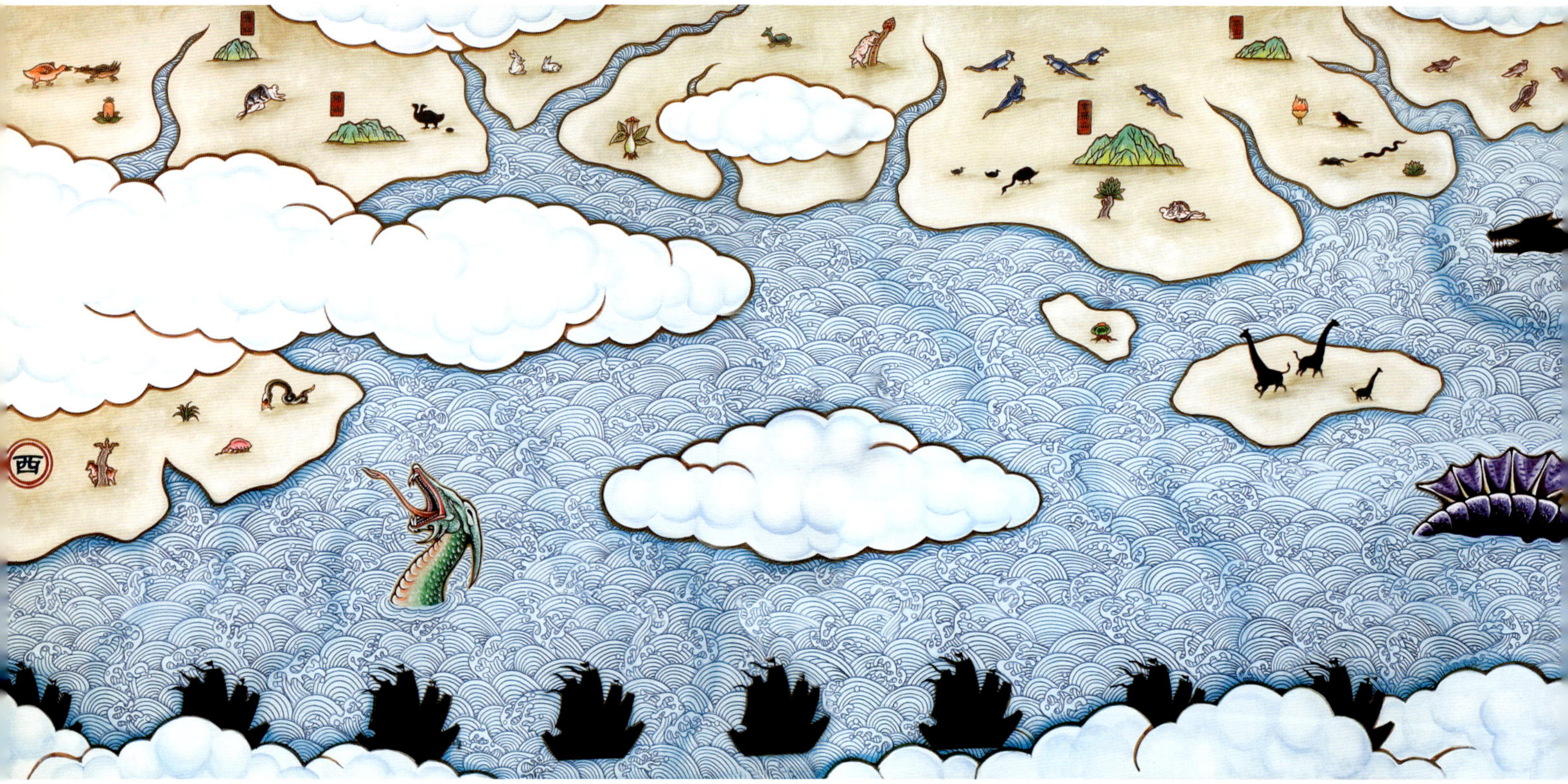
西

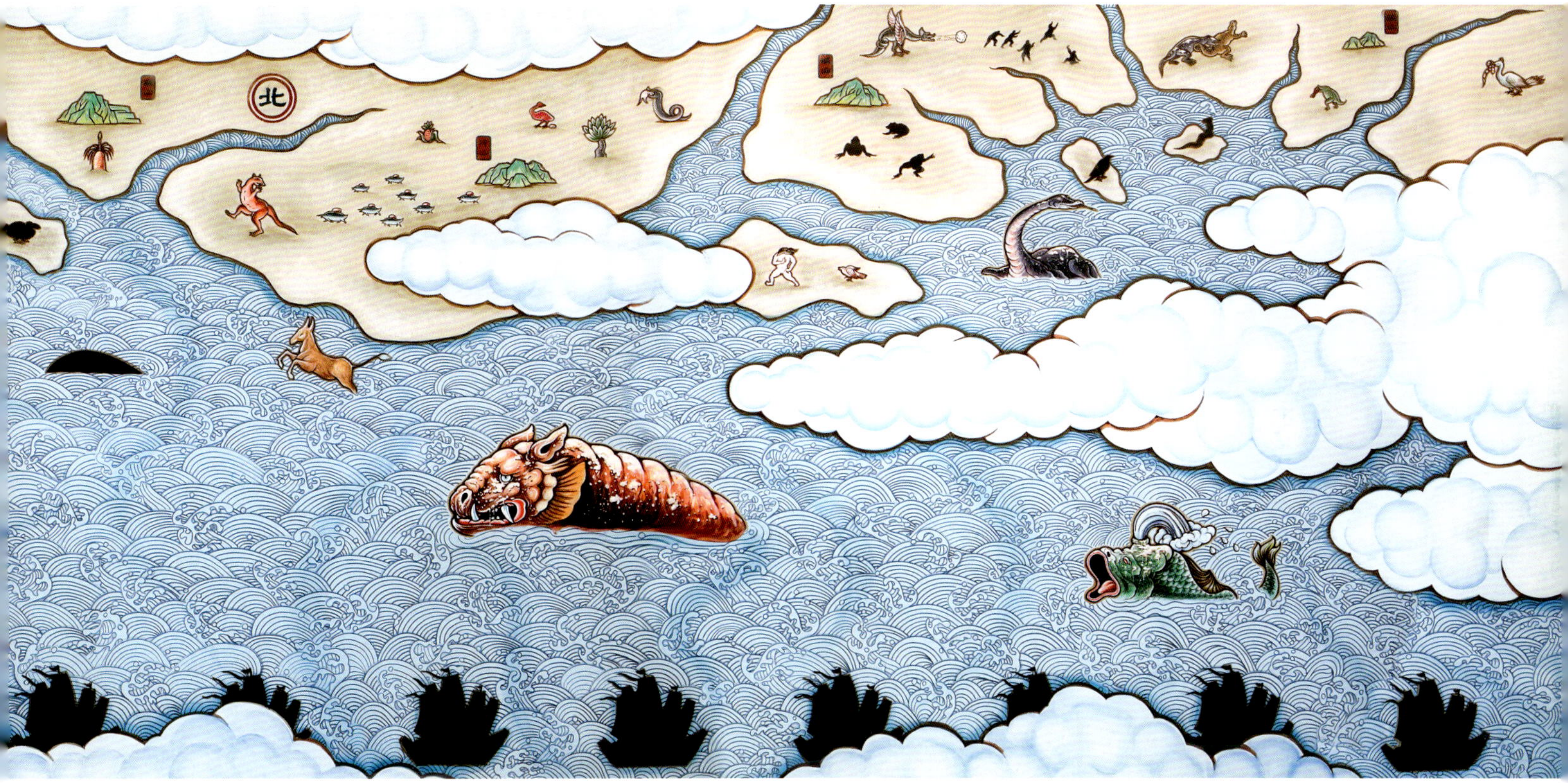

'Treasure Hunt', mural painting.
Photograph: Jean-François Lanzarone, Powerhouse Museum, Sydney.

Treasure Hunt

'The eunuch admiral Zheng He led a legendary fleet of "treasure ships" and thousands of men and set sail for foreign lands. Over nearly three decades, from 1405 to 1433, Zheng He made a series of official voyages, visiting numerous strange and wonderful places.

'Zheng He and his men collected rare spices, marvellous treasures and wondrous birds and animals. They documented the exotic plants, animals and peoples that they saw. On these voyages Zheng He and his crew navigated new ocean routes and created beautiful nautical maps.'

寻宝

三宝太监郑和率领他成千上万的船员驾驶传奇宝船起航，驶向遥远的海外。自 1405 年至 1433 年，郑和先后完成了七次远航，访问了西太平洋和印度洋地区的许多陌生并且令人惊奇的地方。

"郑和与他的船队在异域带回了稀有香料、奇珍瑰宝和珍禽异兽，接触并且记录了海外的植物、动物和风俗民情。在航海活动中，郑和与他的船队探索了新的远洋航线，绘制了精美的海图。"

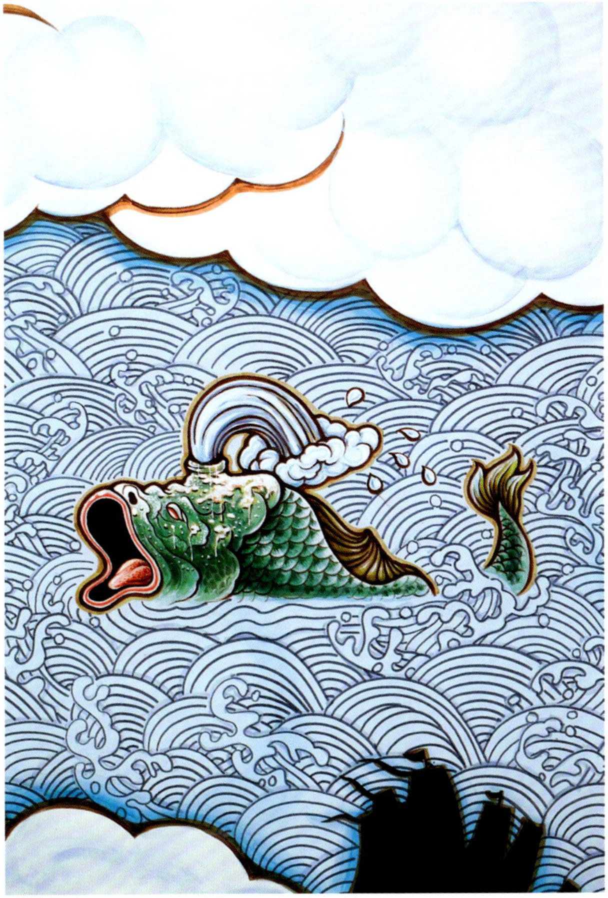

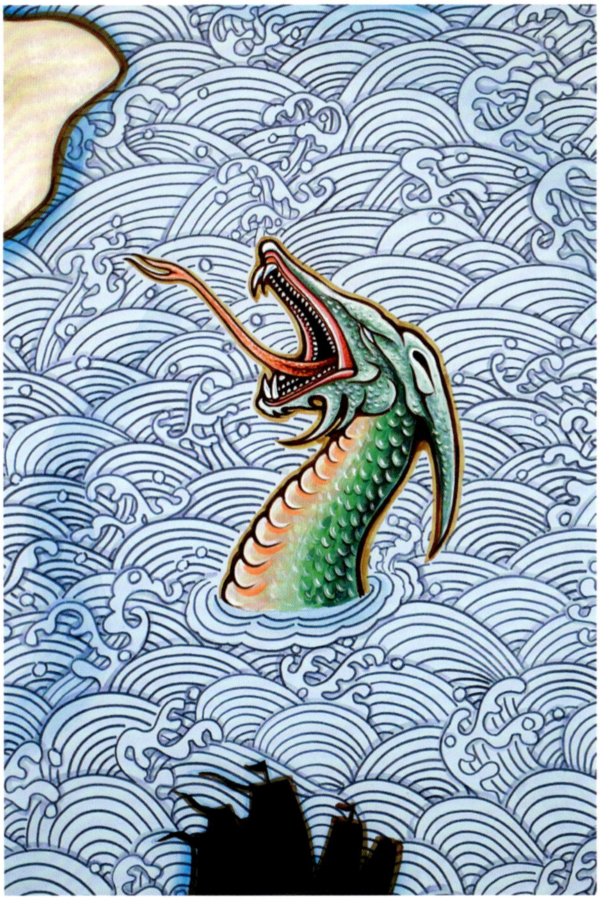

Details of 'Treasure Hunt', mural painting.
Photograph: Jean-François Lanzarone, Powerhouse Museum, Sydney.

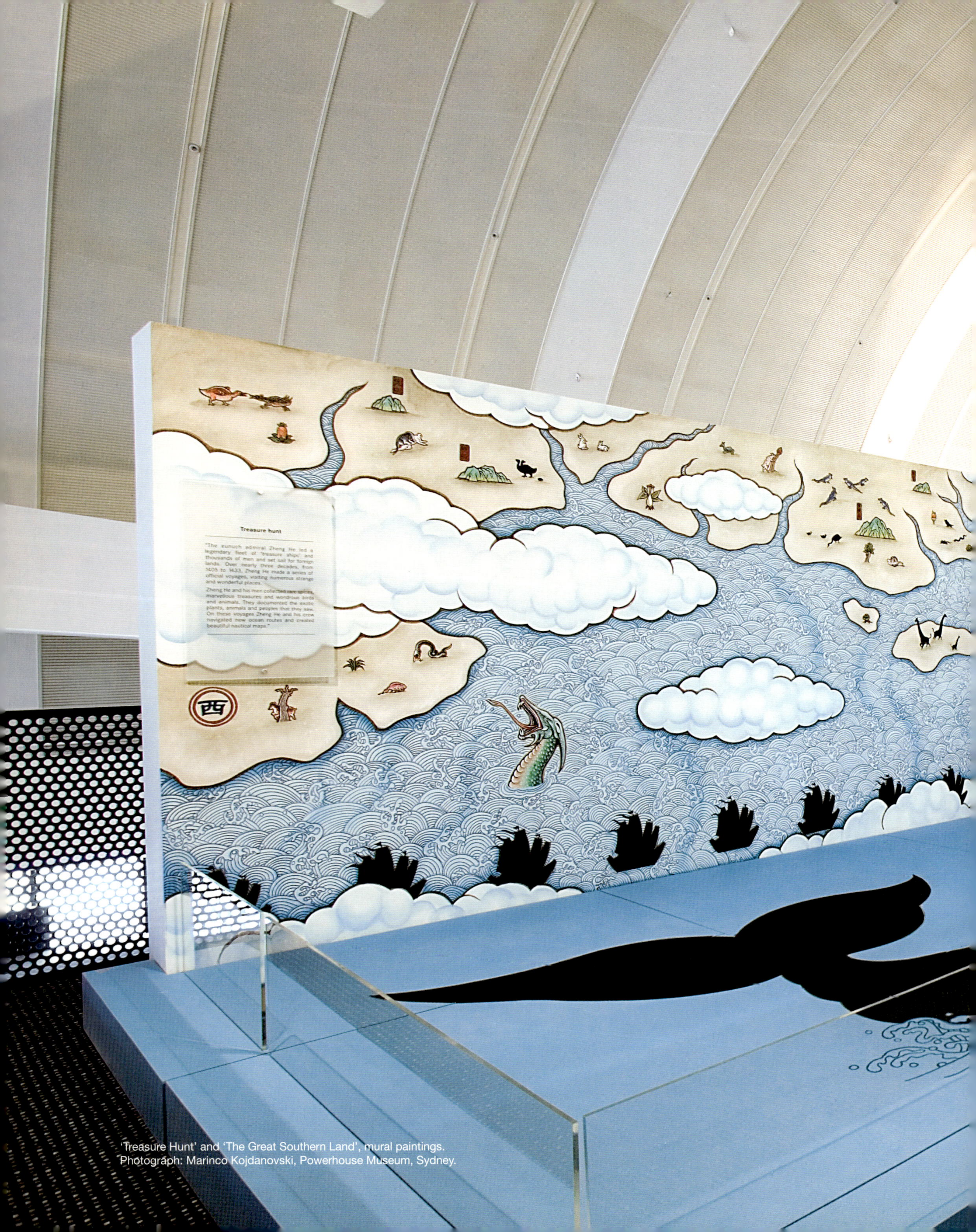

'Treasure Hunt' and 'The Great Southern Land', mural paintings.
Photograph: Marinco Kojdanovski, Powerhouse Museum, Sydney.

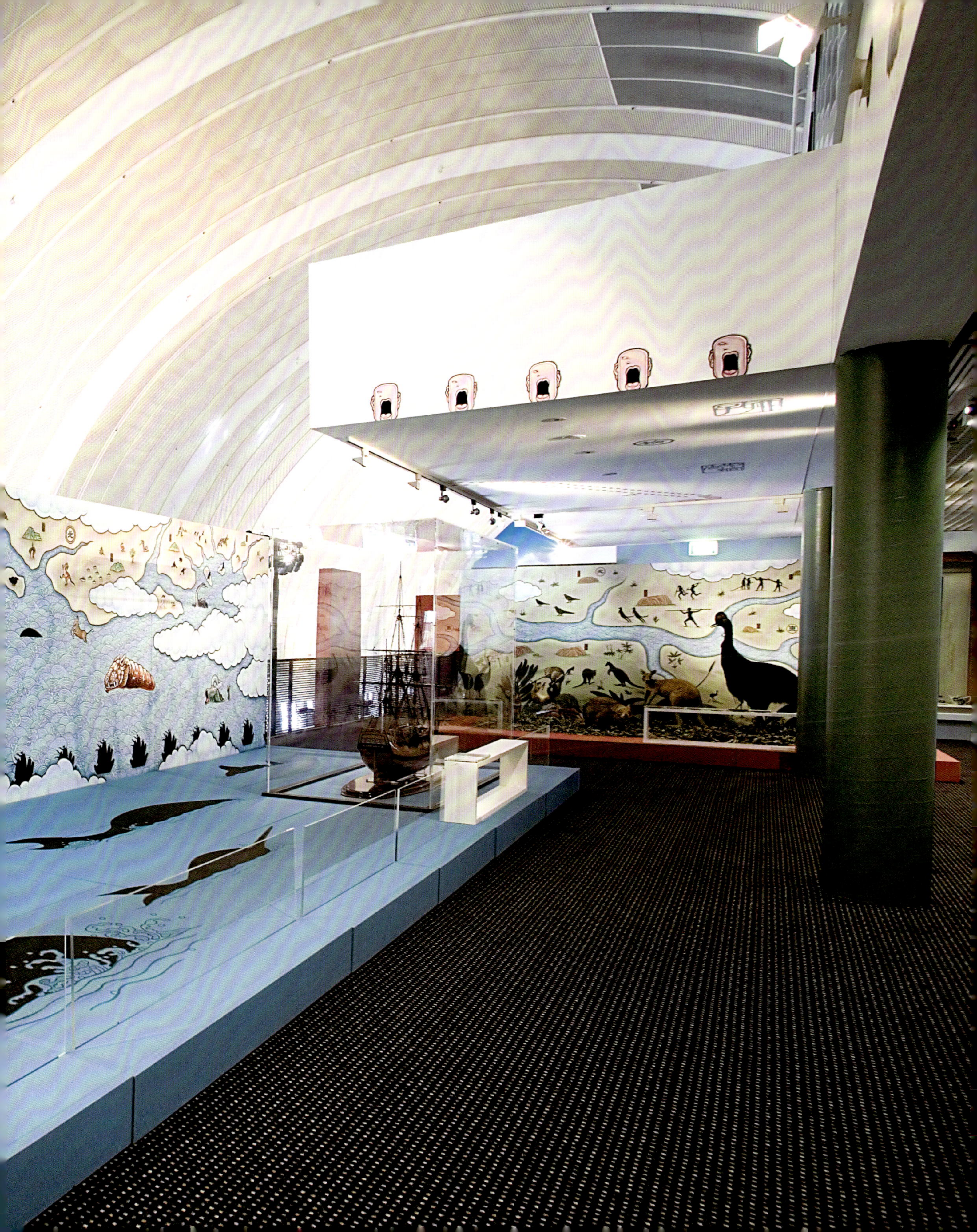

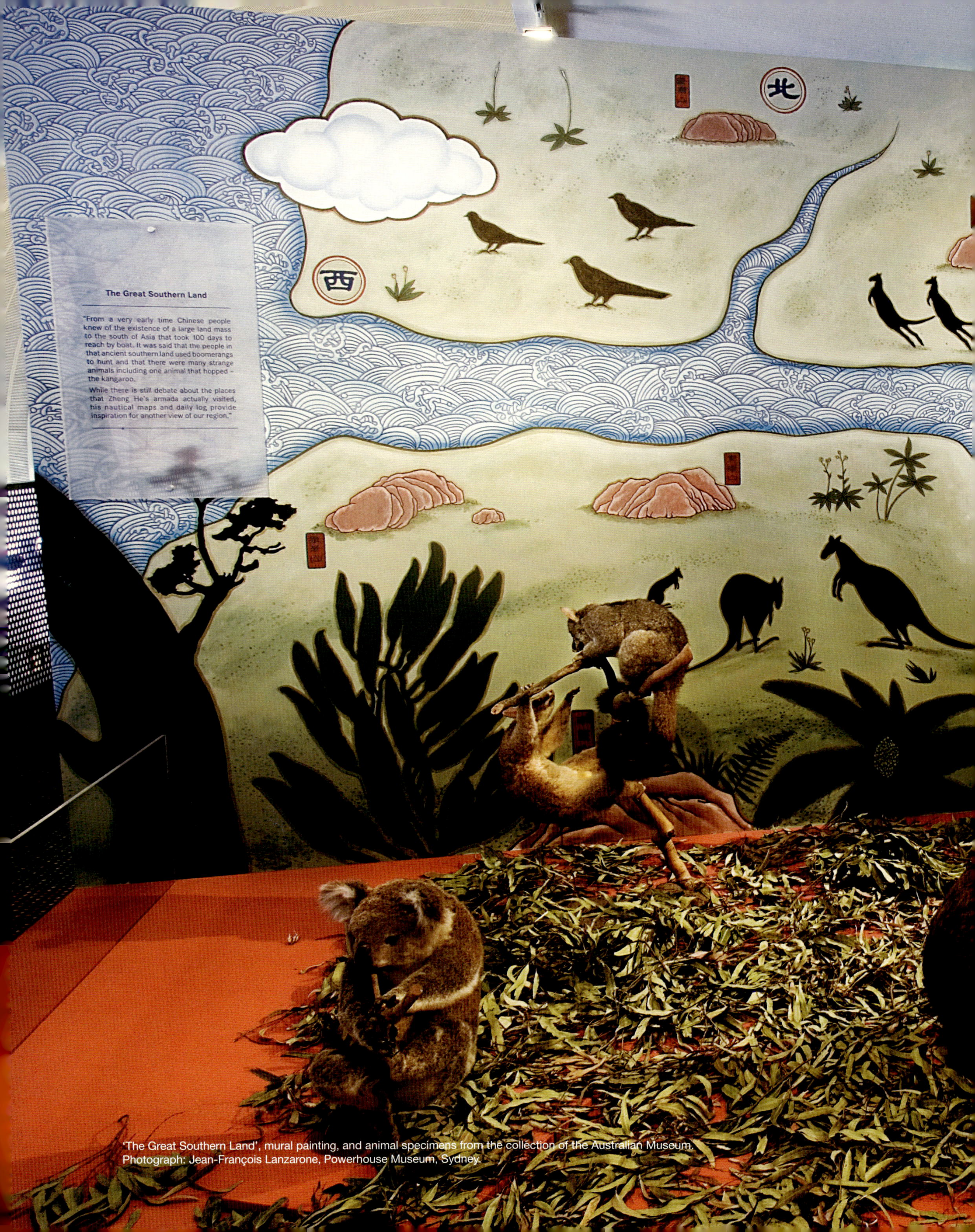

'The Great Southern Land', mural painting, and animal specimens from the collection of the Australian Museum. Photograph: Jean-François Lanzarone, Powerhouse Museum, Sydney.

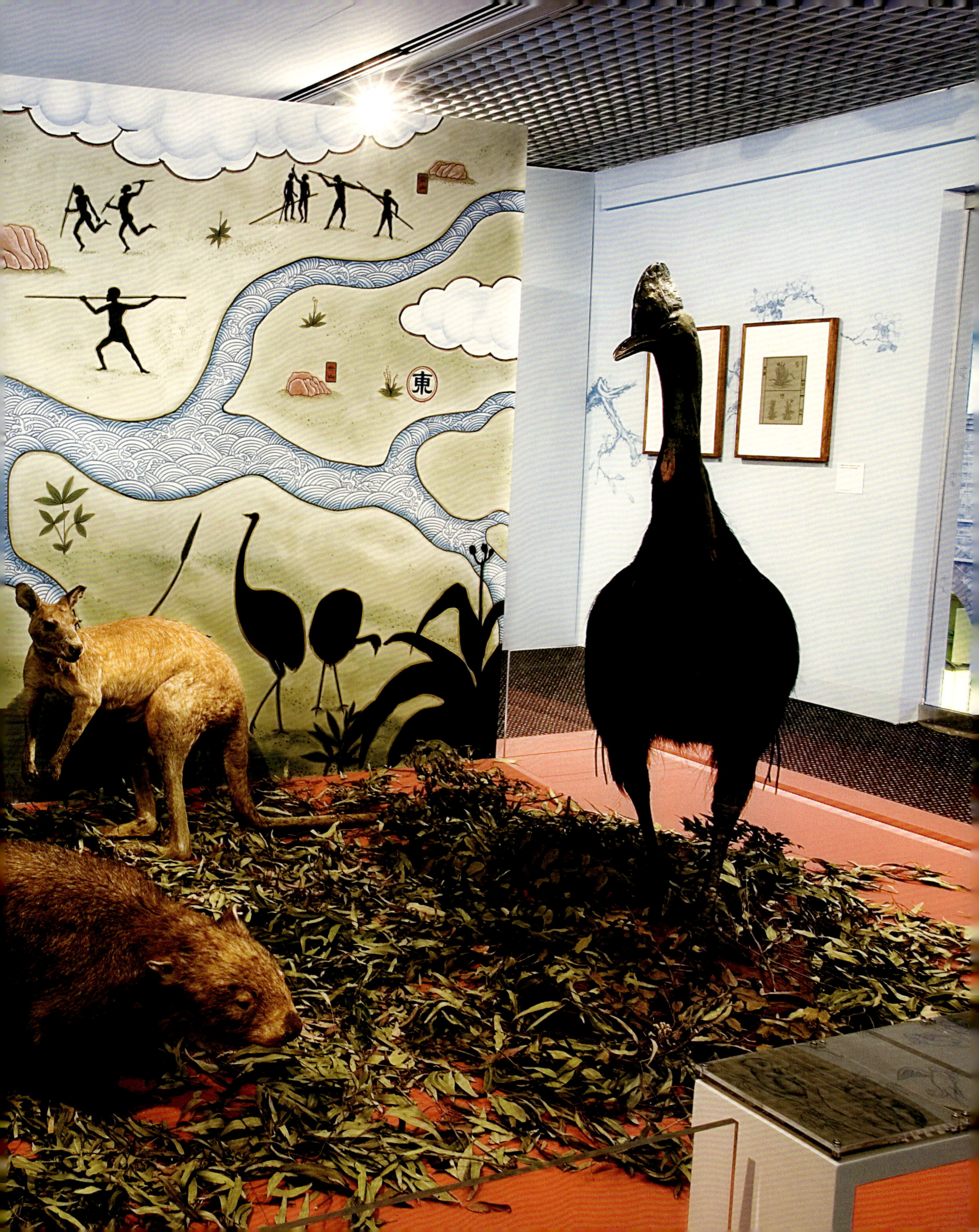
東

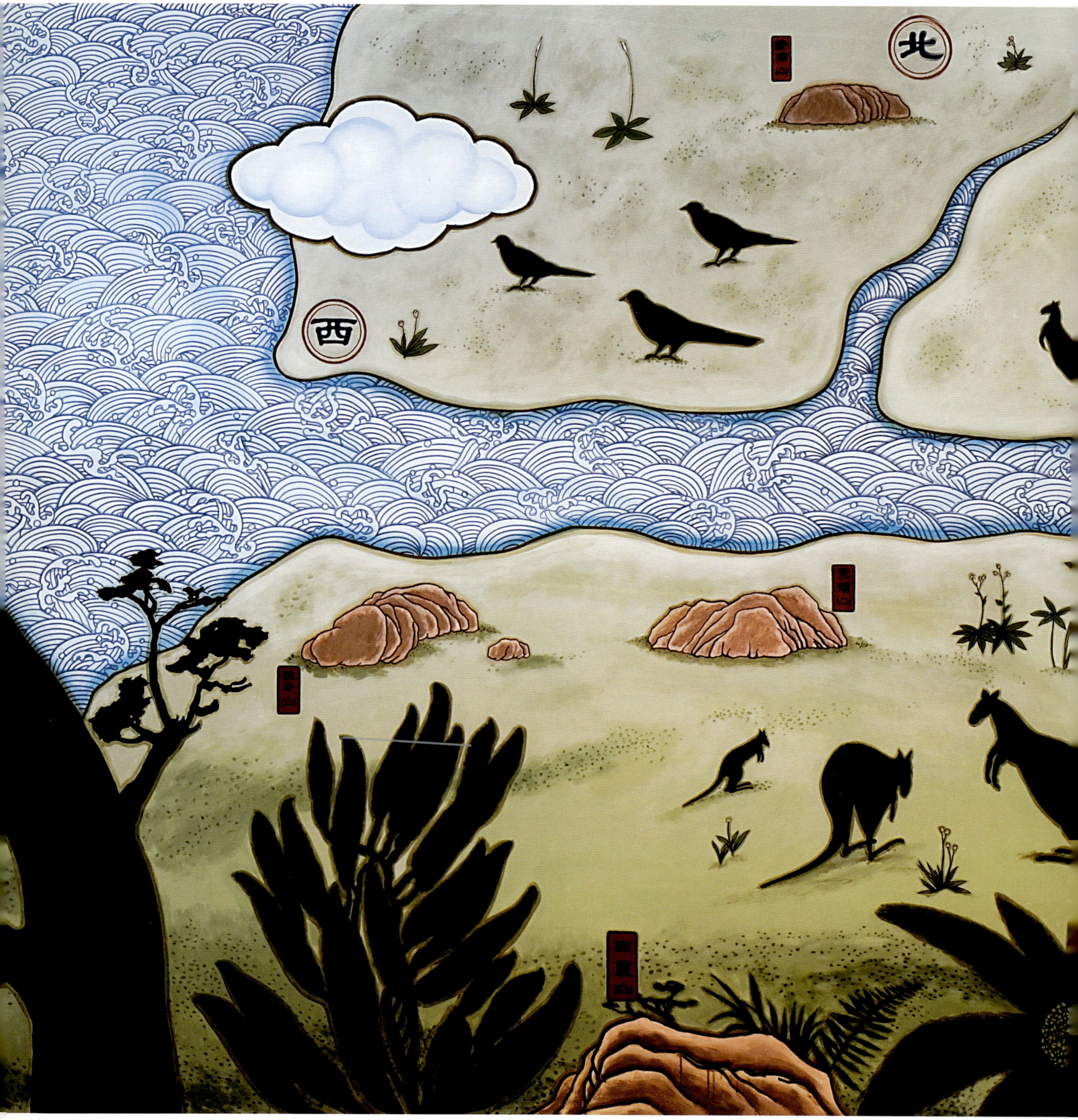
北
西

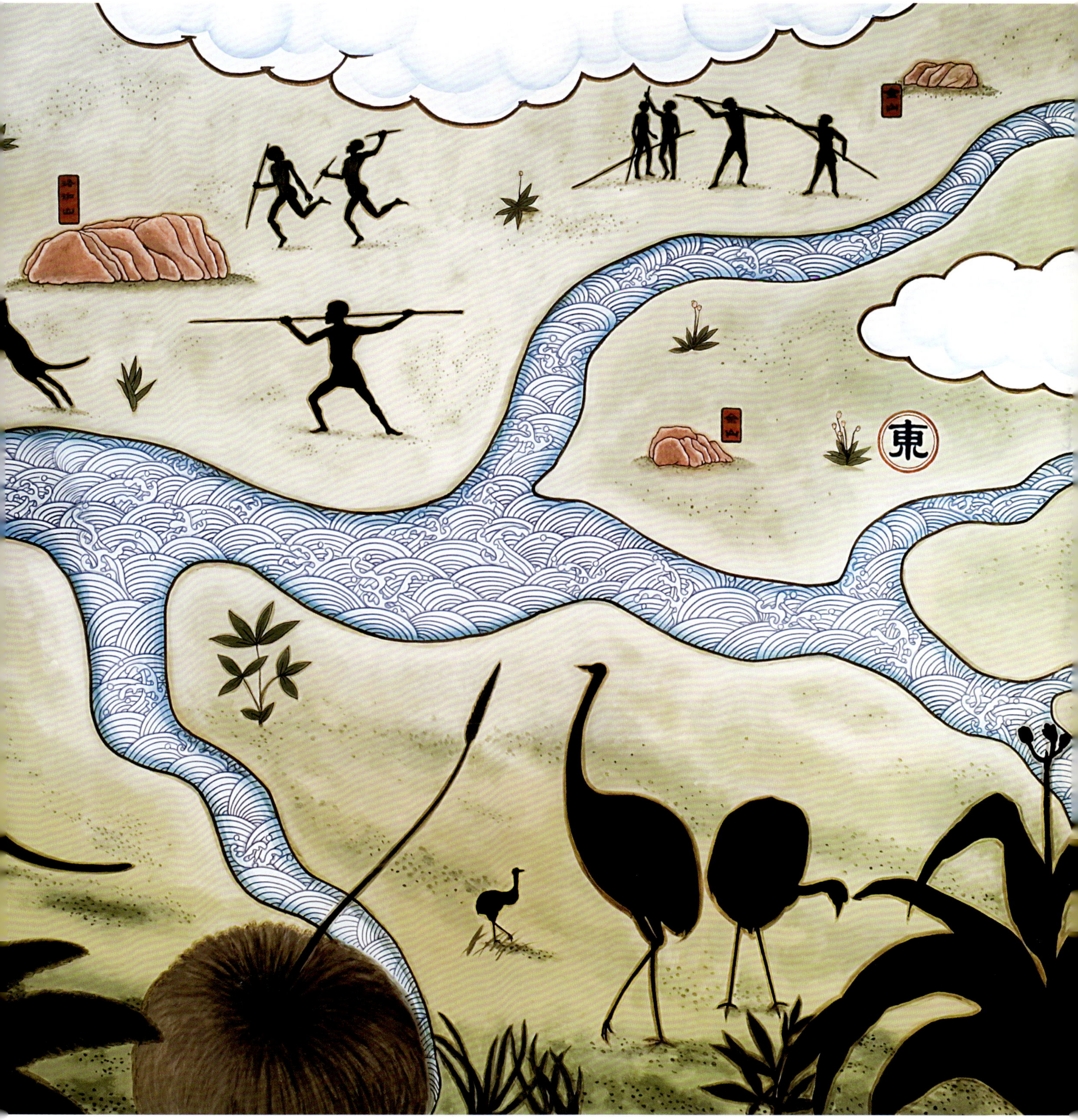

Detail of 'The Great Southern Land', mural painting.
Photograph: Jean-François Lanzarone, Powerhouse Museum, Sydney.

The Great Southern Land

'From a very early time Chinese people knew of the existence of a large landmass to the south of Asia that took 100 days to reach by boat. It was said that the people in that ancient southern land used boomerangs to hunt and that there were many strange animals including an animal that hopped—the kangaroo.

'While there is still debate about the places that Zheng He and his armada actually visited, his nautical maps and daily log provide inspiration for another view of our region.'

辽阔的南方大陆

自从很久以前，中国人就知道在我们的大陆的南面还有另外一块大陆存在，认为从中国的南方沿海到那里需要行船百天。在传说中，自古居住在那片南方大陆的人们会使用飞去来器狩猎，而他们的猎物是对于中国人来说很陌生的动物，包括用后肢跳跃前行的动物——袋鼠。

"虽然人们对于郑和与他的船队是否确实抵达过着这片辽阔的南方大陆存在争议，这些先驱者留下的海图和航行日志却能为我们使用另一种眼光重新观察和构建历史提供灵感。"

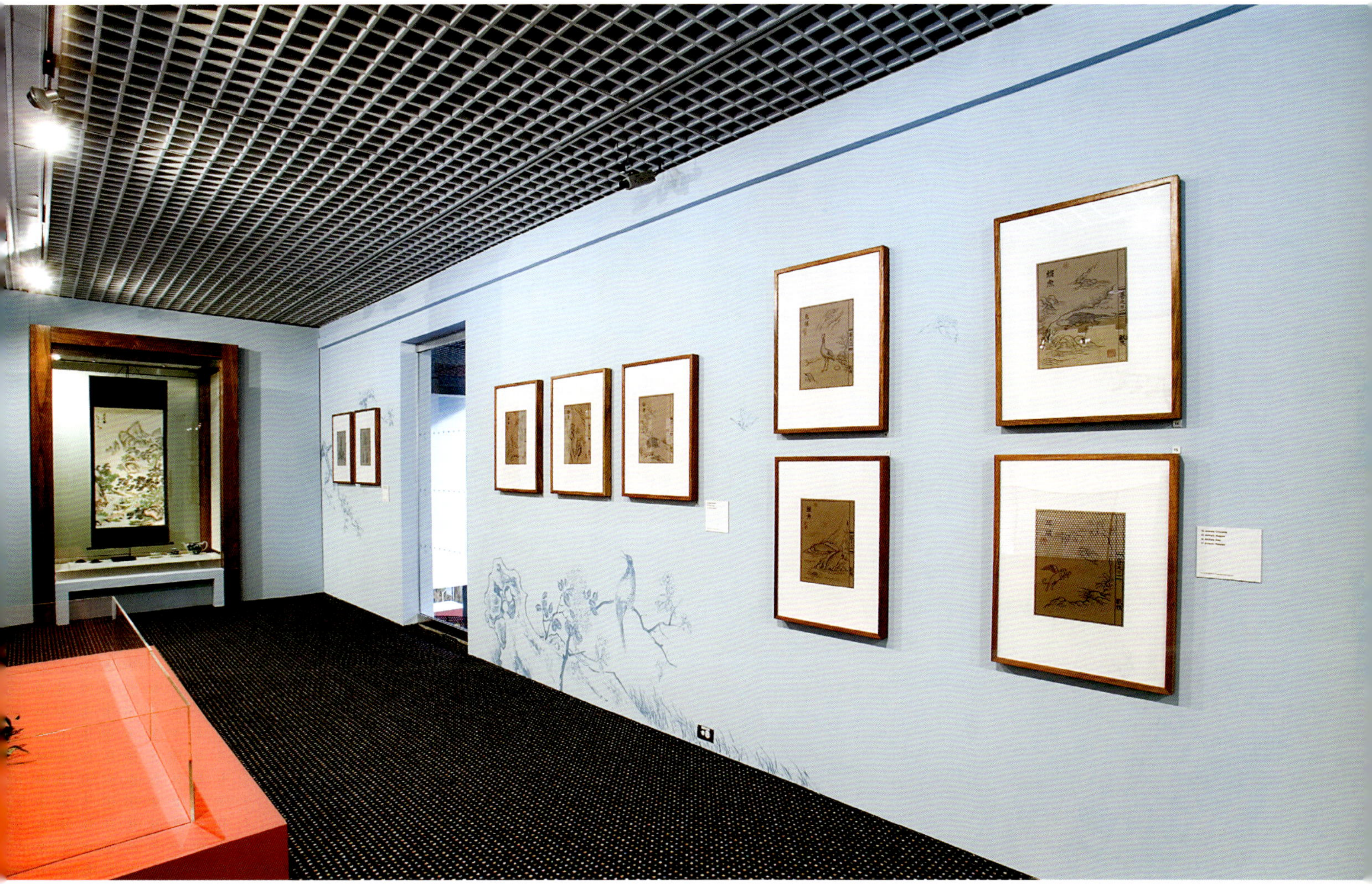

'Animals' and 'Medicinal Herbs', works on paper by Guan Wei.
Photograph: Marinco Kojdanovski, Powerhouse Museum, Sydney.

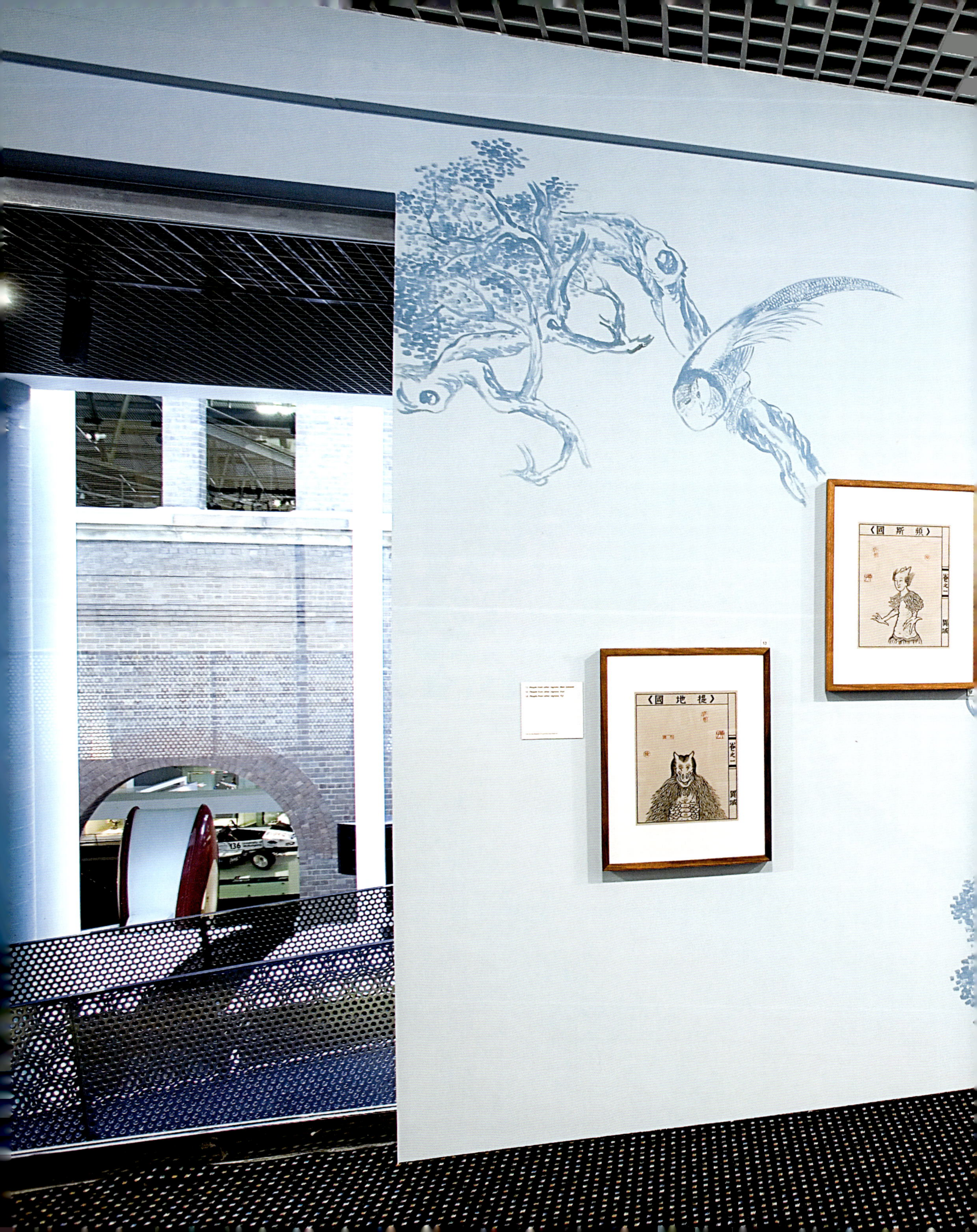

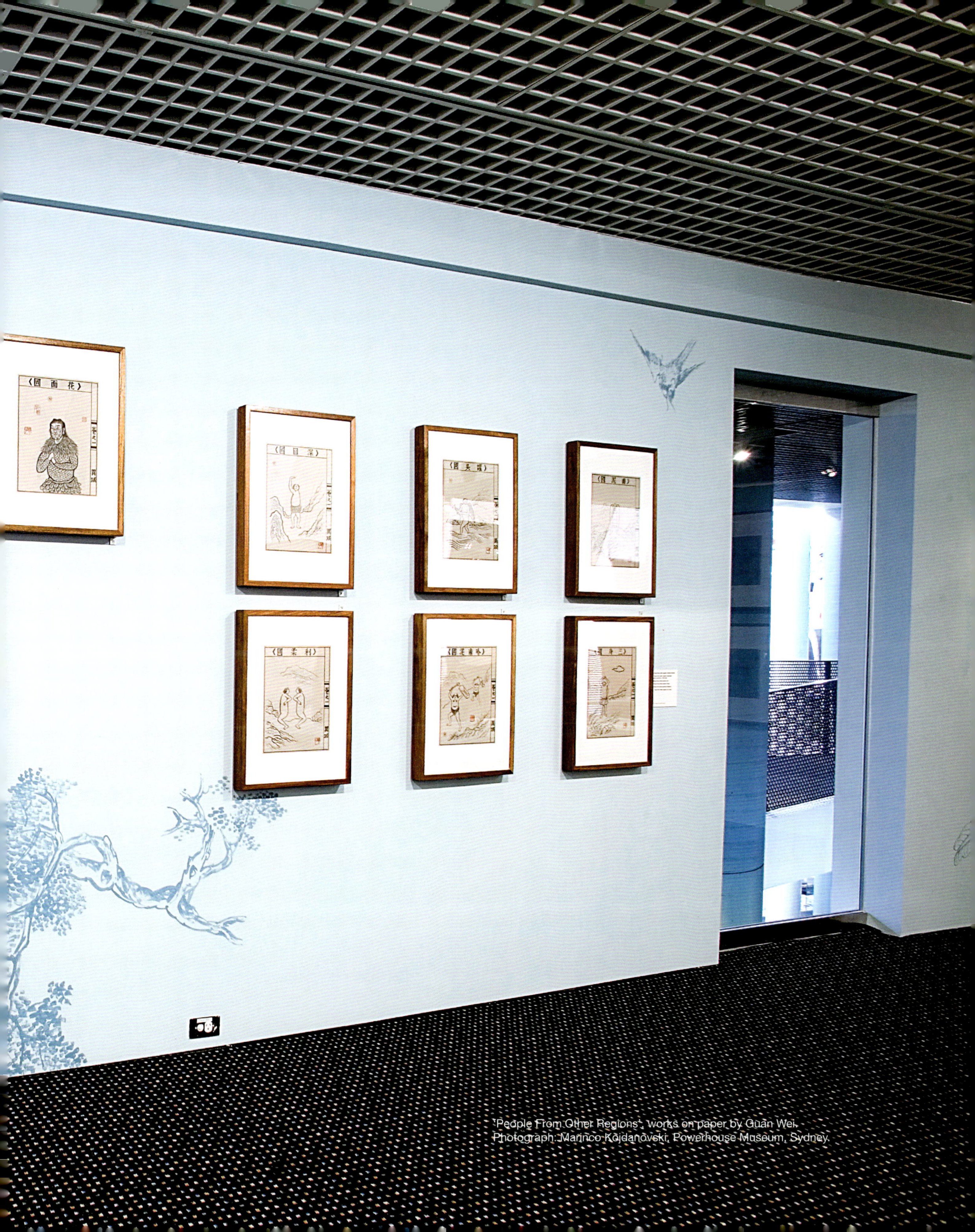

'People From Other Regions', works on paper by Guan Wei.
Photograph: Marinco Kojdanovski, Powerhouse Museum, Sydney.

Unfamiliar Lands

'Ma Huan was a Muslim scholar who accompanied Zheng He on a number of the voyages as an interpreter and clerk. He famously wrote about the exotic sights he encountered in Southeast Asia, recording information about geography, weather conditions, the environment and local customs.

'Some say Ma Huan and Zheng He's treasure ships travelled as far as the Middle East, and even to the Antipodes. Ma Huan's marvellous records written some 600 years ago have the power to fire the imagination and stimulate artistic creation.'

陌生的陆地

穆斯林学者马欢是多次随同郑和出海的译员，在他的著作《瀛涯胜览》中详细地记载着他和船员们在东南亚和阿拉伯地区的各种见闻，以及沿途的地理、气候、环境和税制等情形。

"据说郑和的宝船远航到中东地区之后，曾经横过赤道抵达南太平洋的澳大利亚和新西兰地区。不论如何，马欢 600 年前的杰出著作是激发我们想象和激励艺术创作的璀璨的火花。"

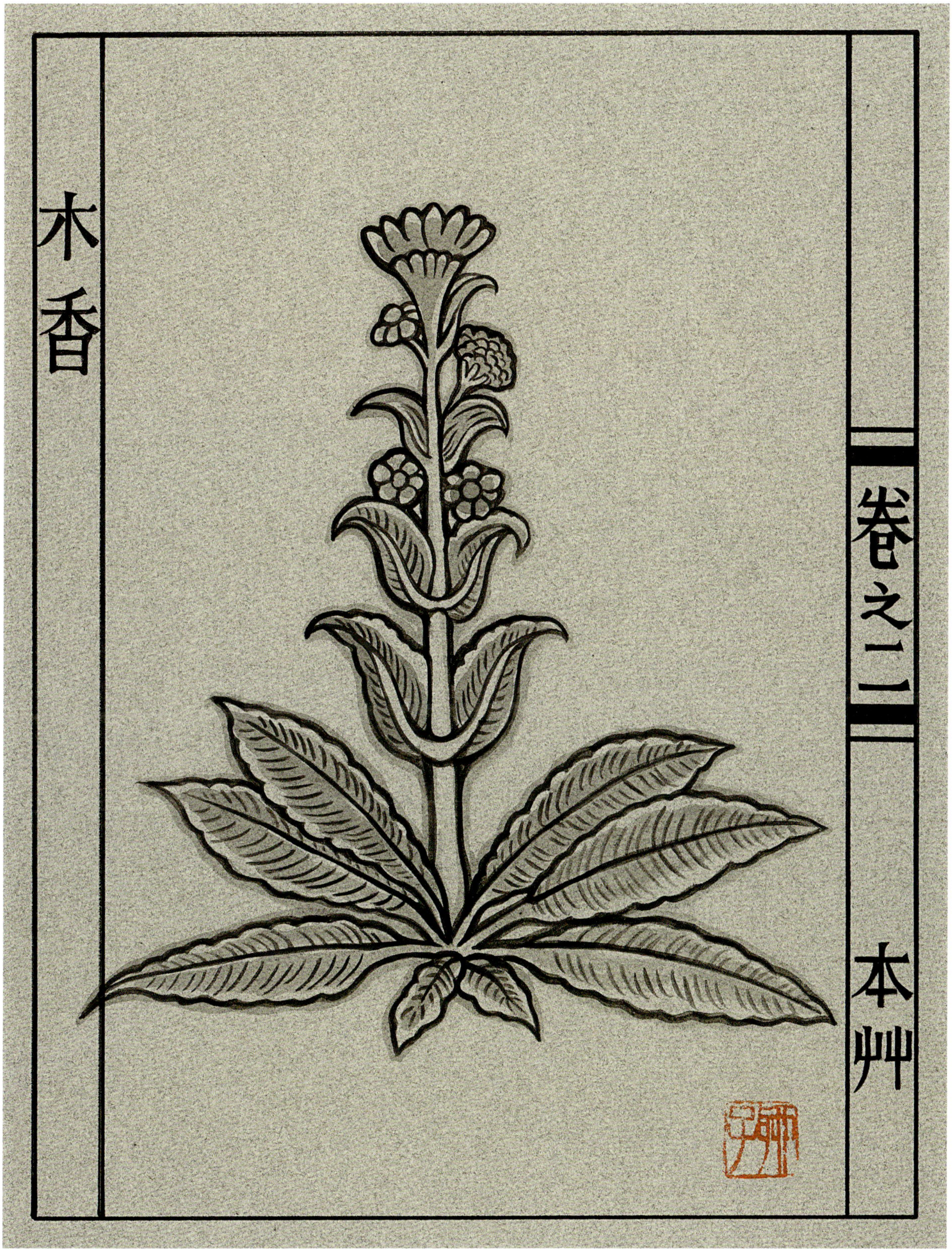

'Medicinal Herb: Aucklandia lappa', work on paper by Guan Wei.
Photograph: courtesy of Guan Wei.

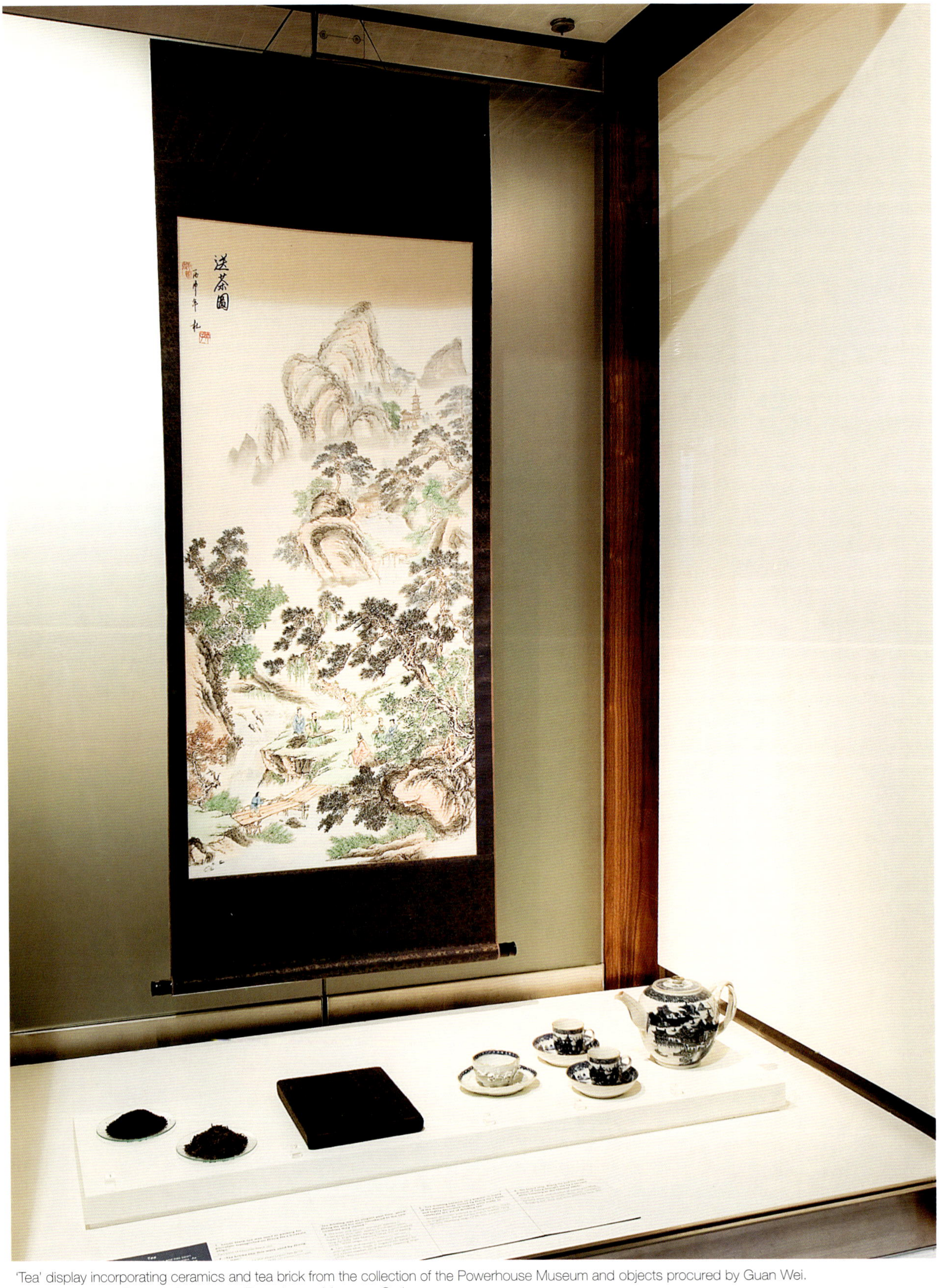

'Tea' display incorporating ceramics and tea brick from the collection of the Powerhouse Museum and objects procured by Guan Wei.
Photograph: Jean-François Lanzarone, Powerhouse Museum, Sydney.

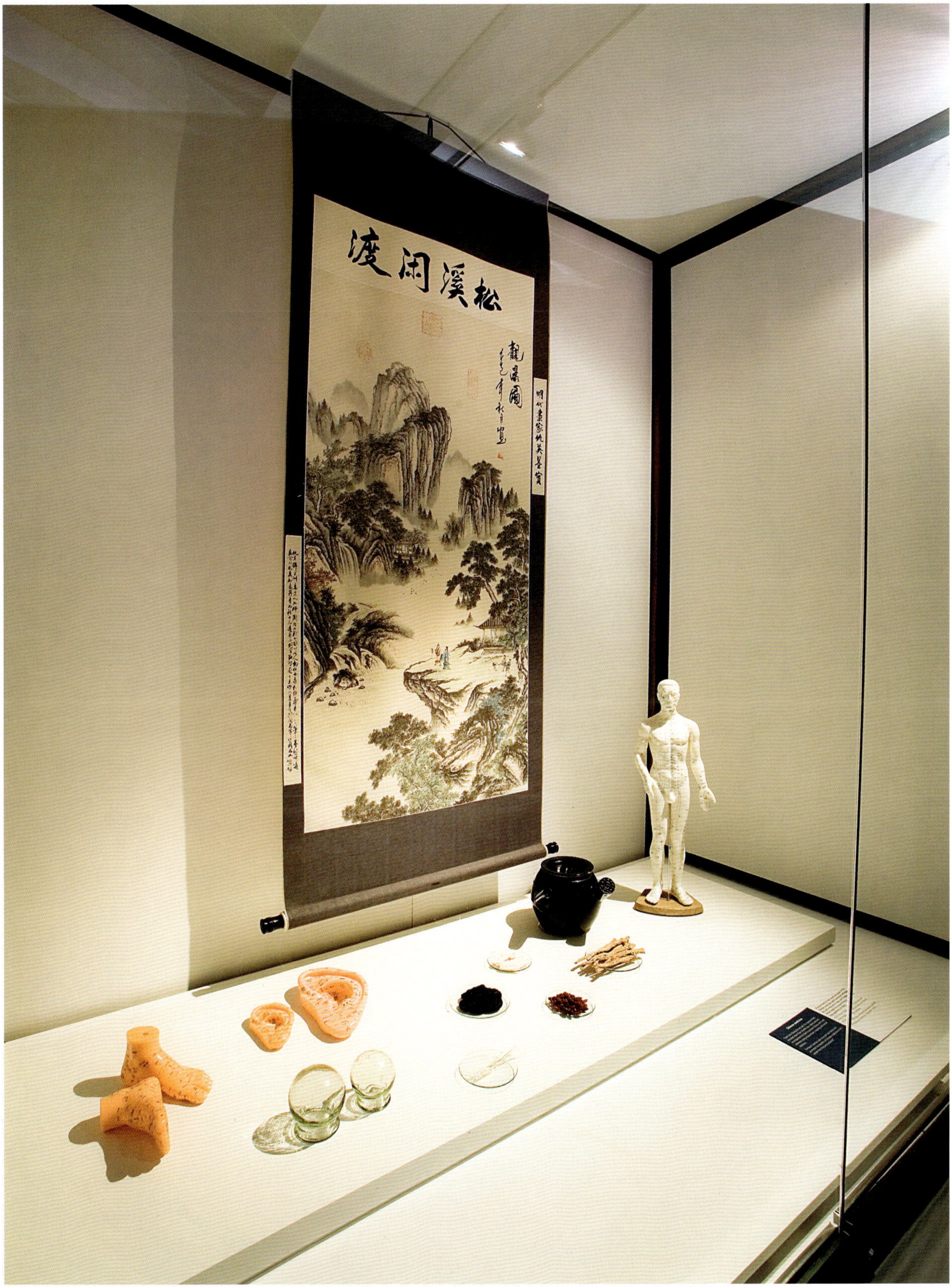

'Chinese Medicine' display of objects procured by Guan Wei.
Photograph: Jean-François Lanzarone, Powerhouse Museum, Sydney.

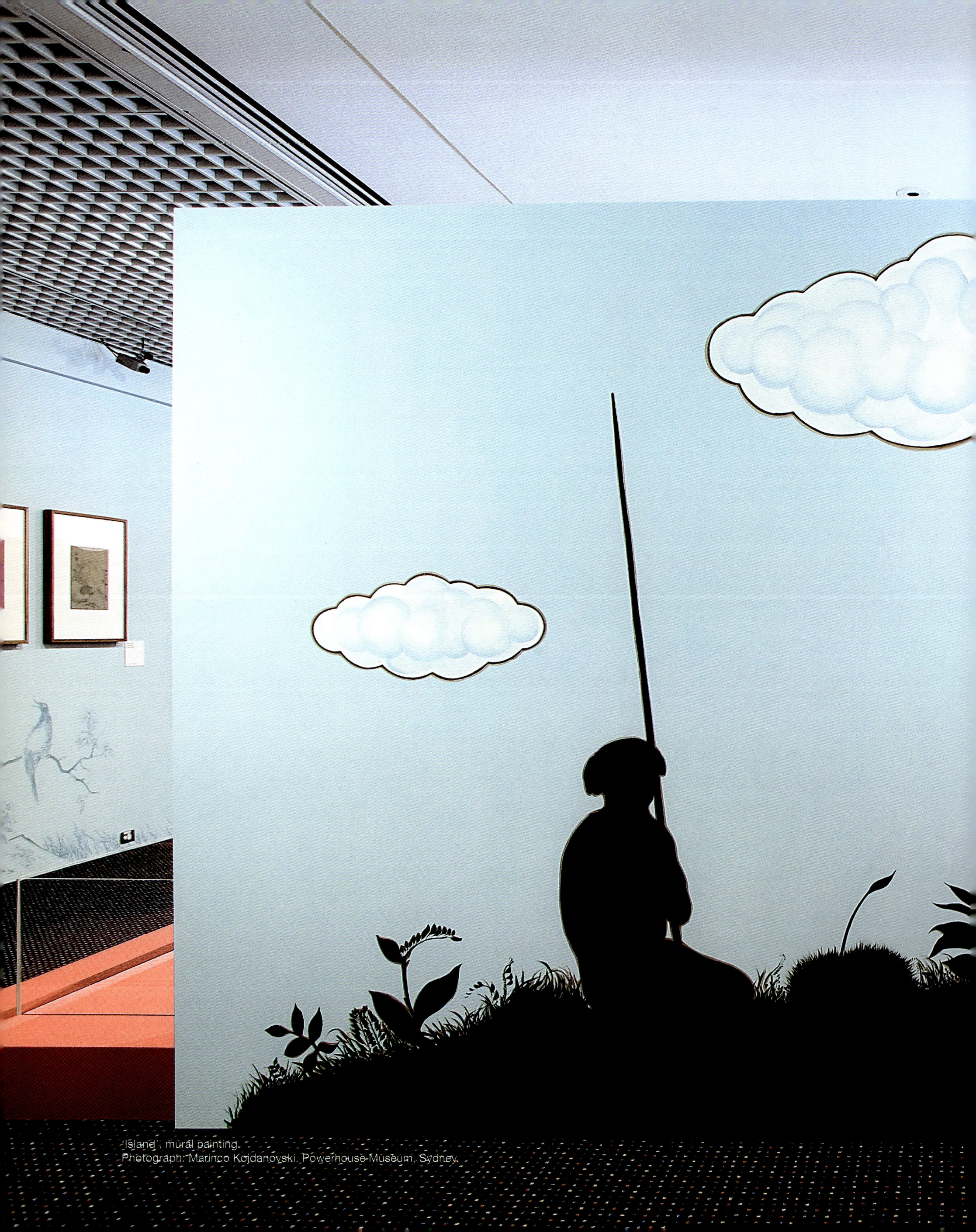

'Island', mural painting.
Photograph: Marinco Kojdanovski. Powerhouse Museum, Sydney.

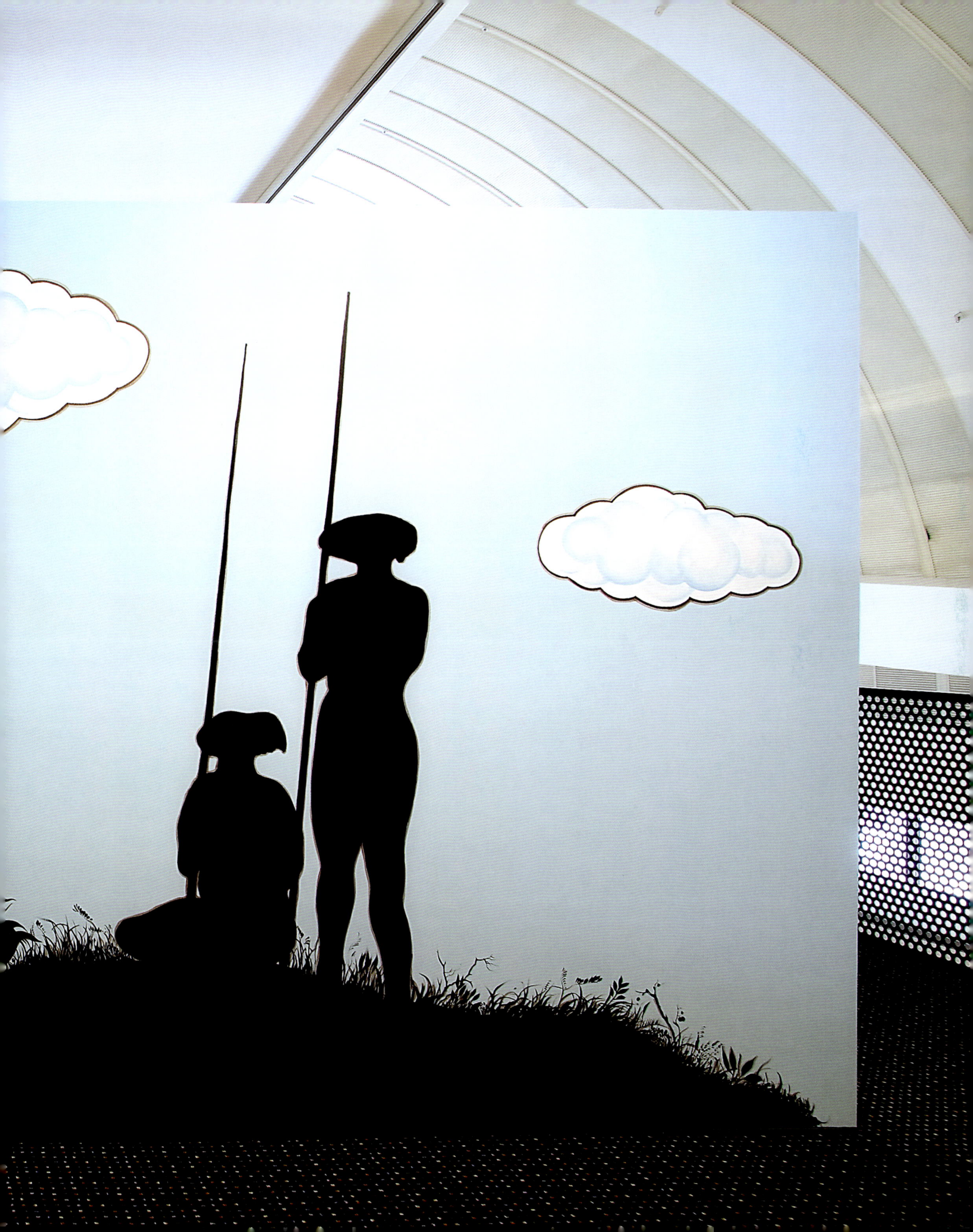

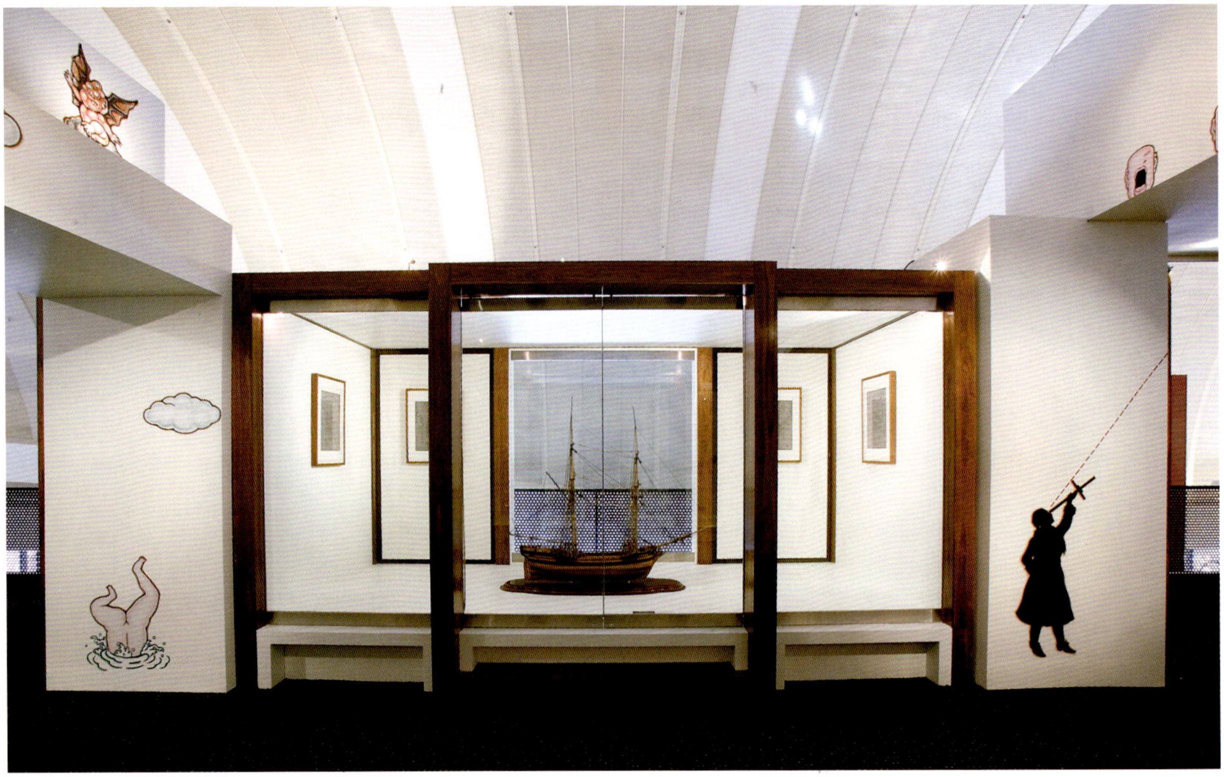

Ship model and works on paper by Guan Wei.
Photograph: Marinco Kojdanovski, Powerhouse Museum, Sydney.

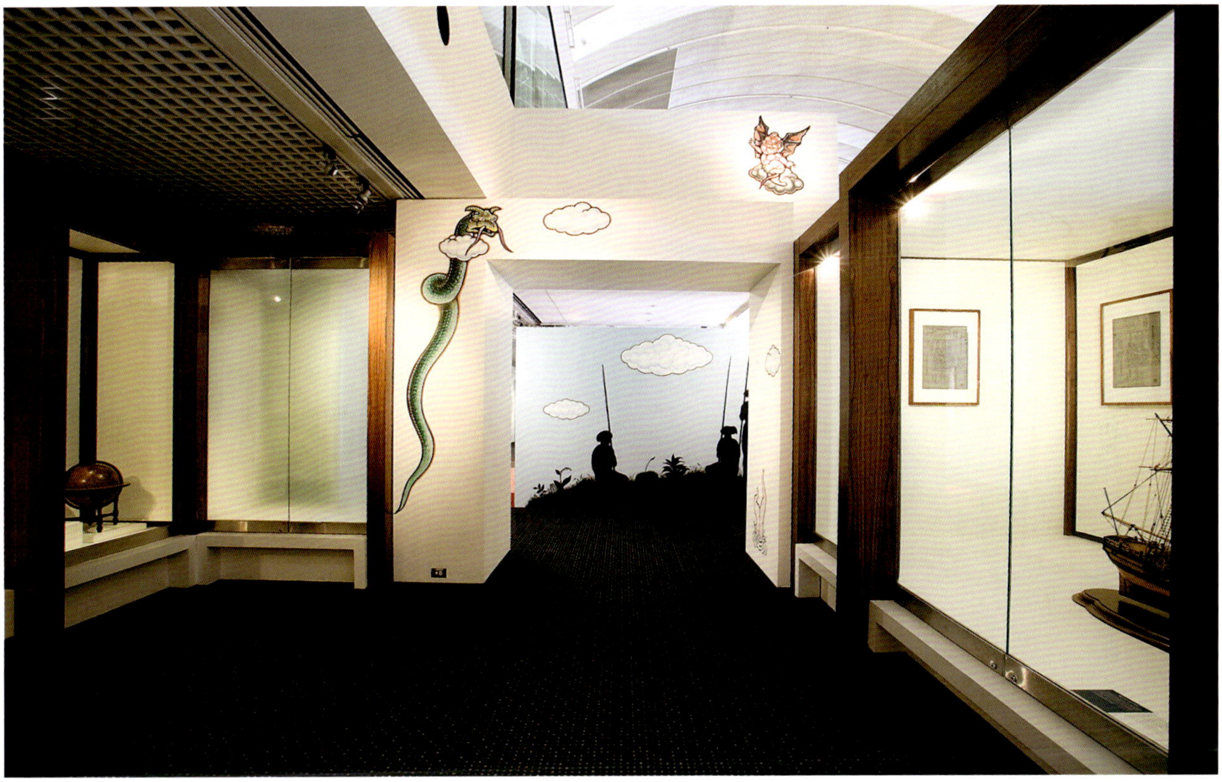

'Island', mural painting, and other motifs.
Photograph: Marinco Kojdanovski, Powerhouse Museum, Sydney.

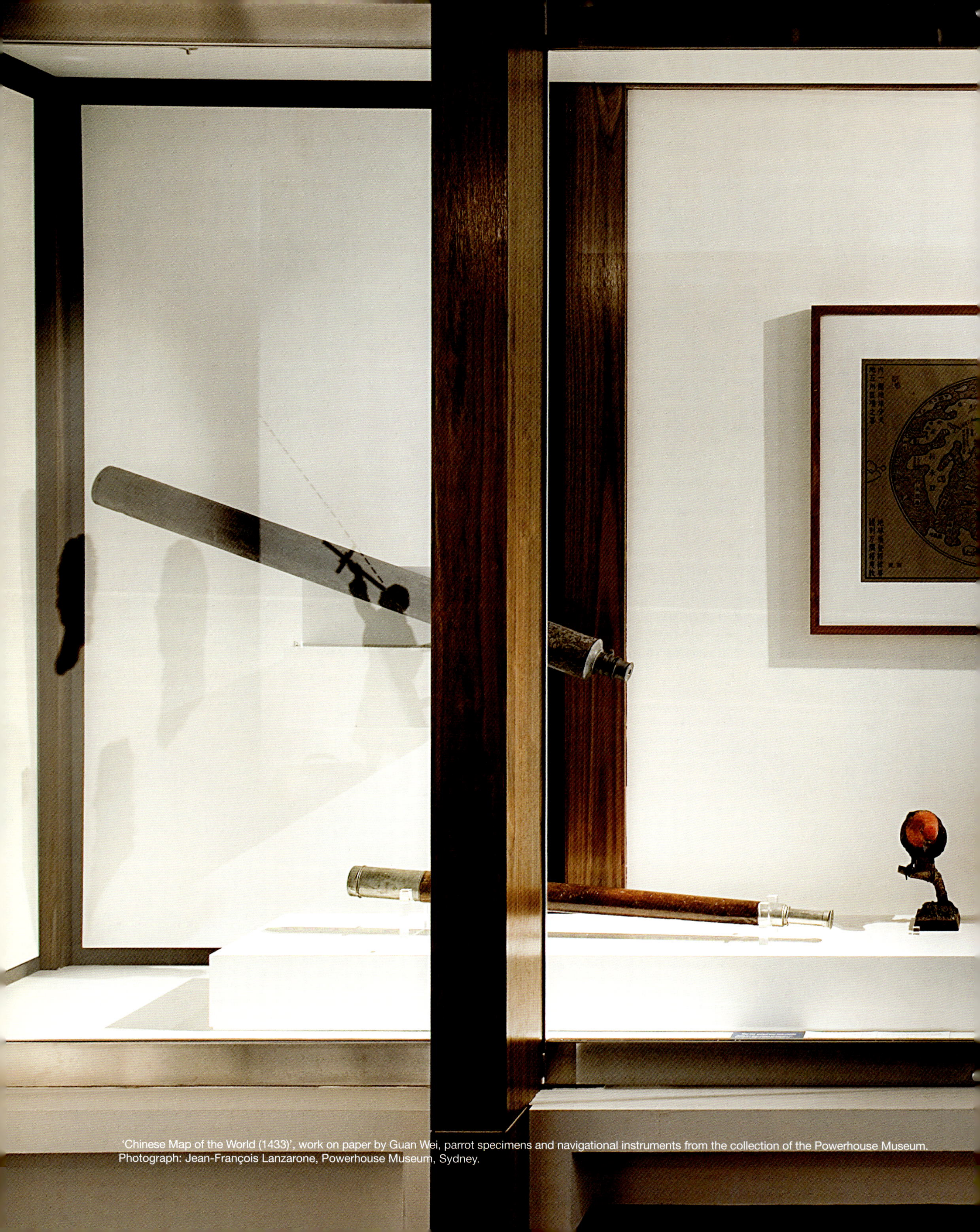

'Chinese Map of the World (1433)', work on paper by Guan Wei, parrot specimens and navigational instruments from the collection of the Powerhouse Museum.
Photograph: Jean-François Lanzarone, Powerhouse Museum, Sydney.

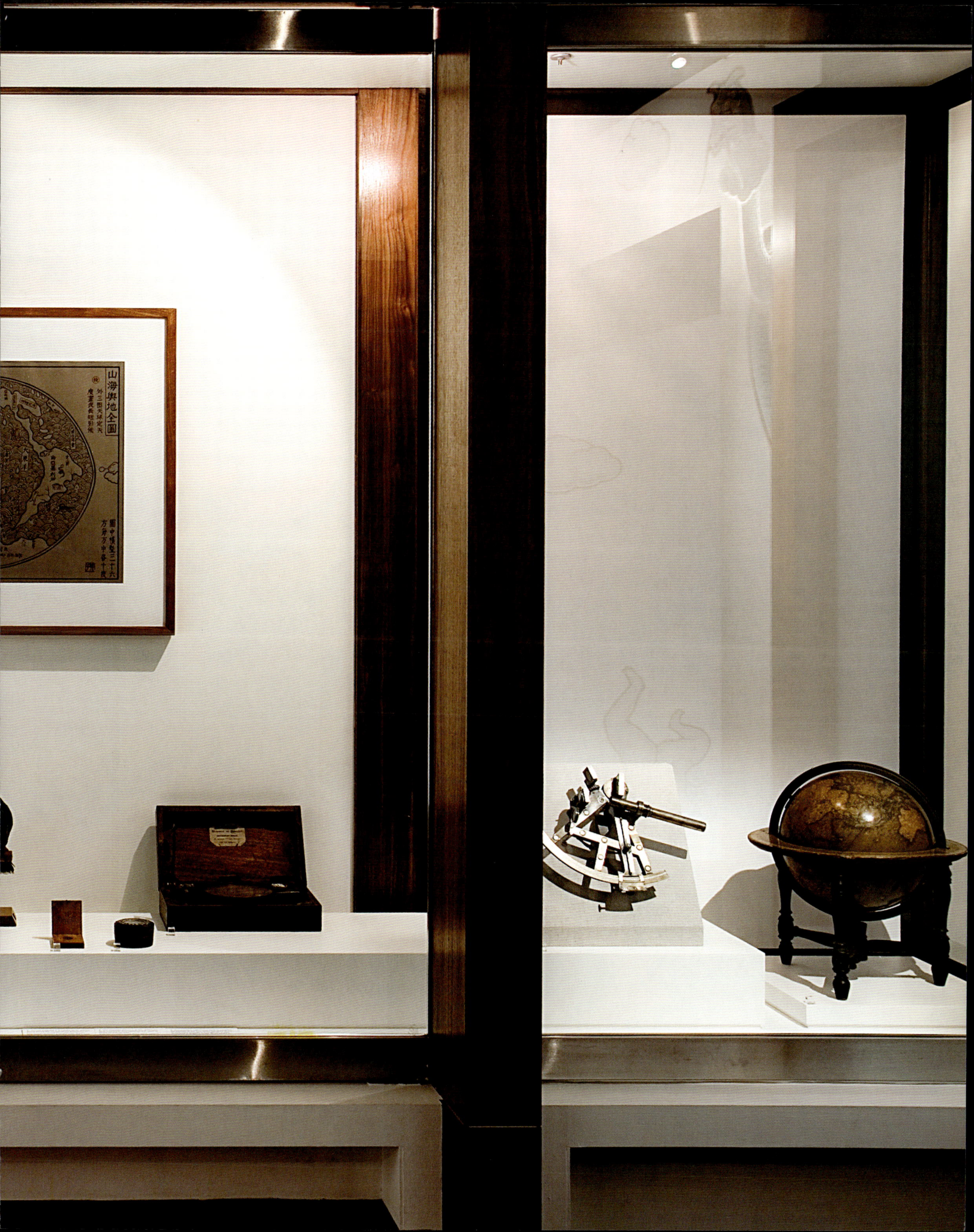
山海輿地全圖

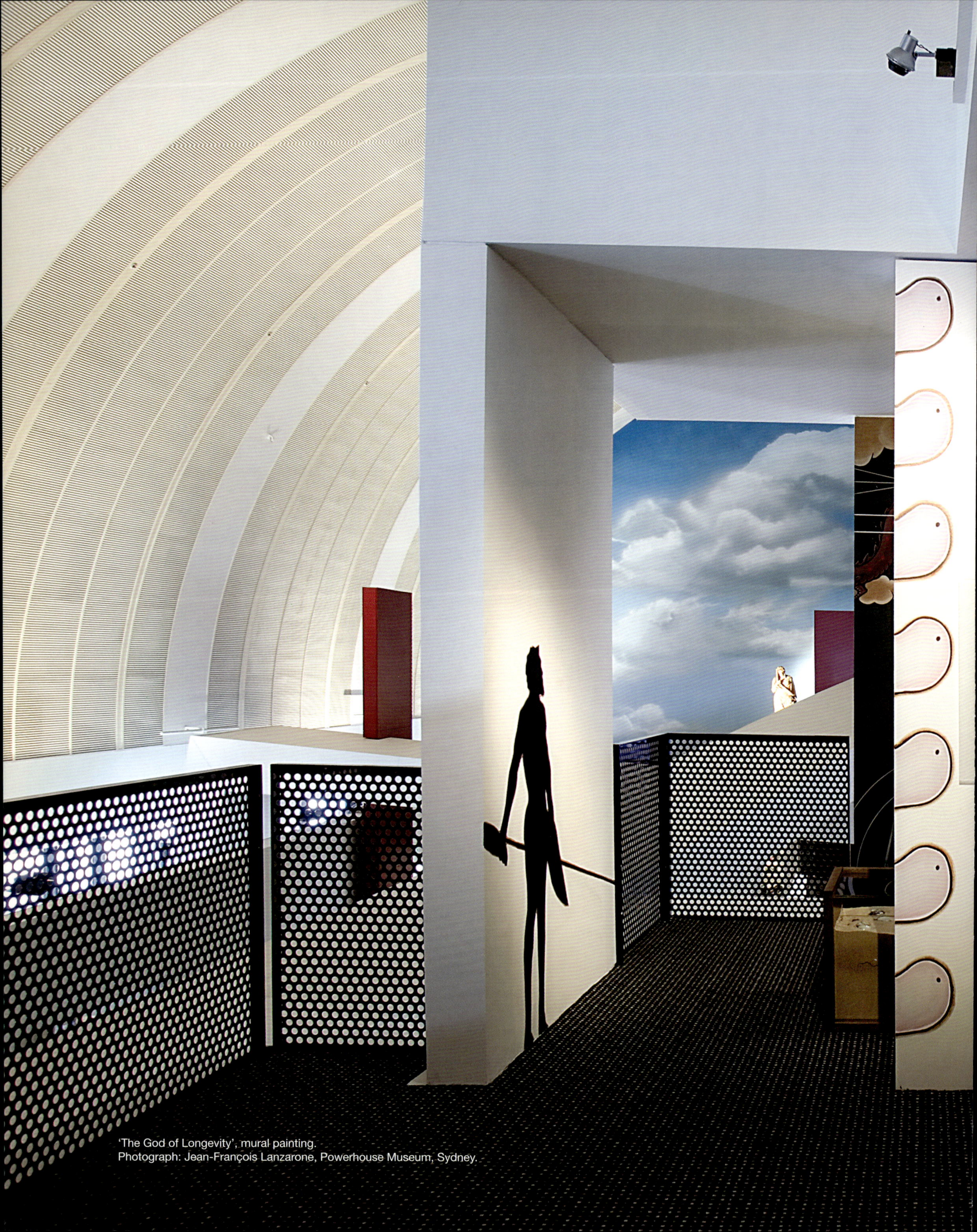

'The God of Longevity', mural painting.
Photograph: Jean-François Lanzarone, Powerhouse Museum, Sydney.

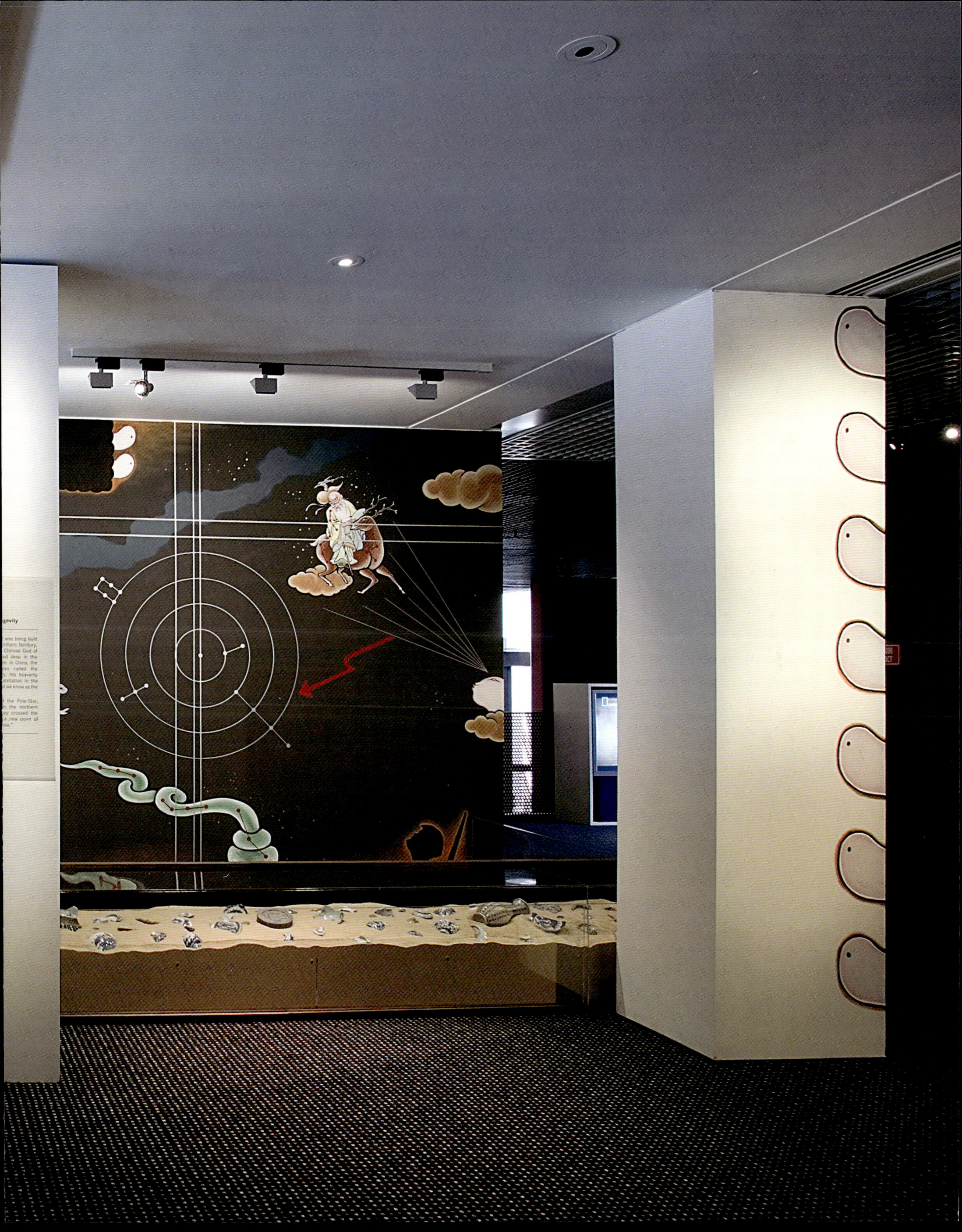

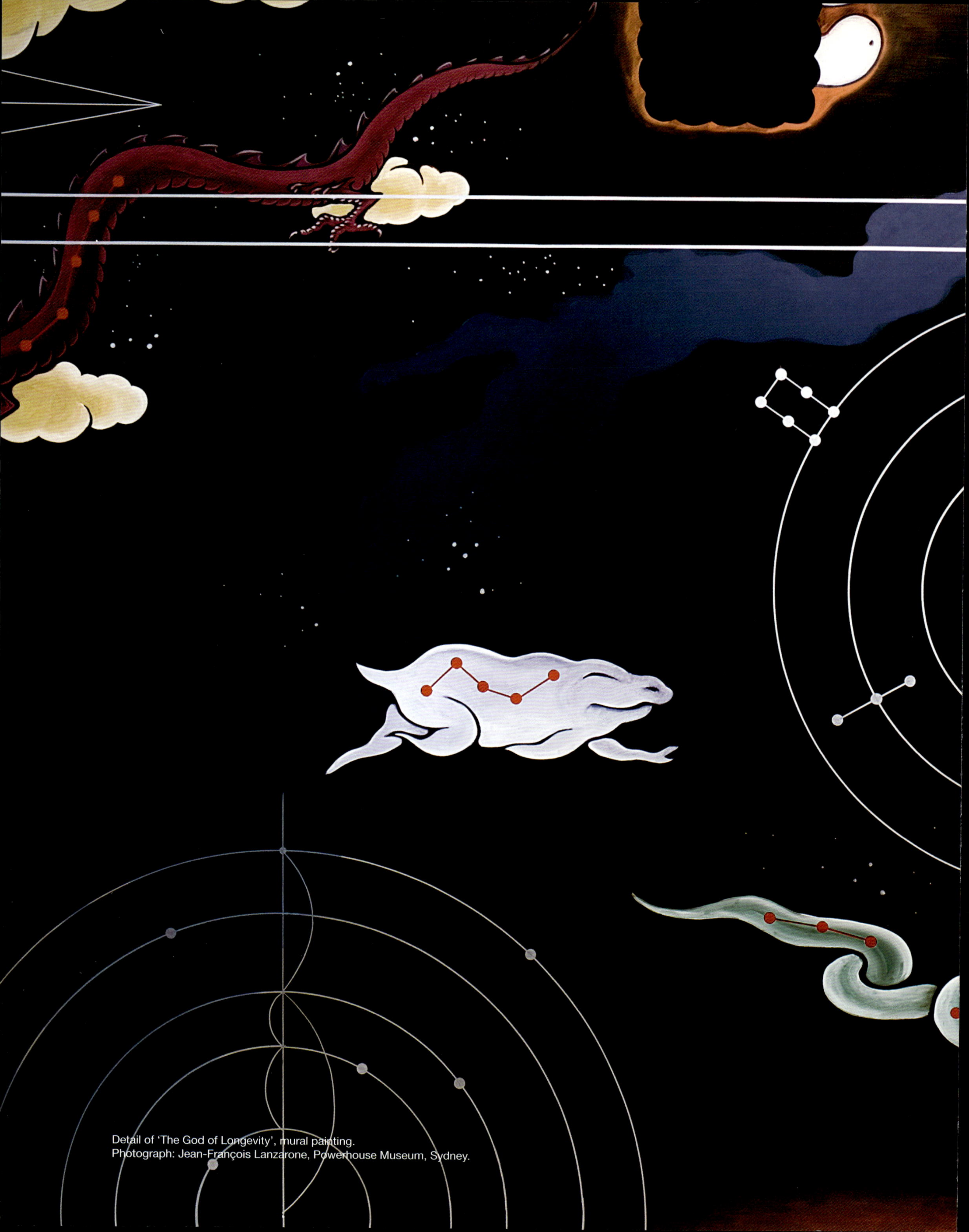

Detail of 'The God of Longevity', mural painting.
Photograph: Jean-François Lanzarone, Powerhouse Museum, Sydney.

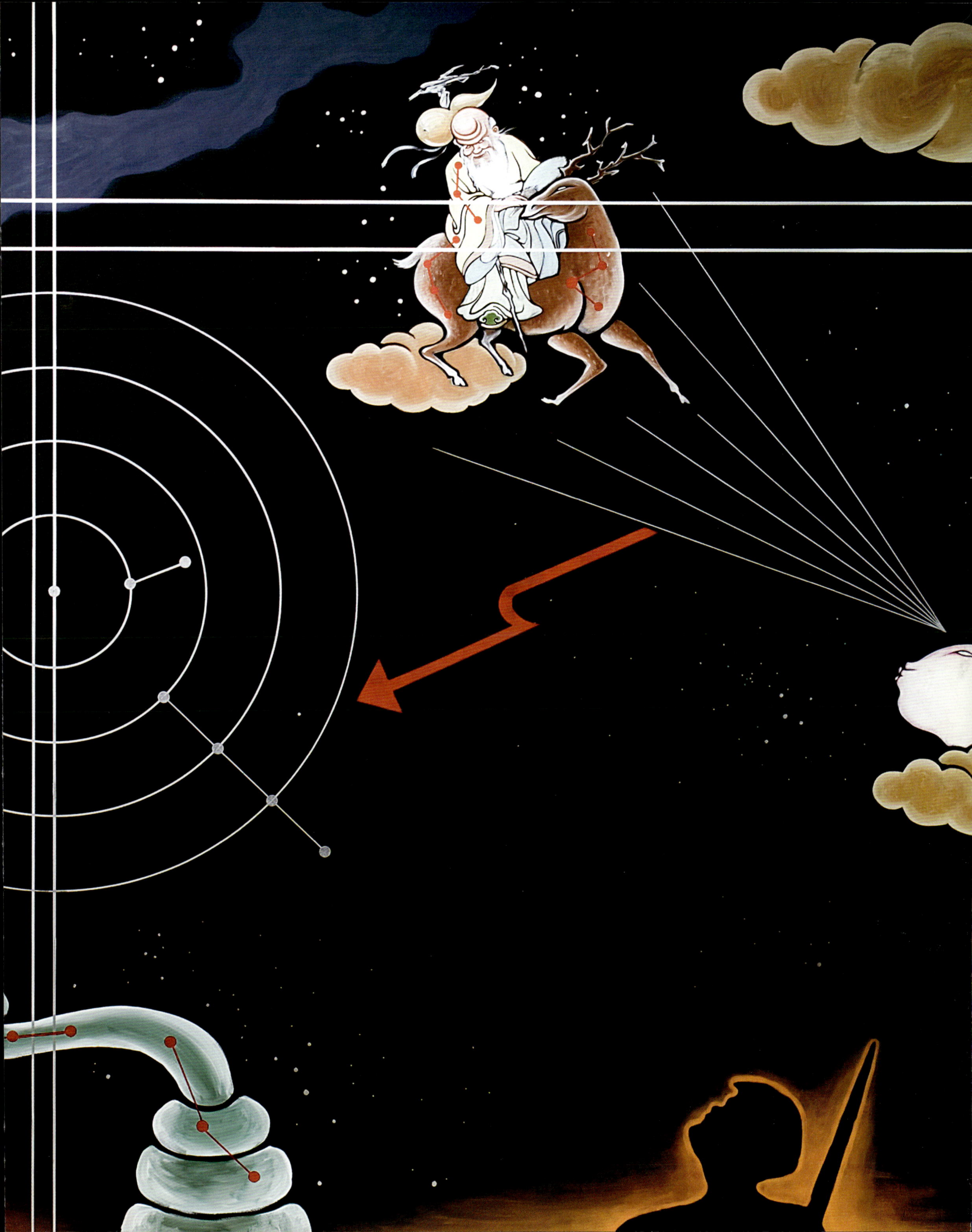

The God of Longevity

'In 1879 when a new road was being built near Port Darwin in the Northern Territory, a Ming-style statue of the Chinese God of Longevity was found buried deep in the roots of an old banyan tree. In China, the God of Longevity is also called the Celestial God of Longevity. His heavenly form is the brightest constellation in the southern hemisphere, what we know as the Southern Cross.

'Zheng He's armada had used the Pole Star, or Polaris, to navigate in the northern hemisphere. But when they crossed the equator they had to use a new point of reference: the Southern Cross.'

老寿星

"1879 年，在澳大利亚北领地首府达尔文附近修筑道路的时候，深埋在古老的菩提树根下的，具有明代风格的老寿星雕像被发现。在中国，老寿星又被称为南极老人，是高悬在天穹南部的一颗明亮的星，是现今被我们称为南十字星座中的一颗星辰。

"郑和与他的船队在北半球航行的时候以传统的北斗星为坐标，当他们穿过赤道之后，船队采用新的坐标，明亮的南十字星座指点着航行的方向。"

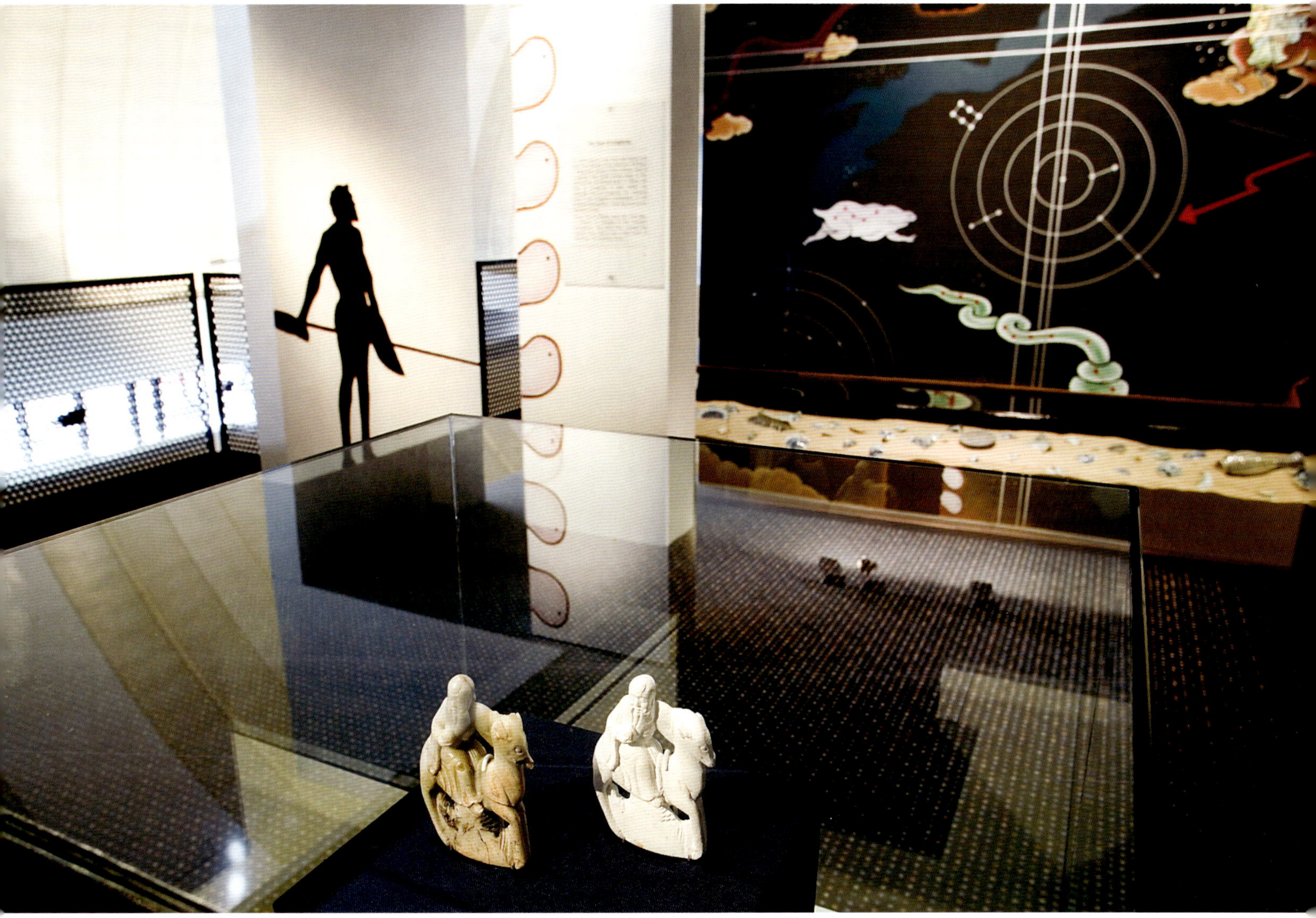

God of Longevity figures and 'The God of Longevity', mural painting.
Photograph: Marinco Kojdanovski, Powerhouse Museum, Sydney.

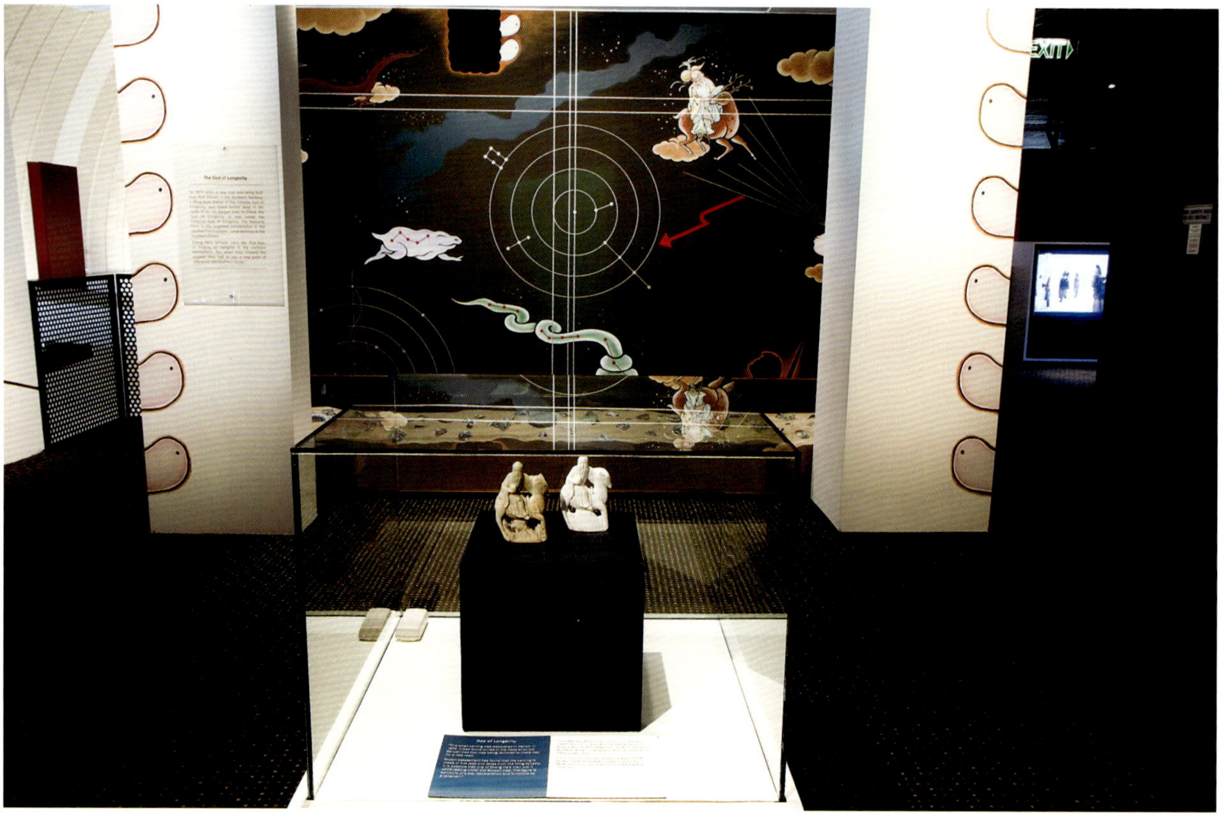

God of Longevity figure and plaster cast from the collection of the Powerhouse Museum and 'The God of Longevity' mural painting.
Photograph: Jean-François Lanzarone, Powerhouse Museum, Sydney.

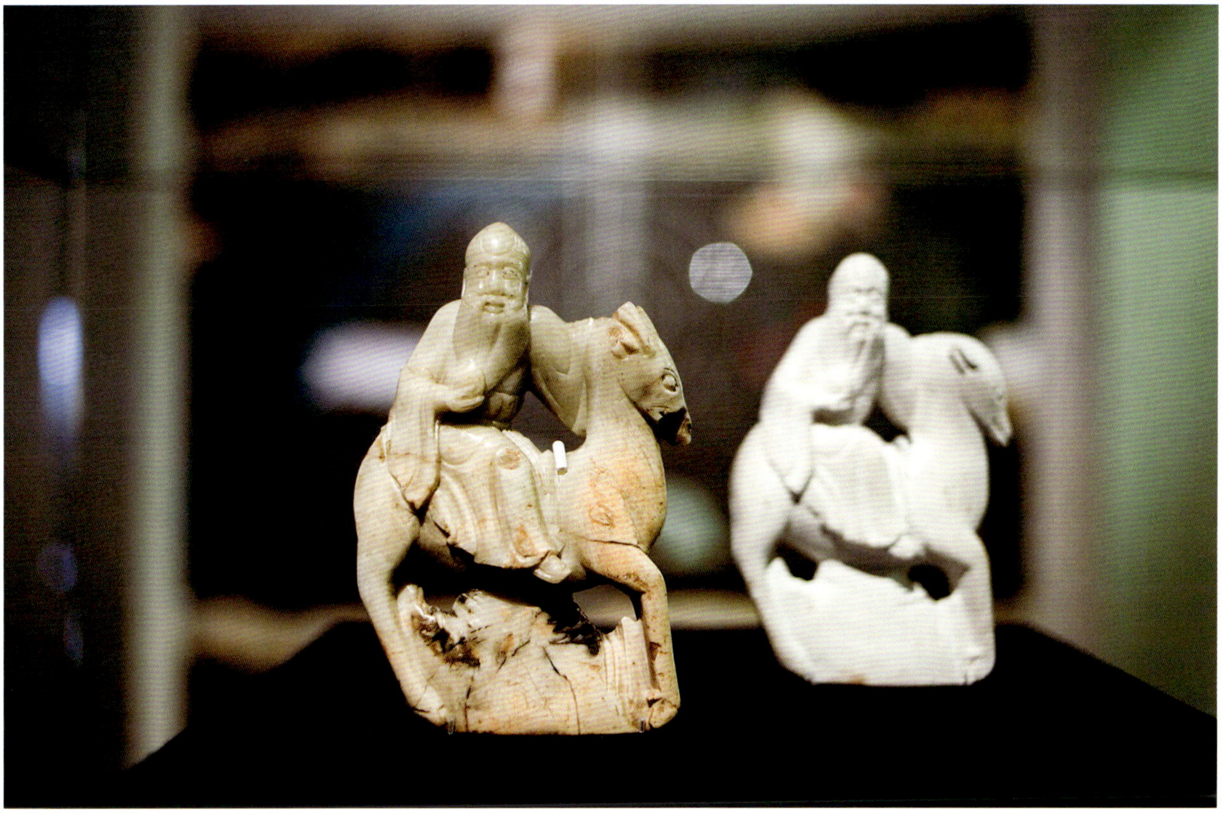

God of Longevity figure and plaster cast from the collection of the Powerhouse Museum.
Photograph: Jean-François Lanzarone, Powerhouse Museum, Sydney.

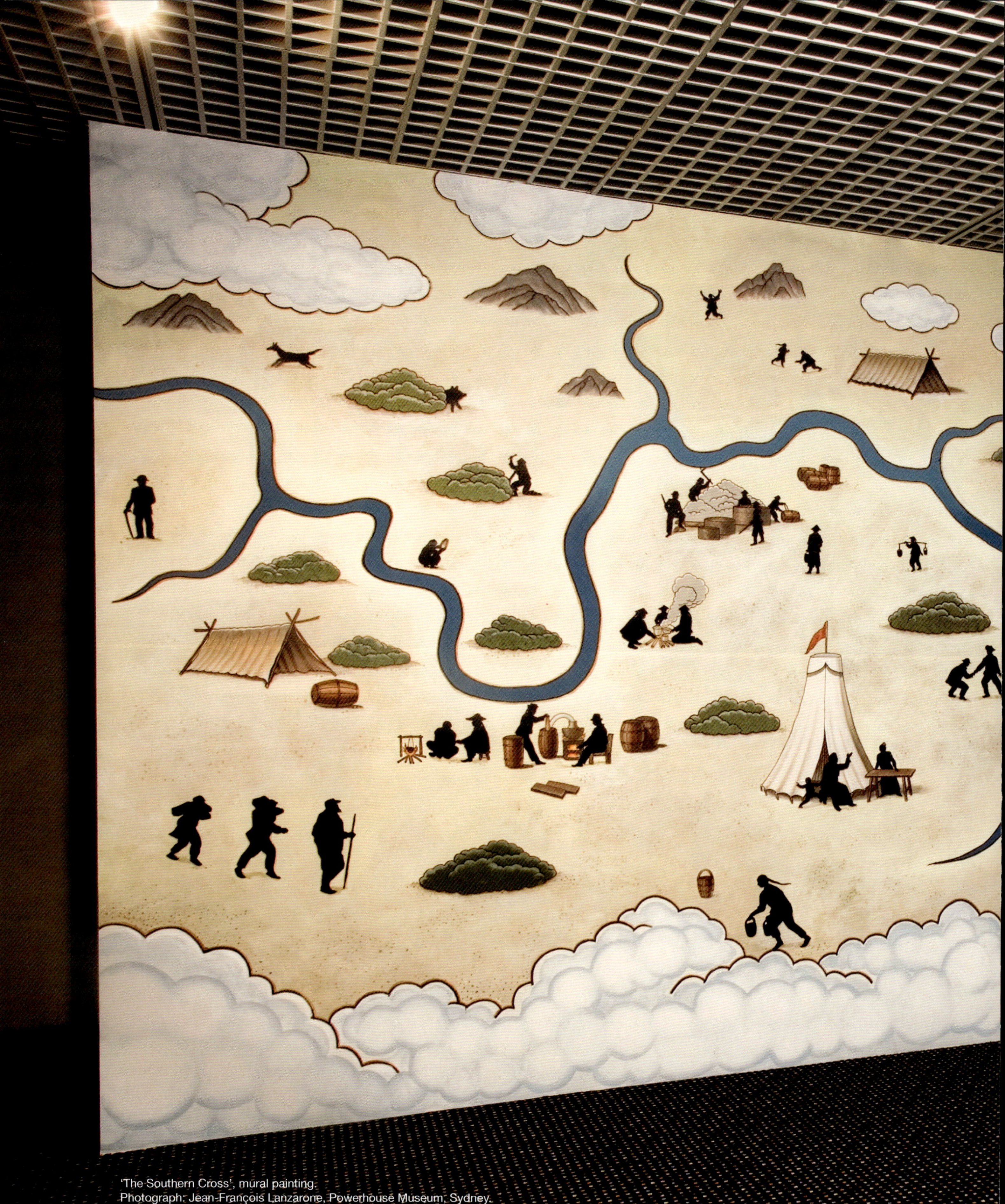

'The Southern Cross', mural painting.
Photograph: Jean-François Lanzarone, Powerhouse Museum, Sydney.

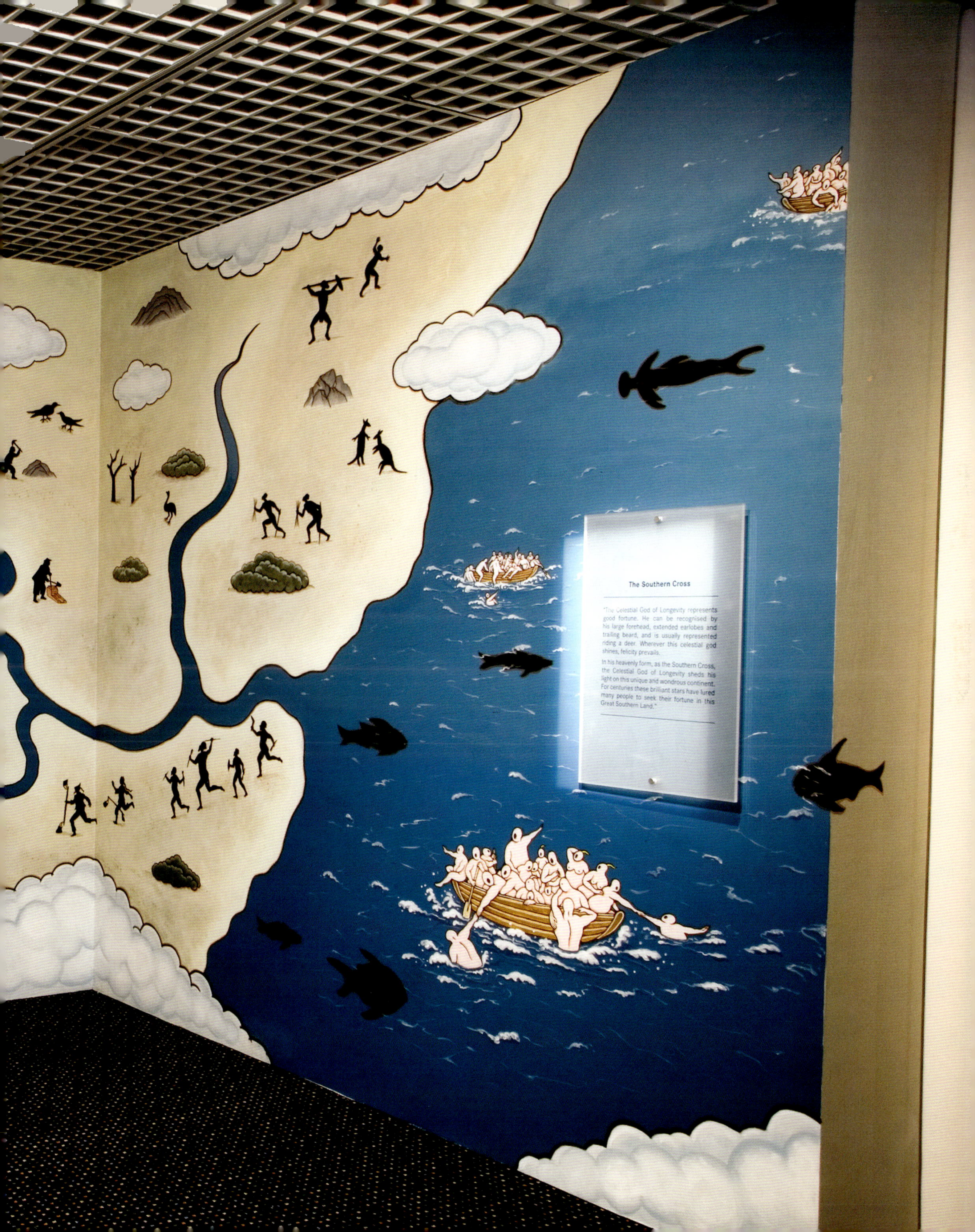
The Southern Cross
"The Celestial God of Longevity represents good fortune. He can be recognised by his large forehead, extended earlobes and trailing beard, and is usually represented riding a deer. Wherever this celestial god shines, felicity prevails.
In his heavenly form, as the Southern Cross, the Celestial God of Longevity sheds his light on this unique and wondrous continent. For centuries these brilliant stars have lured many people to seek their fortune in this Great Southern Land."

The Southern Cross

'The Celestial God of Longevity represents good fortune. He can be recognised by his large forehead, extended earlobes and trailing beard, and is usually represented riding a deer. Wherever this celestial god shines, felicity prevails.

'In his heavenly form as the Southern Cross, the Celestial God of Longevity shines his light on this unique and wondrous continent. For centuries these brilliant stars have lured many people to seek their fortune in this Great Southern Land.'

南十字星座

"老寿星还象征着吉祥好运。老寿星有着宽大的额头，丰厚的耳垂和长长的胡须，骑在梅花鹿上，不论走到何处，人们都在这位天神的佑护之下。

"老寿星的神圣姿态同样地表现在南十字星座，老寿星播撒的光芒照耀在这片神奇独特的大陆。在过去的几百年里，灿烂的星光吸引着无数人到这伟大的南方陆地寻找他们的财富和梦想。"

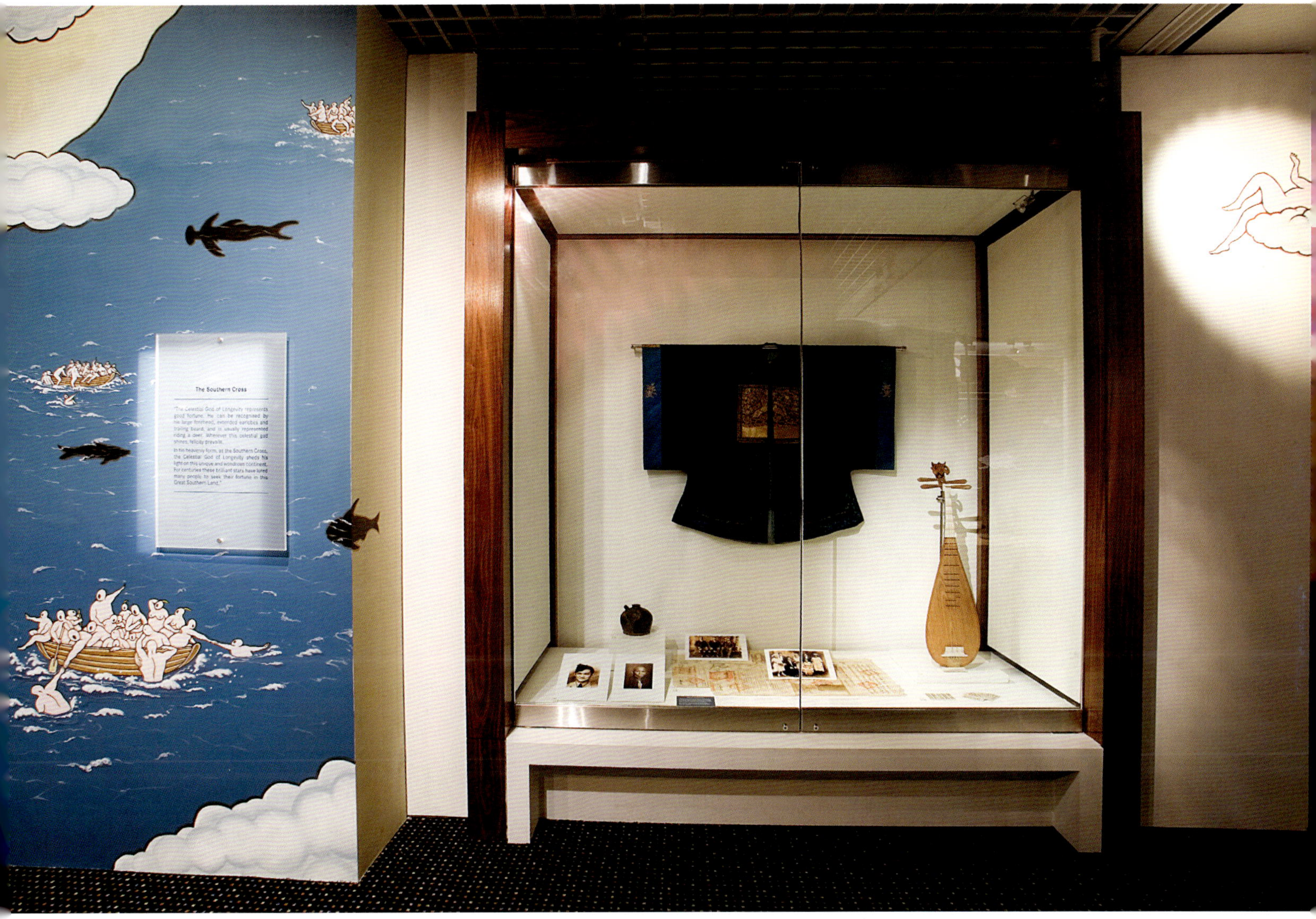

'Chinese in Australia' display incorporating objects from the collection of the Powerhouse Museum and ephemera procured by Guan Wei. Photograph: Jean-François Lanzarone, Powerhouse Museum, Sydney.

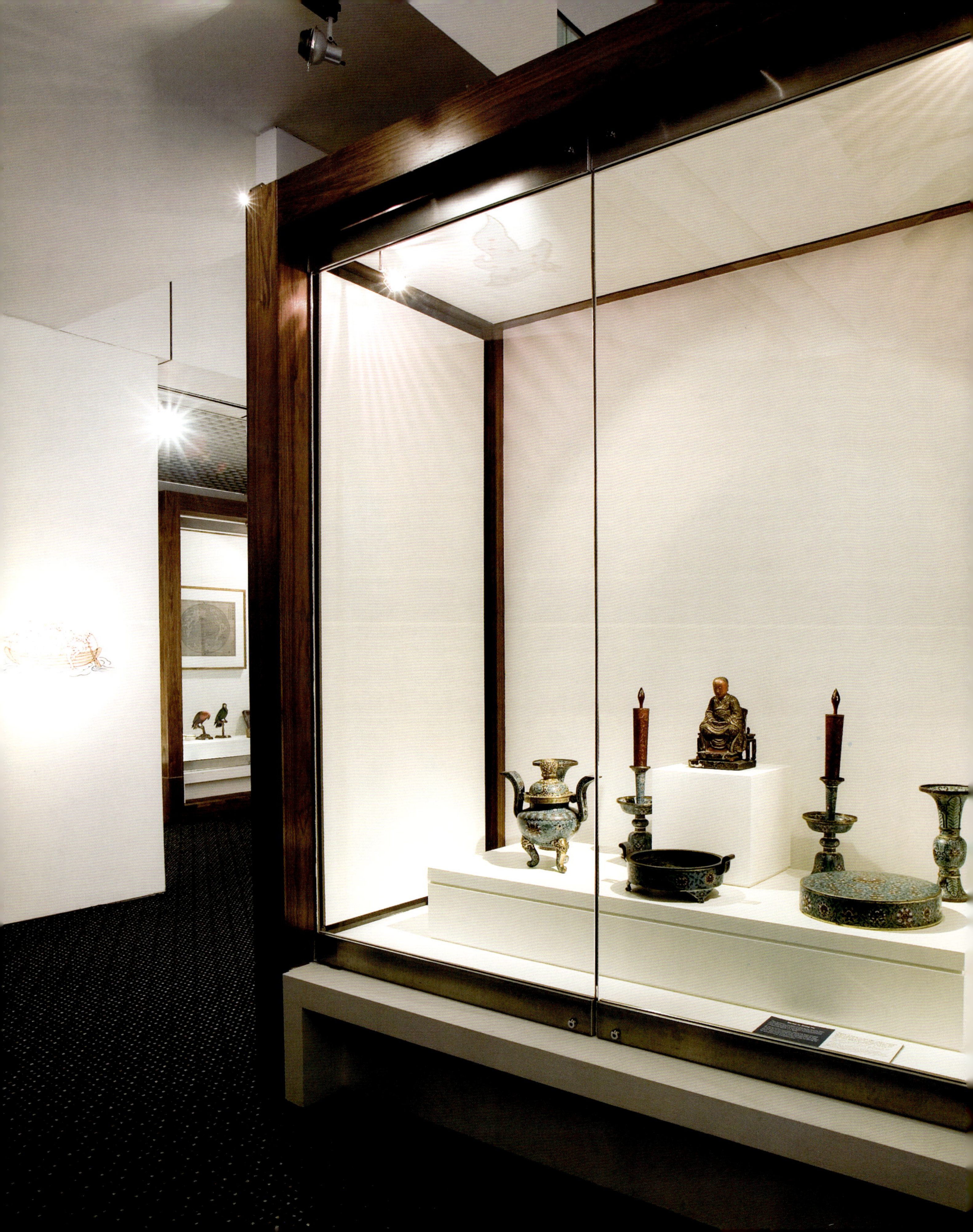

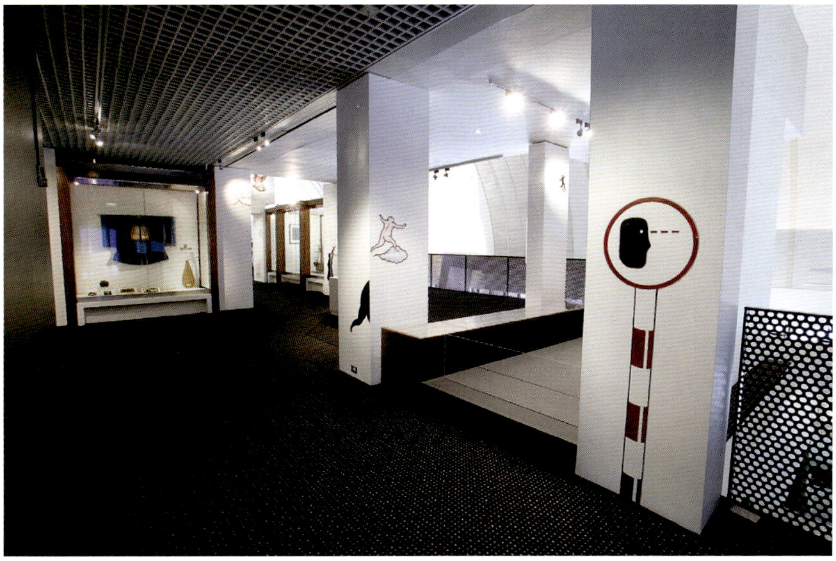

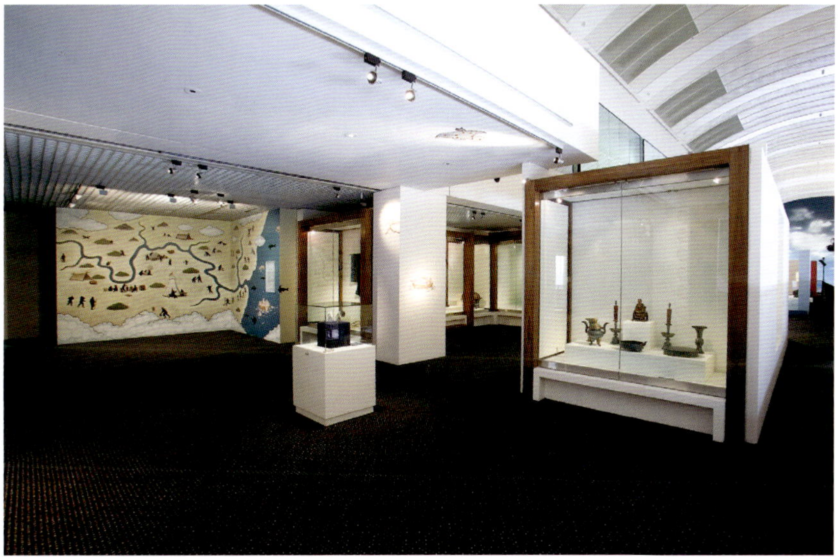

← 'Shrine to Zheng He' display of objects from the collection of the Powerhouse Museum.
Photograph: Jean-François Lanzarone, Powerhouse Museum, Sydney.
↑ 'Chinese in Australia' displays.
Photographs: Marinco Kojdanovski, Powerhouse Museum, Sydney.

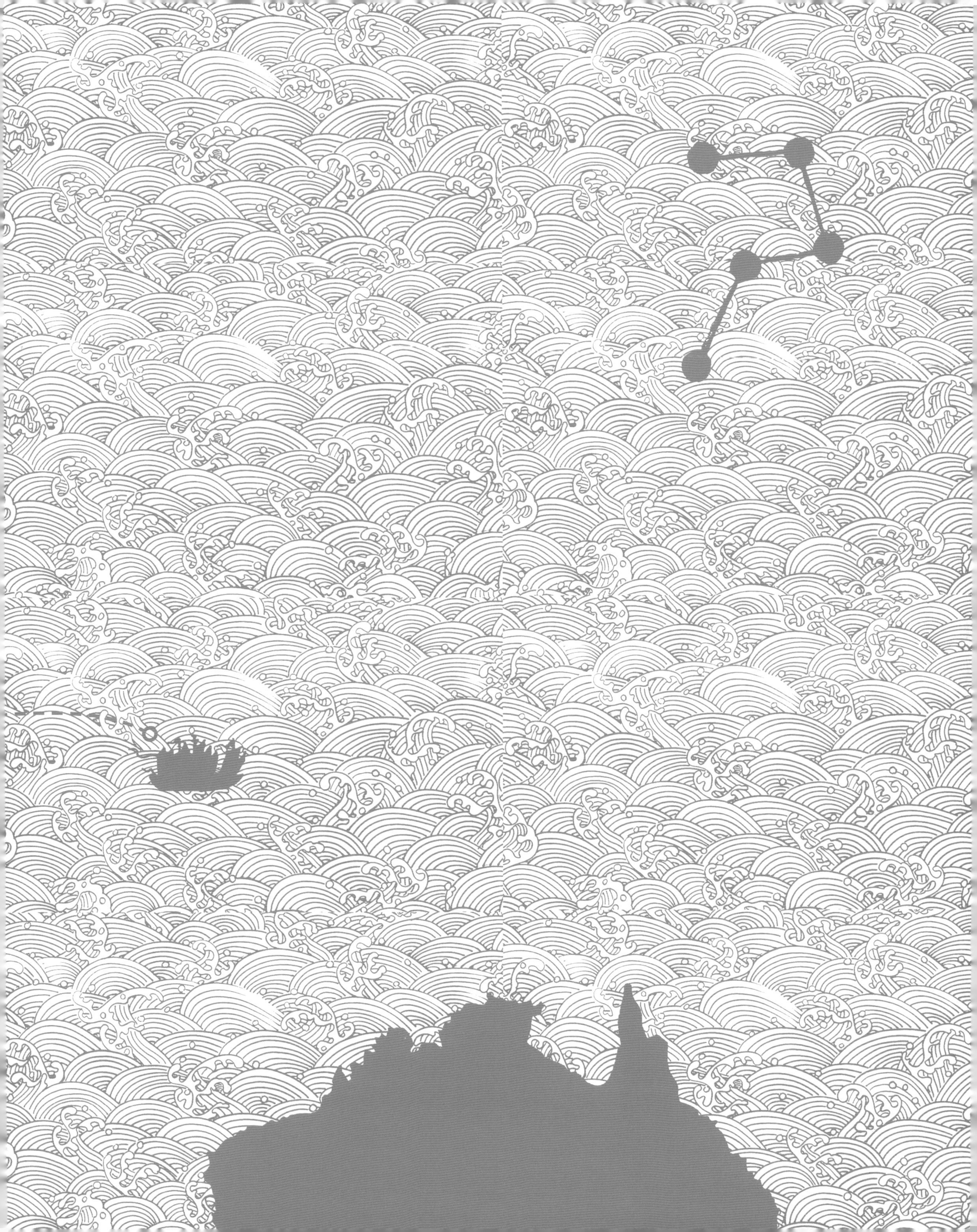

Travels in Guan Wei's Curiosity Cabinet

Geremie R. Barmé

With the welcome incursion of international capital and the radical revivals of numerous eras of history, China has been experiencing an unprecedented concrete re-enactment of its numerous pasts. These are by and large imaginative reprisals in which conservationists have but a weak voice amidst the booming clamour of developers and opportunists. It is in this age of rediscovery, historical re-imagining and the reengineering of China, its times and places, that Guan Wei has created 'Other Histories', his fable for a contemporary world.

Apart from the environment of revivals and cultural tensions in both China and his adopted Antipodean homeland, Guan Wei conceived of 'Other Histories' by taking a page or two from *1421: The Year China Discovered the World*. This best-selling nautical confection by the fabulist Gavin Menzies has been much remarked upon, and lambasted, by scholars in various disciplines.[1] Nonetheless, Menzies' work has been featured in places like China and Singapore, among others, as part of a general move towards creating a more expansive history of how China is presumed to have engaged with the larger world on the cusp of the modern era. While, for the serious reader, *1421* may be little more than pulp fiction, the book inspired Guan Wei to imagine a history in which the worlds of his life, Chinese and Australian, were brought together through an historical sleight of hand.

'Other Histories' created by Guan Wei and guided to realisation by a collective of curators and artists is something of a *Wunderkammer*, a 'wonder room'.[2] Cabinets of curiosity or wonder appeared in the days before a more formal delineation between the sciences, art and the codified appreciation of natural wonders developed. Renaissance Curiosity Cabinets ('cabinet' in the sense of room) were like mini-museums that evolved before the strict taxonomies of the Enlightenment would see objects sequestered from each other in new scientific systems of knowledge. They were individual, and frequently idiosyncratic, displays of rarities, oddities, fascinations, artifices and ephemera, collections of the real as well as the fictitious, assembled for the study and amusement of the avid collector. These crowded spaces inspired speculation in many areas of human knowledge, just as they accumulated the fruits of voyages of discovery, trade and conquest. One such collector was Gabriel Kaltemarckt who, when instructing Christian I of Saxony

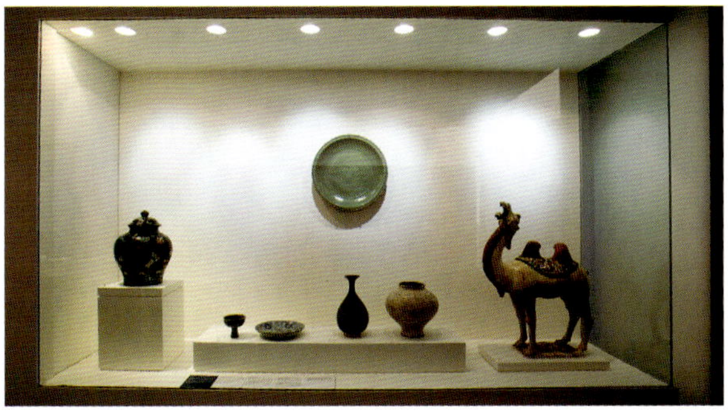

'Chinese Ceramics' display of objects from the collection of the Powerhouse Museum.
Photograph: Marinco Kojdanovski, Powerhouse Museum, Sydney.

in the late-sixteenth century on the creation of an 'art room' or *Kunstkammer*, declared that there were a number of essential items in any such assembly: sculptures and paintings; 'curious items from home or abroad'; and, 'antlers, horns, claws, feathers and other things belonging to strange and curious animals'.[3] With more art than artifice, Guan Wei's 'Other Histories' has reconstituted just such a *Wunderkammer*.

The collection of curiosities also has a venerable history in Chinese culture. Objects of unknown origin, or that would lead to speculation, delight and puzzlement were much favoured for being 'extraordinary'. Stones of mysterious form dredged from the depths of lakes where tides and eddies had done the work of sculpting them, vegetal shapes that suggested otherworldly mystery, ancient inscriptions that hinted at unknown auguries, hoary bones that seemed to be those of mysterious dragons, all were collected assiduously, shared sparingly with friends and cognoscenti and marvelled over in private delight. Many early encounters with the post-Renaissance European world led Chinese collectors to delight at oddities of what was called the 'Far West'. For a culture that had been endlessly inventive, the intricate workings of clocks, the quaint use of chiaroscuro in painting human faces, the bizarre ability to make water betray its nature and flow upwards in fountains were all tricks of great ingenuity. One of the great emperors of the Qing dynasty, Qianlong (r. 1736–1795), would delight in these curiosities and he made them a feature of his palaces at the Garden of Perfect Brightness (Yuanming Yuan) to the northwest of Beijing.[4]

It has been observed that the Western 'discovery' of China and Columbus' voyage of expansion are linked through interpretations of Marco Polo's travel account of his time in the Mongol capital and the imagination of a distant Cathay.[5] In his own way, Guan Wei perhaps saw

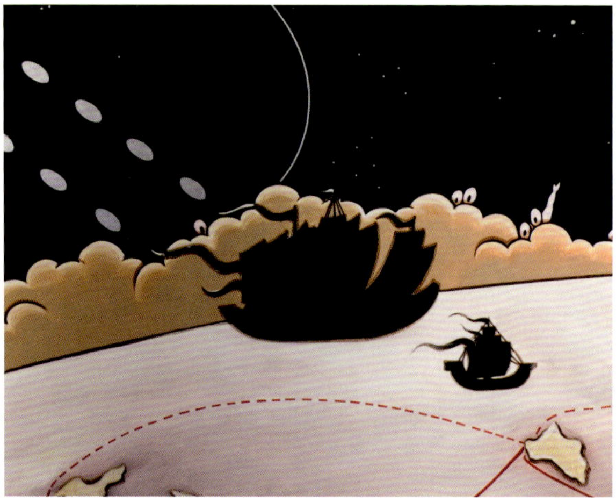

Detail of 'Zheng He and Columbus', mural painting.
Photograph: Jean-François Lanzarone, Powerhouse Museum, Sydney.

in his early encounters with Australia something of an El Dorado, as did many people who came to Australia from South China in the late-nineteenth century.[6] It is here that he and other Chinese cultural figures active in the international arts scene have been encountering and creatively embracing the voyages of discovery of Europe. Guan Wei takes his own trip through history collecting and displaying the essentials for a modern Cabinet of Curiosities, one that he calls a 'Fable for a Contemporary World'. In 'Other Histories' Guan Wei celebrates Australia and the friable possibilities of an Antipodean land whose people, flora and fauna enthralled early visitors, and eventually its conquerors. It is a work that Guan Wei has spoken of as being a 'floating poetic corridor in which history and memory, fact and fiction are blurred'.[7]

Guan Wei has woven around the person of the Ming dynasty Yongle Emperor, the eunuch admiral Zheng He and the Southern Seas an imaginary tale of travel, encounter and enrichment to produce a monumental mural installation. As Claire Roberts notes in her essay in this volume, 'Responding to queries about the conceptual veracity of his portrayal of the historical events and mythology surrounding the voyages of Zheng He—said to have involved an armada of "treasure ships" and some 27,000 men who travelled a distance of 70,000 nautical miles, over 28 years—and the idea that they might have reached Australia more than 350 years before Captain Cook, Guan Wei is reported to have said: "It doesn't matter, I am an artist."'[8]

'Other Histories' also found inspiration in the mysterious origin of a small statue of the Chinese God of Longevity.[9] That object, unearthed in the northern Australian city of Darwin in 1879, belongs to the collection of the Powerhouse Museum. No one knows how the little figure arrived in Darwin. Some have suggested that it may well prove that Zheng He's fleet reached Antipodean shores long before James Cook. In his book *1421*, Gavin Menzies provides an illustration of the object to bolster one of his many extravagant claims. In 'Other Histories', however, Guan Wei launched his own imaginative investigation, making the God of Longevity part of the constellation of the Southern Cross (emblematic of Australia) that Zheng He had used to guide his fleet, leading later immigrants from China south to this island continent.

Guan Wei's artistic trail is laid out through a series of relationships between the diminutive statue and other objects from the Museum's collection. Some are real, while others are masquerading in different roles, yet others are cheap commercial manufactures introduced into the museum space as part of the divergent narratives of Guan Wei's history of the Chinese encounter with the southern hemisphere. By travelling not only in time, but also through space—by literally 'displacing' himself as a Chinese artist—Guan Wei gives himself room in which to think and imagine. By this means, he creates a narrative initially about China, then about Australia and then further on about China's place in Australia, as well as Australia's place in the world.

This new fable starts with the usurpation of the imperial throne in the Ming dynasty by Zhu Di, the Yongle Emperor. Taking as a departure point objects related to the Great Wall, imperial palaces and trade, Guan Wei creates the context for Yongle's most abiding creation, the expanded imperial city of Beijing. Yongle overthrew his nephew the Jianwen Emperor (r. 1399–1402), Zhu Yunwen, and sacked the capital of Nanjing. Jianwen would disappear and rumour held that he had fled the country. Some would even claim that Zheng He's expeditions were launched, in part, out of the Yongle Emperor's desire to track down his dethroned nephew.

This northern city was Zhu Di's base, and after he took the throne he moved the dynastic centre there, naming it Beijing (the 'northern capital' in contradistinction to Nanjing, the 'southern capital'). It was not only a power base, but the place from which the emperor effectively staved off the invasions from the north-east and began work on strengthening the border defences known as the Great Wall. Guan Wei chooses the moment when Zhu Di usurped the throne to become the Yongle Emperor as the starting point in his own narrative. The Ming 'civil war' is represented in Guan Wei's account by a full-wall schematic painting of the territory of the Ming Empire

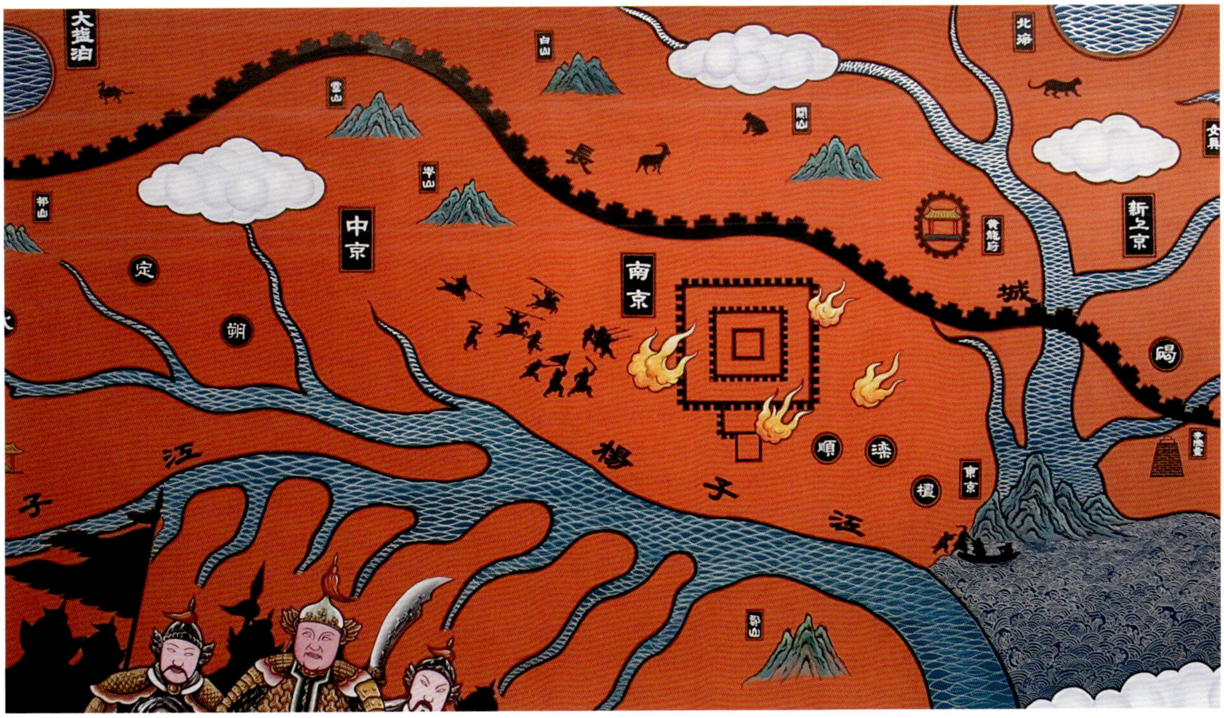

Detail of 'The Ming Dynasty: A Battle for Power', mural painting.
Photograph: Marinco Kojdanovski, Powerhouse Museum, Sydney.

featuring Nanjing in flames, a sinuous Great Wall, the mighty Yangtze River snaking with dragon scales through the landscape and the images of battles, confusion and flight. The move of the imperial centre to Beijing is the event that then gives the artist, and his Powerhouse collaborators, an opportunity to create a new story about what happened when Yongle took the throne. 'Other Histories' continues its narrative combining murals, vitrines and three dioramas. Guan Wei and his team of painters create a series of wall paintings that tell a story that is then reinforced and juxtaposed with displays of objects carefully selected from the Museum's collection. These items are imaginatively reassigned meanings that reflect the complex history that now unfolds.[10]

The design and construction of the imperial city Beijing also gives particular inspiration to Guan Wei. That city and its history are important for the artist not only in the re-imagining of the past in 'Other Histories', but also in the context of his own life, for he is from a lineage of lived history. His surname is a Han Chinese abbreviation of a Manchu clan surname Guwaligya; he is the scion of the Qing imperial clan. His great-great-aunt was the daughter of Ronglu, a military figure who famously conspired with the Empress Dowager Cixi in 1898 against the Guangxu Emperor. Guan Wei's great-great-aunt married into the imperial family, and her husband Prince Chun was the regent who oversaw the empire in the first years of the Xuantong reign (1909–1911), their son, Puyi, being the last Qing emperor.[11]

In his work Guan Wei shows the Yongle Emperor and the eunuch general Zheng He against the backdrop of the newly created imperial palace in Beijing. The artist then

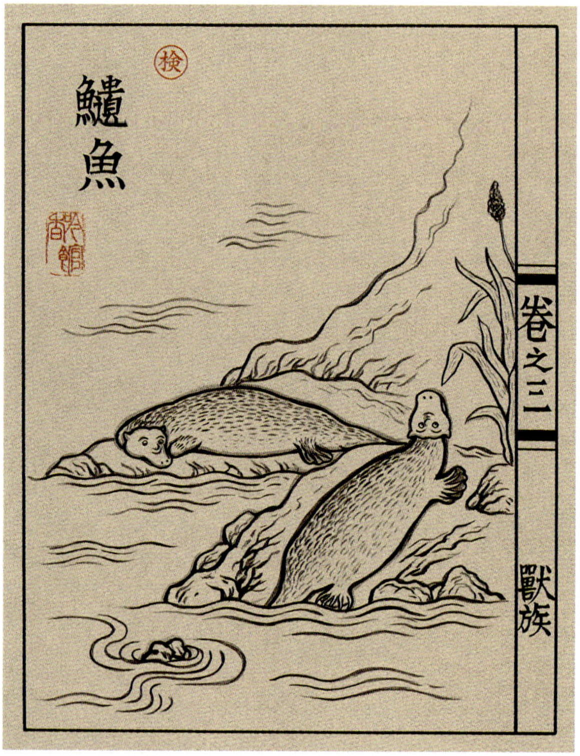

'Platypus', work on paper by Guan Wei.
Photograph: courtesy Powerhouse Museum, Sydney.

traces one particular journey of Zheng He's armada as they move along an imaginary timeline and through a partially fictional geography to travel to the south-sea islands and eventually to the shores of a massive southern continent. This pictorial travelogue leads to Australia, but it carries the viewer/traveller along a trajectory that is never far from Guan Wei's abiding concerns with the Chinese world, the issues of encounters with non-Chinese 'Others', and the question of how a non-confrontational engagement with the foreign might look, and even feel. Guan Wei's story of cultural adventure and sea-bound exploration comes at a particularly fraught period in the history of contemporary Australia, one during which politicised debates about border security, ethnicity and inclusivity have repeatedly threatened the very fabric of society.

During what has been the long decade of conservative rule in Australia, race politics has been used to narrow the national vision and incite public vigilance. While the country has become ever-more enmeshed with the economies of the Asian and Pacific region—profiting in particular from a resource boom fuelled by China's expanding economy—the previously more relaxed and expansive attitude to the cultures and peoples outside Australia has been paradoxically stymied.

At the outset of this era that has seen the narrowing of national vision and increased anxiety about the outside world, the historian and diplomat, Stephen FitzGerald—one of the pioneers of Australia's contemporary engagement with China—warned against Australia loosing its way in dealing with the rising powers of Asia. He was also aware of how the blandishments of economic wealth could easily blind people to the rich possibilities of cultural growth that a booming Asia could offer. Over a decade ago Stephen FitzGerald expressed his concerns in a provocatively entitled book, *Is Australia an Asian Country?* In it he wrote of a transformation of the national ethos and spirit in response to the rise of China and other Asian economies. FitzGerald warned also that

> The mythologizing of the history and culture and values of Asian societies is not... confined to Confucianists. It is more widespread. It is ahistorical. And it contains some dangers, because there are some signs that the emerging Asian 'Asia' could go the way the West did and make such myths about itself that it comes to believe it is the ultimate and only repository of virtue and good behaviour. In some quarters this already had the flavour of political orthodoxy. But a united Asian region driven by such political orthodoxy is a united region to be feared, and for Australia it is critically important that we work for the maintenance of regional pluralism as the guarantee of heterodoxy and independence.[12]

It against the backdrop of the newly expansive economies and polities of Asia that Guan Wei has created for a contemporary Australian audience his own story of Chinese adventure and encounter with the 'Other'—that is, Australia. Although conceived by Guan Wei and created with a group of artist assistants, 'Other Histories' is, as you might have gathered, also the result of an extraordinary collaboration. It is a collaboration of the order and significance of which Stephen FitzGerald also wrote in his book, for he ended his discussion of Australia's new engagement with Asia on a positive note. He foresaw the possibility of the melding of people, ideas and cultures in Australia that would create a place where multiplicity would not be the source of racial tension and political exclusion. He hoped for an engagement with the world outside of Australia, and with the country's immediate neighbours, and that Australia would evolve into a country where difference allowed for possibility, one in which the 'Other' found a homeland. He was himself most at home when discussing and imagining how in the new millennium a deeply engaged, enriching and culturally resonant interaction with a nation like China could well work if it were a collaboration across nation-state divides that reached beyond received notions of exclusivity. In some ways, vital ways, Guan Wei's creation resonates with that home for this millennium.

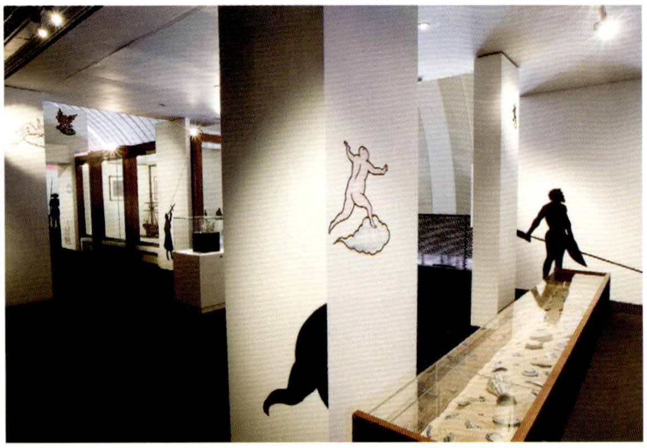

Exhibition view.
Photograph: Marinco Kojdanovski, Powerhouse Museum, Sydney.

The poetic tradition of imagination and otherworldliness makes 'Other Histories' a story of the spirit as well as being a confabulated narrative of movement and interaction. It is also a work that, through the engagement of both Guan Wei and the curatorial team of the Powerhouse Museum with China and Australia, and the powerful and rich distance between them, uplifts and expands the possibility of a more relaxed, fruitful and enjoyable cultural intertwinement. While China's continued economic rise and a heady Australian prosperity heightened by the mineral boom could lead to clientism, the grounded yet unfettered vistas featured in Guan Wei's curious cabinet of created history show that there are richer possibilities. For beyond the mutual pursuit of profit, the increased appetite for the consumption of material goods, the intermeshing of China with a wider world, something that has taken place as many people in Australia have reached out in unprecedented ways to their neighbours near and far, allows for a more mature appreciation of what individuals with shared human concerns can do across cultures, as well as across time. Re-enactment, historical fantasy and lived artistic reality work to make 'Other Histories' appeal as a history to which we can aspire, rather than just being a nostalgic account of a history that wasn't. It is a history in which narrow nationalisms are recognised but which do not dominate the stories of people, the movement of ideas and the connection of lives. It is a history that finds future vistas in which common concerns are addressed and resolved through an appreciation of how individuals in the past have attempted to reach out beyond themselves.

Known for the airy humanoid figures that populate many of his works, and for a sardonic humour that eschews the irksome irony that still marks so much Beijing-generated art, Guan Wei has a more expansive sensibility. He works from a bold palette to create an engaging world that is neither confronting nor repulsive. Nonetheless, it is a realm that can, upon closer inspection, and introspection, prove to be haunting. It is a place in which whimsy often masks disquiet, one in which the artist favours a lightness of touch to deal with lurking menace.

Thus there is a sombre side to Guan Wei's lightness of touch. The first time I encountered his work was in Beijing in 1987, when I was introduced to him by the artist Ah Xian (now celebrated for his extraordinary porcelain sculptures). Guan Wei was creating a series of works inspired by acupuncture. They showed featureless grey and muted figures with acupoints (some real, others of Guan Wei's invention) highlighted with red circles and labels; many were fractured creatures, others carried chiding messages of warning. They were a ghostly evocation, slightly humorous, also haunting. In our anthology of non-official Chinese writings *Seeds of Fire: Chinese Voices of Conscience* (1988), in a section entitled

'Pressure Points', John Minford and I refer to what we called 'the Chinese Velvet Prison', stating that at the time the independent cultural creator, be he/she an artist, writer or intellectual was 'faced with a choice of suffering complete cultural ostracism or accepting the State's efforts to incorporate them in a new social contract, one in which consensus replaces coercion, and complicity subverts criticism.' In commenting on Guan Wei's work we said that, 'The paintings also evoke the nightmarish world of the artist as inmate.'[13] It is in the artist's striking southern journey to the Antipodes, a new path leading out of this landlocked condition, that Guan Wei offers a different vision of how imaginative territory can be negotiated by a transnational cultural creator like himself. 'Other Histories' thus provides Guan Wei with a different territory, and therefore new perspectives, from which to consider his place of origin, as well as his adopted home.

'Other Histories' is thus an exemplary work in which a creative Chinese mind long nurtured in Antipodean reality embraces and enmeshes itself with local anxieties while speaking to wider, human concerns. Artists like Guan Wei who remain engaged with their place of origin while finding meaning in their domicile of choice enrich the scope of a world Chinese culture, contributing to it with an ambition that speaks to human reality, and possibility.

---

1. For an internet site devoted to debunking Menzies' book, see http://www.1421exposed.com/.
2. This point is also made by Michael Goldberg in his review 'Other Histories: Guan Wei's Fable for a Contemporary World', *Object Magazine*, 52 (April-July 2007): 48.
3. B. Gutfleish and J. Menzhausen, 'How a Kunstkammer Should be Formed', *Journal of the History of Collections*, 1 (1989):11, as cited at http://en.wikipedia.org/wiki/Cabinet_of_curiosities
4. See *China Heritage Quarterly*, 8 (December 2006) at www.chinaheritagequarterly.org
5. See Peter Hulme, *Colonial Encounters: Europe and the Native Caribbean,1492-1797* (London: Methuen, 1986), pp. 20-22.
6. In contradistinction to this, it is useful to follow the history of perceptions of China in Australia since WWII. See Timothy Kendall, *Ways of Seeing China: From Red Peril to Shangrila* (Freemantle: Freemantle Arts Centre Press, 2005).
7. Guan Wei, quoted in Claire Roberts, 'The Artist as Storyteller', in the exhibition booklet *Other Histories: Guan Wei's Fable for a Contemporary World* (Sydney: Powerhouse Publishing, 2006), p. 3.
8. Claire Roberts, 'Guan Wei: Artist as Storyteller', in this book, p. 51.
9. See Claire Roberts, 'The Artist as Storyteller' and Guan Wei, 'Other Histories', in the exhibition booklet (Sydney: Powerhouse Museum, 2006).
10. The objects carry two labels, one indicating their location in the Museum's collection, the other written by Guan Wei and his collaborators to reflect the narrative that he has created and the part that the objects play in it.
11. See my 'Serious Manchu Whimsy: What Goes Around Comes Around', a catalogue essay written for Guan Wei's exhibition at the Sherman Galleries in Sydney, 30 October-22 November 1997.
12. Stephen FitzGerald, *Is Australia an Asian Country? Can Australia Survive in an East Asian Future?* (Sydney: Allen & Unwin, 1997), p. 145.
13. Geremie Barmé and John Minford, *Seeds of Fire: Chinese Voices of Conscience* (New York: Hill & Wang, 2nd ed., 1988), pp. 386, 387.

The Swift Might Speak of its Flight, if Stories Are No Longer There . . .

Alexis Wright

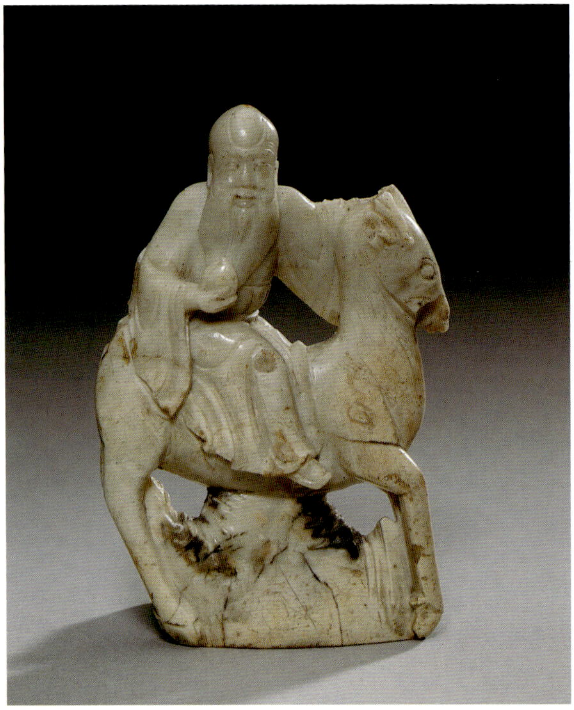

God of Longevity figure. Collection: Powerhouse Museum.
Photograph: Scott Donkin, Powerhouse Museum, Sydney.

I imagine when thinking of spirit fish making stories in the sea that there were days when grand scenarios occurred, that might even have involved how the little statue of the God of Longevity reached our shores centuries ago.

A school of huge fish, trevally perhaps, was once corralled in a wall of water building off the coast of Darwin. Hour after hour, the trapped fish were thrown around through rough waves, until they reached the sea's end, and were hauled up through an almighty tide thrown over the coast, along with everything else the cyclone had collected and stirred up through the vast distances it had travelled across the sea.

The statue was shaking about in the stomach of one of these fish which had snatched it long before from a string hanging down into the water that had been worn around the neck of a fishing man who had always carried it on his journeys to the sea. It was the fisherman's loss for bending so close to a hungry fish whilst at sea in his boat. Now, it was the fish's loss when the special treasure was spat right out of its mouth, as it tried to swim backwards to the sea, while caught in the hell of the tide.

The fish could have been killed, but, having been blessed by this god, lived. Unharmed, it swam even faster to save itself, as it sped off in a flash of silver through the flow rolling back to the sea. The statue was not broken when it was thrown clear from the water, and it ended up laying on the ground until it was found by the local Indigenous people who owned this part of the land. Then as time passed, the statue once again belonged to many people who liked the kind face of the foreign spirit god who was sitting on his deer and holding a strange piece of fruit in his hand.

The spirit god could not be carried around forever for he served no practical purpose other than offering a mystery, so he was eventually placed in the shade to rest, in a nook among the aerial roots of an old man banyan tree, by the hands of people who believed that ancestral spirits lived forever. Or, perhaps a different story was told where the old spirits were sorry for this god straying on their land, and had asked the visiting turtles and dingos to dig a big hole to bury the statue under the banyan tree, which after all also belonged to a similar legendary spirit of longevity in another world. The local ancestral spirits holding the wisdom of eternal knowledge for this land kept feeling sorry, and, saying—let the tree grow, let it grow, until one day..., created a small refuge for the statue that had originally come from the stomach of a fish. The statue was long forgotten when over time it became entangled in the roots of the tree.

More likely though, there might have once been a man of dreams, because there have always been men of dreams, those who seek adventure and fortune in faraway places. He believed in his own gods, so he took on his long sea voyage a treasured possession, a beautiful carved statue of his God of Longevity. The statue is creamy white of a man with a long beard who wears a cap, long robes and slippers. He holds a peach in one hand and with the other hand pats the head of a deer on which he sits. The seaman travelled by boat from China, bringing only what he could carry, perhaps some clothing, a compass, money or some items to trade and vegetable seeds, and if he arrived safely, he came ashore in northern Australia, to a coastline of

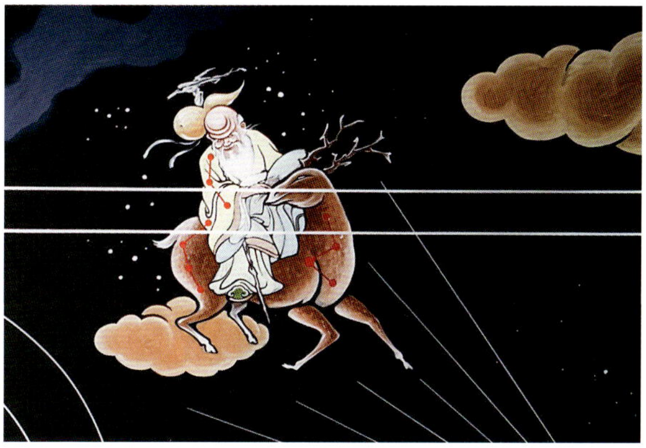

Detail of 'The God of Longevity', mural painting.
Photograph: Jean-François Lanzarone, Powerhouse Museum, Sydney.

pandanus trees and mangrove in a place that is now the city of Darwin.

I wonder if the man touched the power of his god while searching for answers about his life, if he felt lonely in this land laced in a tropical Top End wet season storm? Had he thought of flying home in dreams of Chinese deer, or on a free flight of a migrating swift, swallowing back through a land where forests were laden with snow, back through to the summer of ripe fruit falling straight into his hand from a peach tree that might have grown in him from childhood where storks danced like brolgas do, and, through these memories, thought of much else that represented a longing for his homeland? I wonder if this man returned to his country or stayed behind with his god, both abandoned and buried next to a banyan tree.

We may never know how the statue of the God of Longevity became embedded in the roots of a banyan tree where it was found four feet underground in 1879, during the construction of a road from Gwoomrajamurk[1] (Doctor's Gully) to Point Emery, near present-day Darwin. I have imagined that the statue was originally brought to our shores by a Chinese mariner, an ordinary man whose

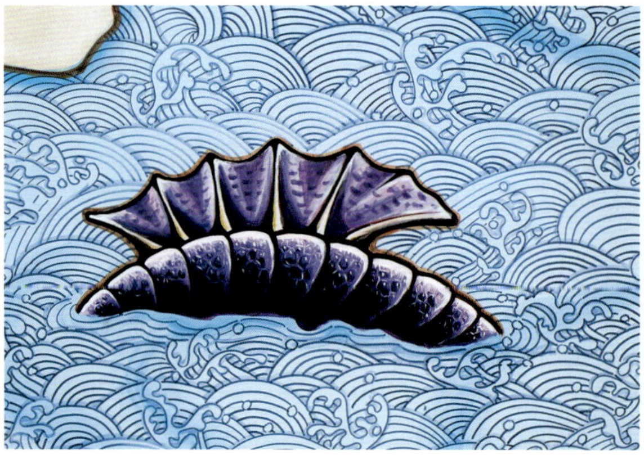

Detail of 'Treasure Hunt', mural painting.
Photograph: Jean-François Lanzarone, Powerhouse Museum, Sydney.

story was lost once he landed on the northern coast of Australia. It was not odd that he travelled this way, since he was following routes charted by his people centuries before through the sea to this part of the world.

Perhaps the mariner's father felt deeply worried about the dangers his son was taking in this long voyage to a foreign land, and knew that only a god made safe pathways possible to and fro across the sea. A good father might have carefully placed the statue of his God of Longevity in a silk bag with a cord attached so that it could be worn around the neck. He might have given this gift to his son on his departure from China. Indeed, this god is known in Chinese mythology as Canopus, which is the second brightest and a major navigational star in the sky at night.

The truth of a story can only reside in the statue that continues to represent its esteemed role of longevity through the safe hands of those who have cared for its safety ever since it was unearthed. Yet in the realm of long cultural tradition that is indigenous to this land, there are more ways of viewing truth. The story of how the statue was found, its symbolism, and the associated symbolism of a banyan tree are fascinating. It is a good story that allows us to open up our imagination to wonder at the possibility of other ways of understanding what can happen in our world, to surpass the mixed feelings that are produced in the harsh realities of our modern world. And it is a continuing story. One that increases our knowledge and scholarship of the statue's place not only in Chinese culture, but how it is also thought about through the multi-cultural, layered matrix of how thoughts are formed and grow in the mix of all of our

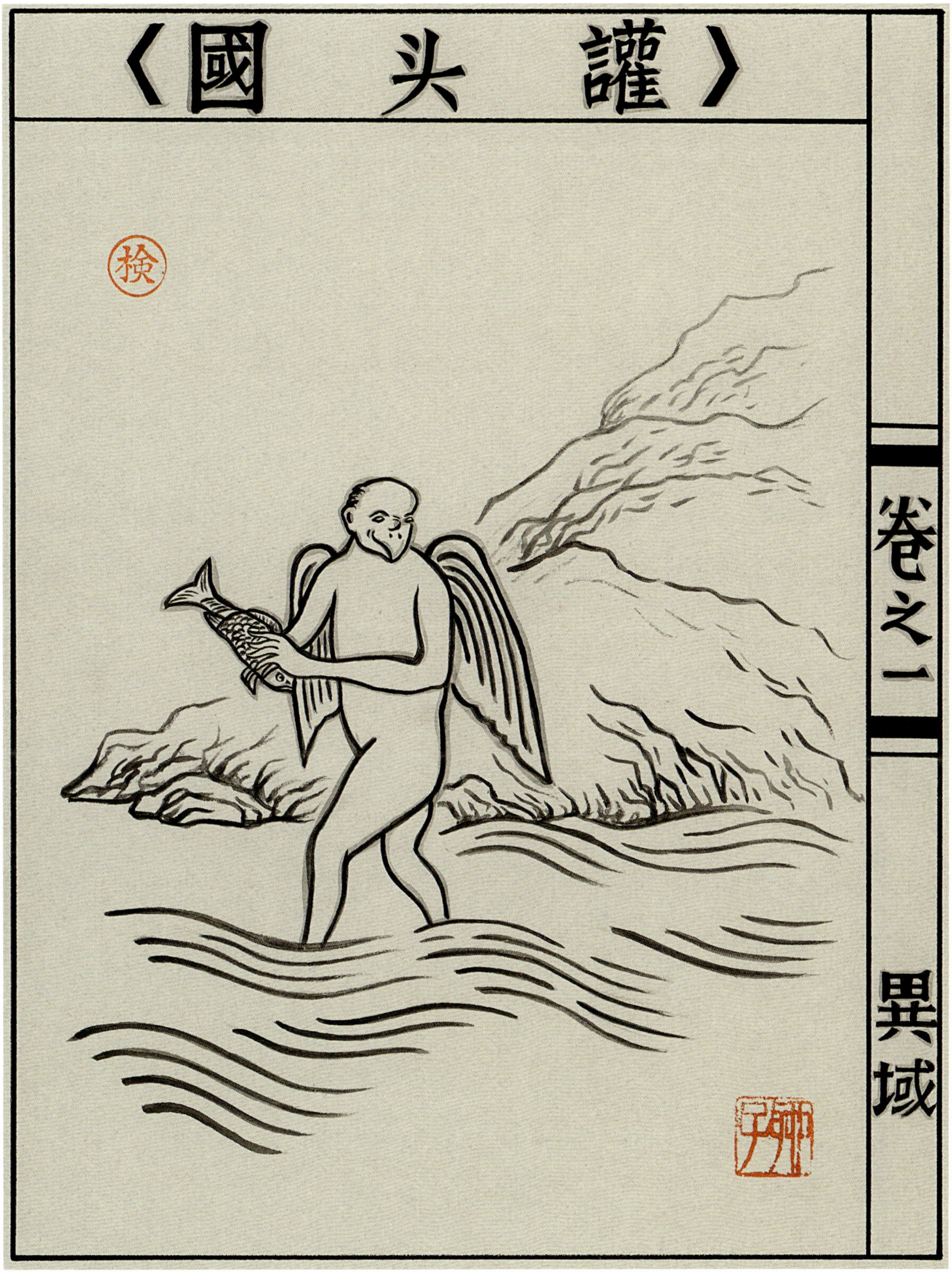

'People From Other Regions: Java', work on paper by Guan Wei.
Photograph: courtesy Powerhouse Museum, Sydney.

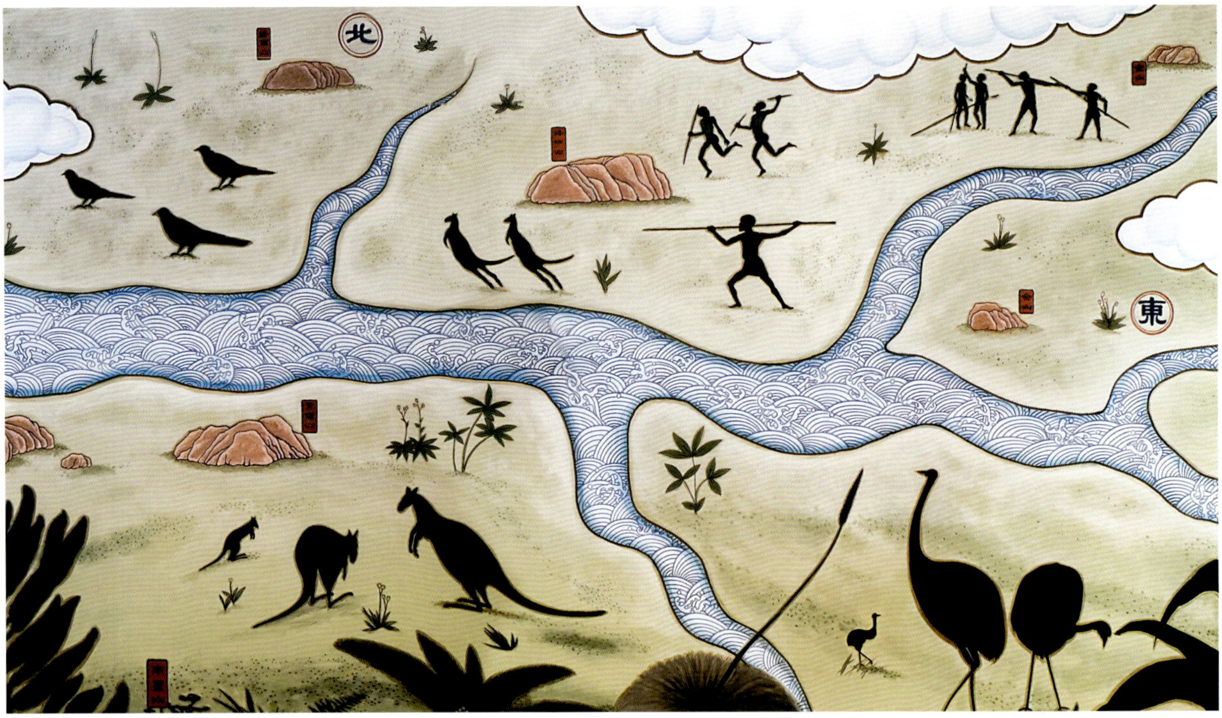

Detail of 'The Great Southern Land', mural painting.
Photograph: Jean-François Lanzarone, Powerhouse Museum, Sydney.

diversity as Australians. In the statue's prestigious home in the Powerhouse Museum in Sydney, it can no longer be simply viewed as a remnant of history, although this is part of a lingering true story too, that it belonged to a culture that was scarcely glorified or celebrated in the early years of colonisation in Australia.

The mariner's story, as he might have wished when he died, should live with his people through the spirits of his own country. The statue was left to live alone, in another symbol of longevity—the banyan tree where flocks of birds feed on its red berries, and the Indigenous people of the Larrakia might have sat under its branches as the traditional proprietors of this land and holy people of their nation, perhaps speaking of an important matter to the tree that might have been recognised as a stranger. They might have spoken about how the tree might be adopted, or incorporated into their law, like donkeys and feral cats could be in other parts of the country, and sometimes, visitors sat there too, who celebrated the tree's mythology that belonged in far away lands.

The tree itself may have found its life through a seed dropped by a white bird, a sulphur-crested cockatoo known by his traditional name in different Indigenous languages across Australia, and as Barrawa in the Waanyi language of my homeland whose ancestral spirit is represented in the Aboriginal law for this land, and is also associated with creatures of long life that the Chinese mythology for the God of Longevity gathered around him. The tree might not even have been a stranger to the Top End of Australia. Yolngu elder Mungurrowuy Yunupingu of the Gumatj clan in Arnhemland, and father of the esteemed Indigenous leader Galerrwuy Yunupingu, had once stood in front of a banyan tree with an axe and his young son Galerrwuy to prevent the tree from being destroyed by a bulldozer clearing the site for the Alcan Alumina Plant at Gove. The elder believed that the tree was sacred because it was the home of the spiritual guardian of the rain forest that once surrounded this tree in ancient times.[2]

I think something amazing happened in the hugely unrecorded history of Chinese contact in this country through this little statue. It helped to break the code of silence about whose history should be written in Australia, by insisting we recognise the existence of someone who once brought the statue here. This knowledge will live and grow for as long as people try to unfold the mystery of the statue, and this in itself helps us to connect not only with the spiritual ancestry of the natural world, but to more strands in the history of other people who once visited this land. The spirit breathes air charged with the power of creating the changing face of 'contact' history for the future, through the imagination of those visiting the statue, that might find within themselves a good spirit of mind, simply by looking through the smile of this ancient god that was left behind.

The statue could have been buried under the banyan tree for safekeeping, just as members of my own family once had a habit of burying something important in a tin container that was so secret, no surviving member of the family would ever find the rumoured money etc., that was buried somewhere. Or, more fantastically, an aerial root of a banyan tree had carried the statue sunk underground into the earthly darkness, where nature applied its own magic, and the statue became entangled in the roots of the tree, until dug up by Chinese workmen building a road in the Port of Darwin in 1879. The statue might even have continued to live with nature indefinitely, never being discovered, if the road being built by the colonial government of South Australia had the capacity to bend, to encompass the spirit of the tree.

My great grandfather Sam Ah Bow, who was a gardener, arrived in the Lawn Hills area in the Gulf of Carpentaria via Darwin in 1883, according to Queensland police district records.[3] I wonder how long he might have spent in the old Port of Darwin before he took the overland journey to the Gulf country. Perhaps, he had originally spent time working in the Chinese market gardens that were already established in the area of Doctor's Gully when the tree was being excavated, and possibly he knew of the story about how the statue was found in the roots of the tree. Could the Chinese workmen employed in the hard 'pick and shovel' physical labour to uproot a landmark in the natural and spiritual worlds, the mythically packed banyan tree, for a road that must be linear and straight, feel blessed with good luck, or cursed when the statue was found?

Ah! But, the statue was found, and it lives, the swift replied, and flew home with an empty seat, but had a lot of stories to tell …

---

1. The Larrakia nation name for Doctor's Gully as I heard it spoken by Larrakia traditional landowner Mr Koolpinyah Richard Barnes, Chairman of the Larrakia Development Corporation Pty Ltd, in our telephone conversation on 3 October 2007.
2. This story is told by Galerrwuy Yunupingu in Bob Beale, *If Trees Could Speak: Stories of Australia's Greatest Trees* (Sydney: Allen & Unwin, 2007), p. 230.
3. www.archives.qld.gov.au/downloads/ Indexes/Asiatic_aliens/no_surname_ah_way.pdf. This document records that Sam Ah Bow arrived at Louie Creek in 1883 from the Gregory Downs district. However, this could be wrong, as he might have been at Lawn Hills where he worked as a cook for Frank Hann earlier. According to records from my cousin, Phyllis Ah Kit, my grandmother's birth certificate states that her eldest brother was born seventeen years (1886) before her birth in 1903.

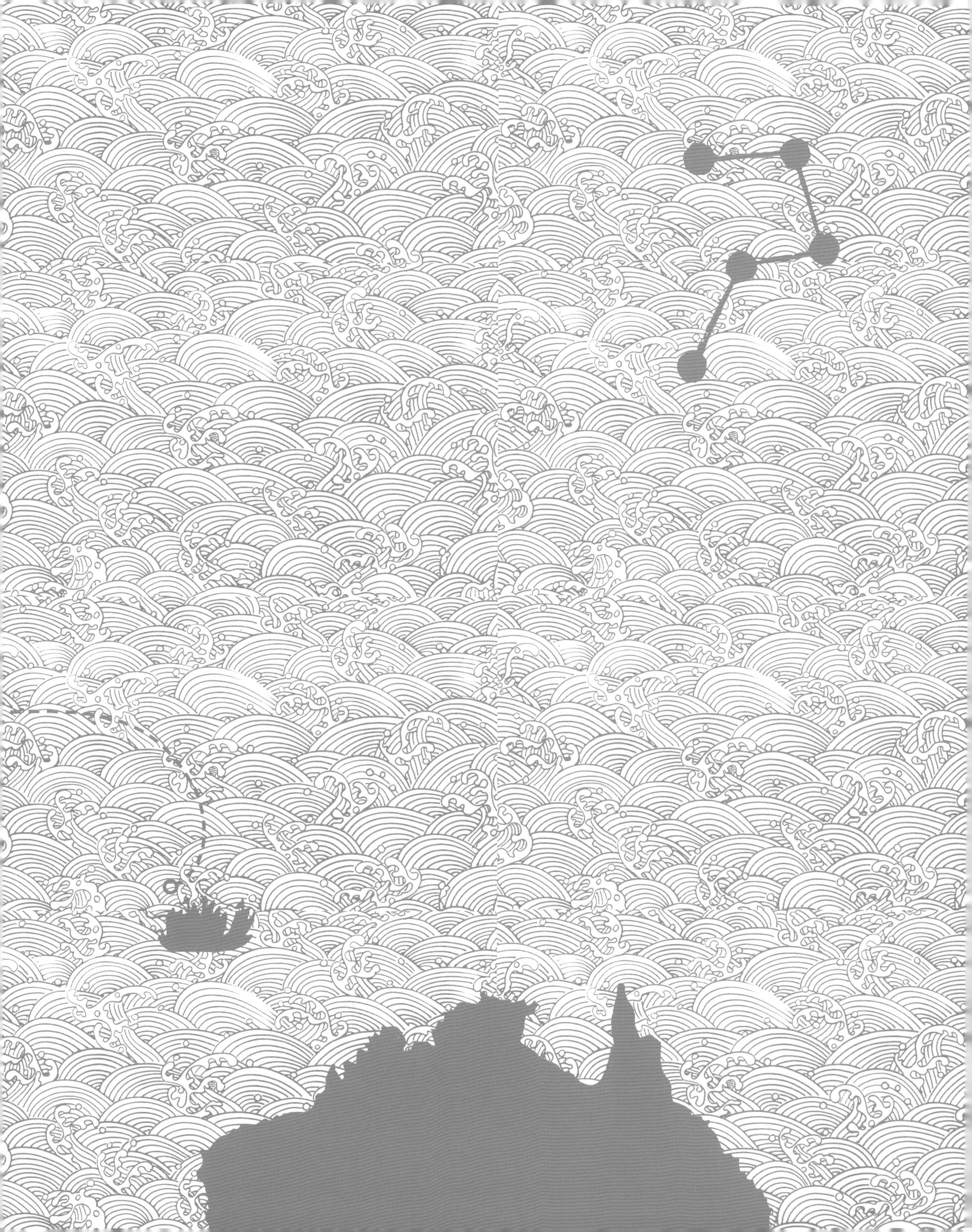

另一种历史的呈现：起因与创作心得

关伟

经过历时两年的精心筹划与创作，我的大型壁画和装置艺术展《另一种历史——关伟的现代寓言》自 2006 年 10 月起至 2007 年 4 月在澳大利亚悉尼动力博物馆举办。在这个展览中，我综合运用了多种艺术形式，呈现另一种历史——中国明代的伟大航海家郑和率领他的船队在将近六百年前抵达现今被称为澳大利亚的这片辽阔大地的辉煌历程。

奉明永乐皇帝朱棣之命，郑和率两万七千余人组成的庞大船队扬帆出海，先后七下西洋，历时 28 年，航程共计 7 万多海里，相当于环绕地球 3 周有余，陆续访问了几十个国家和地区，与当地居民在贸易和文化等方面进行了广泛的交流，建立和加深了中国与这些国家与地区的相互了解。郑和首次奉诏出海是永乐三年六月十五日，即公元 1405 年 7 月 11 日，比哥伦布发现美洲新大陆早 87 年，比达 · 伽马经过好望角早 92 年，比麦哲伦开始他的环球航行早 114 年；此后不久，在我的这个展览中，他又先于库克船长大约 350 年抵达了澳大利亚。

2002 年 3 月，英国退休海军军官加文 · 孟席斯在伦敦宣布他的研究成果说：是中国人最早绘制了世界海图，郑和的船队先于哥伦布到达美洲大陆，郑和是环球的航行第一人；同年，他出版了《1421 年：中国发现美洲》，并在 2003 年将这本书更名为《1421 年：中国发现世界》再版发行。加文 · 孟席斯在他的书中提出：最早发现美洲和澳大利亚的都是郑和，郑和在将近六百年前就已经踏上了澳大利亚的土地，并且在澳大利亚和新西兰建立了殖民点。作为支持上述观点的证明，加文 · 孟席斯展示了他在十多年的研究过程中找到的海图、罗盘和另外几件文物。数量很有限，而且还存在争议的这几件文物能否证明他所说的这段历史事件，是否足够支持他的惊人论断，以及如何认定和怎样解释这几件文物等等，无疑是非常有趣的问题。

我认为可以将历史学家和考古学家们对于既往事件的研究和呈现视为解码与编码的过程。他们对新发现的文物所进行的分析和鉴定的工作，实际上是发掘与认定这些文物所携带的密码的解码过程；然后，他们将这些被他们赋予了相应身份的文物放在博物馆的相应位置进行陈列，实际上是将它们归入早在此前就已经被制定完成，并且被多数人所接受的历史程序的编码过程。因此，当观众们被展出的这些文物所吸引，并且由此联想到某个特定的时代，对历史的恢宏油然升起景仰与怀念之情的时候，其实也就是他们接受别人的解码和编码，而且顺服于这个程序的被动过程。

那么，作为当代艺术家，我是否可以通过创作对这个解码与编码的过程进行逆向操作，先从艺术的角度出发制造出一些文物，完成艺术家的编码，然后通过在博物馆的展出呈现给观众，由他们对这些艺术化的文物进行解码？我认为我完全可以进行这样的尝试，完全能够以文物艺术化的方式为博物馆观众这个很广大，但是非专业的人群提供主动参与的机会，从而共同创造艺术化的历史。

郑和下西洋这段历史年代久远，可供征引的文献不多，可资证明的文物也很少。对于历史学家来说，这是非常遗憾的事情，但是这种缺失却给我提供了一个非常巨大的空间，我因此可以发挥更多的想象，更自由地去构建郑和的壮举，让我的郑和船队在澳大利亚登陆，呈现辉煌的另一种历史。

中国文人存在着一种比较独特的气质，对于一件作品的创作，他们既有严肃地精雕细刻的一面；又有幽默地举重若轻的一面，并且通过这两者的融会贯通，达至完全的审美快感。这也是本展览所要遵循的宗旨之一，我要求自己在展览的构成与制作上既要精细耐看，又要幽默轻松，就是说既要经琢磨又要很好玩儿。于是，就大结构而言，我把展览分为既对立又和谐，既严肃又活泼的三个部分：一，皇帝与太监；二，寻宝与海图；三，老寿星与南十字星座。

展览中共有九幅大型壁画。最初的几幅，分别展现了明朝初年的历史、永乐皇帝与郑和的生平等等，也就是早已被制定完成，并且被多数人所接受的正统历史。紧随其后的几幅，则是带有很强烈的个人想象成分的出海寻宝、抵达澳大利亚，以及跨越时空的，实际上发生在清朝的中国人来到澳大利亚淘金的画面。除了这九幅大型壁画，我在可供利用的展厅其它平面上，比方天花板、地面平台、立柱和一般观众意想不到的其它角落里，还绘制了许多小幅画面。这些画面的图幅很小，但是非常引人注目，与大型壁画构成在意象、色彩、内容等方面既疏离又紧密的联系，给人以整体的视觉冲击。

我在最近的几年里创作过很多大型壁画，积累了丰富的经验。大型壁画的特点一是空间不受限制，可以自由自在地发挥；二是因为是现场制作而带有比其它形式更大的即兴与变通成分；三是这些作品通常都是临时性的，展览结束后会被全部涂掉不留痕迹。作品并非天长日久的现实，会对艺术家的心态产生巨大的影响，艺术家在创作时会因此更加专注于纯艺术的思考，摆脱作品商业化的干扰。这个展览中的壁画，可以说是我这几年在壁画创作方面的总结，创作规模大，绘制时间长，在我的艺术家朋友与助手赵葆康、金沙、杨熹发和侯松鹤的协助下，我用了整整一个月的时间才全部绘制完成。

除了壁画，在展览中我还利用了动力博物馆收藏的古钱币、古陶瓷、古家具等大量文物，以及另外一些实物展品。我对进入展览的这些馆藏品进行了重新编排和命名，也就是赋予它们新的身份，让它们参与叙述另一种历史。例如老寿星和它的故事：礬石雕刻老寿星是悉尼动力博物馆在上世纪五十年代征集到的文物，据记录，它的出土时间是 1879 年，出土地点是澳大利亚达尔文港附近一棵年代久远的大榕树下，出土时被树根紧紧缠裹。有关这件显然产自中国的文物为什么会在澳大利亚出土，是郑和船队还是别的什么人在几百年前把它带到澳大利亚等等，至今还是谜。既然它的身份至今还是谜，我就干脆用它重新编排了一个有答案的故事，请它在另一种历史中现身说法——在中国典籍中，老寿星号称南极老人，是夜空最南端的一颗星；于是我把它和澳大利亚天顶的南十字星座相结合，让我的郑和船队在北半球航行时以他们所习惯的北斗星为坐标，穿过赤道进入南半球航行之后，以他们眼中的老寿星，也就是南十字星座中最亮的恒星 Acrux 为坐标，向着南极老人照耀下的土地前进，终于抵达了澳大利亚……然后，一代又一代的中国移民沿着郑和开辟的航线，仍旧是在老寿星的引导下踏上了这块神奇的南方大陆，开始了昔日的淘金、寻宝和今天的求学、就业。老寿星和它的故事被我安排在展览的第三部分，通过两张大型壁画和老寿星展柜，以及放置在另外两个大型展柜中的其它移民文物，集中呈现郑和船队前往澳大利亚的经过和由此开始的南北交流，中澳交流。

将馆藏文物引进当代艺术展览，并不仅仅是对博物馆资源进行再度开发与利用，也不仅仅是单纯地增加了博物馆的参与程度；把获得了新身份的文物作为既是艺术的又是现实的装置作品整合于当代艺术的空间，这本身就是一项新的试验。

通晓阿拉伯语的学者马欢是郑和船队的随行翻译，他的著作《瀛涯胜览》出自他参加郑和船队远航的沿途见闻，对现今为越南、马六甲、斯里兰卡、印度尼西亚、阿拉伯等地的风俗和特产有着图文并茂的记载。以马欢的文字和明清两代的多种《山海经》绘本为参考，我为另一种历史创作了三十余幅以人物、植物、动物、地图、海图和牵星图为内容的仿古图画。这些用镶框悬挂方式展出的单幅图片使用了考古、历史、航海、气象等诸多方面的人文与自然因素，就形象而言又均有澳大利亚特有物种为蓝本，全方位地展示了郑和下西洋这个历史事件所带来的地理大发现。仿古图画的使用，在很大程度上丰富了展览的内容，有效地调整了节奏，同时也大大地提高了局部观赏性，从而有节制地拓宽了基于博物馆空间的展览范围。

真文物与被视为文物的仿古图画的同时空展示，在观念上打破了传统展览类型的界限。概念和作品的真伪并存，造成了难以给我的这个另一种历史明确定位的现实，观众们可以把这个展览看成是考古与历史文物展，可以把这个展览看成是工艺美术及民俗艺术展，也可把这个展览看成是平面与装置结合的当代艺术展，而这正是我在这个展览中所追求的另外一个目标。

在另一个历史的呈现过程中，我还充分地注意到了澳大利亚的文化资源。从社会历史、人与自然的关系等因素，我引申出原住民文化、殖民文化、多元文化等内容；从海洋、岛屿、内陆荒漠的再现，联系到航海、探险、寻宝、移民，直至全球化的影响和应对……这是一个非常丰富的资源，它的存在，有力地推动我探索新的视觉表达方式。

不论郑和下西洋的历史还是郑和下西洋的意义，都存在着超出于事件本身，超出于航海之外的解读。这些解读都是解读者使用他所处的那个时代的观念对郑和的再认识，并且通过自己的解读给予作为符号的郑和众多的新意。作为出生在中国，生活在澳大利亚的当代艺术家，我所创作的这个作品是以个人经验为出发点：起初，我把自己的创作活动置于郑和下西洋这个事件之中，使创作成为这段历史的组成部分；然后，随着事件情节的展开，艺术创作本身的规律又促使我必须对正统历史进行颠覆；最终，我的郑和船队终于抵达了澳大利亚，对除原住民外是英国人首先抵达澳大利亚的传统说法提出了挑战，构成了具有关伟特色的另一种历史。

另一种历史未必就是历史，呈现另一种历史的目的是不过是颠覆单一的意识形态，释放自由的想象。今日的我们生活在充满紧张焦虑的环境之中，我衷心地期望我的郑和船队所带来的另一种历史能够促进不同种族，不同文化背景的人们相互交流，互施友爱，和谐共存。

关伟：艺术家和传奇的讲述者

罗清奇

关伟是属于我们这个时代的艺术家。他的许多作品是以见多识广的过去经验为源泉，但他同时又敏锐地瞄准并且融合当前的情绪。在他以往的创作主题中包括移民和难民的境遇，恐怖与战争，环境与污染。关伟所遵循的表达方式是回避诲人不倦的说教，宁肯采用幽默和简约的艺术语言帮助我们认识我们的道路，从而更明朗地鉴识我们所共有的人性。澳大利亚艺术评论家约翰 · 麦克端纳认为关伟最近的作品"另一种历史"或许是关伟的杰作[1]，他通过这个大型装置作品叙述了他自己版本的中国历史和中澳关系史，这可能是个人对历史的理解，可能是同样私人的形式的再设定。他对公认的历史进行再选择，以高度的观念主题结合回顾的形式，轻捷地穿行在娱乐和实验的过程之中。这是起源于深层意识的历史，他采用以自己的过去映射当今的冲突，显示着乌托邦理想的姿态[2]。

"另一种历史：关伟为当代世界创造的寓言" 于 2006 年 10 月 11 日至 2007 年 4 月 22日 在悉尼动力博物馆举行。这个展览基于明代历史和中国航海家的史诗，或者说由明代历史和中国航海家史诗抒发开来的假想。关伟出生在北京，1990 年移民到澳大利亚，他在这个展览中继续展示他既是艺术家同样又是传奇讲述者的角色，创造将他的壁画与博物馆藏品作为装置艺术相结合的，叙述将风雅的消遣实体化的假定性历史。这个展览的推论性命题是明朝的穆斯林太监和航海家郑和的旅行，他从大明帝国前往陌生的南方大陆，最终抵达澳大利亚。关伟希望这个展览能够呈现"在历史和记忆中蜿蜒流动的诗廊，将事实和虚构交融并且模糊化"的意境[3]。

面对有关他所描述的历史事件真实程度的质询，尤其是关于概念上的真实与表层所呈现的神话的关系，关伟的回应是：郑和与他的船队所进行的大航海是千真万确的事实，参与航海的大约有 27,000 名船员，宝船在太平洋和印度洋总共行驶了大约 70,000 海里，先后长达 28 年左右，他们有可能先于库克船长 350 年抵达澳大利亚。至于是否真地抵达了，关伟说："这是无关紧要的，我是艺术家"[4]，所以他是在自由地创造着他自己版本的历史。

"另一种历史"的筹划过程很长，在这个项目的孕育期间，关伟由起初的想法不断地延伸和发展。他的方案初稿写作于 2002 年，标题是"遗物的再创造：发现澳大利亚的中国先驱"。这个想法部分地来自于加文 · 孟席斯在 2002 年出版的，富有争议的著作《1421 年：中国发现世界》。这本书引起关伟兴趣的是孟席斯依据历史遗物想象郑和"发现"澳大利亚的途径。在这个最初的方案里，关伟抓住了孟席斯带来的那些迷人的设想，但他怀疑这些很有限而且有争议的古代遗物是否可以满足将这段历史具象化的要求；与其说这段隐秘的历史深藏在那些遗物之中，不如说更紧要的是如何认识和解释这些遗物。在稍后的接触和交谈中，关伟和我反复讨论了什么是他需要面对的关键，关键是如何推定和解释历史[5]。因此，展览方案最核心的要素是他自己所特有的见解，包括对这些历史遗物的认识，以及对海图、地图和标本等可资利用的实物的再创作方式。他说："这将是有计划的另类考古发现展，采用博物馆风格进行陈列，整体设置在用壁画的暗红色和光点耀斑所营造的环境，从而建立起神奥和隐密的氛围”[6]。由此可见关伟着迷于通过汇合“证据”和使用清晰的博物馆式装置构成他自己版本的历史的概念。

关伟与悉尼动力博物馆联系，希望在2005年实现这个展览，该年是郑和航海600周年，中国将为此举行官方纪念活动。关伟在此时已将他的方案修订为预期目标是：对博物馆功能的重新分析，对博物馆展览障碍的突破和化解，对博物馆藏品的再解释，以及关于澳大利亚历史主流理论的质疑[7]。展览设置在博物馆环境的预期，以及与专业人员在大的公众事业机构协同工作的愿景，锐化了他的创作焦点。

也正是在这个阶段，关伟由绘制画板拼接作品转移到创作大幅壁画的试验。2003年下半年和2004年，他最初的壁画作品出现在柏林、墨尔本和悉尼[8]。壁画形式之所以吸引了关伟，很大成分在于他因此得以在现场直接实现自己的想法，轻捷地在大尺度空间穿行，不必顾及有关作品运送和画布处理等问题，也不必考虑作品的出售。

壁画是位置特定的，尺度巨大的，毫不胆怯的强烈形式。敦煌莫高窟的古代佛教壁画是关伟的灵感来源之一[9]。莫高窟壁画绘制在保存着沙岩雕刻和彩塑的洞窟的四壁、窟顶和佛龛，以佛像、史迹、经变、供养人等为题材，还有表现狩猎耕织等社会生活的画作。敦煌位于中国西北的戈壁沙漠，是古代丝绸之路的重镇，曾经有无数的商旅和大量的朝圣者穿过沙漠到达这个绿洲。在目前，辉煌精美的莫高窟壁画多数保持尚好，敦煌已是旅行者所向往的胜地，但关伟从未获得亲见原作的机会，一直是在观摩复制品。

在20世纪的中国，不朽的传统壁画艺术被变更到顺应那个时代的需要。文化大革命期间，也就是关伟成长的时代，曾有大量的宣传画和标语直接涂写在建筑物的外墙，向所有经过它们的人宣示政治教条。在今天，除了偏远市镇的人迹罕至之处，我们已经很难到看到这类当年遍及各处的宣传品的痕迹。目前残存于社会角落里的那些，则透过粉刷在它们上面的白色涂层的遮盖，鬼魂般地在旧建筑的表面寂静地显露出模糊的面目——这种残余的政治符号，也是激发关伟灵感的源泉[10]。

自1970年代末开始，壁画在中国被赋予当代建筑的室内装饰功能。其中著名的示范是1979年北京国际机场的壁画，方式是谨小慎微的自由。机场壁画中的一幅是先锋派艺术家袁运生（生于1937年）因云南西双版纳傣族泼水节而获得灵感的，包含三个裸女形象的作品“泼水节——生命的赞歌”。这幅壁画完成后，因裸体女人形象的出现在1980年初引发了激烈的辩论，甚至有官员声称壁画中傣族形象有损于民族团结，终于在五讲四美的道德运动中先是被纱帘然后是隔板隐蔽。

在对当代艺术的表现和艺术家立场达致全面控制的空间里，如果该作品不被接纳，壁画的生命通常是朝生暮死。这种形式仿佛体育竞赛或歌剧表演，它的所有细节，不论展示时间和表现空间都是一个受限过程并且因而变得戏剧化，是艺术家挣脱自身的束缚和他们惯常创作模式的释放。此外，壁画的展示一般的会随同展览的结束而结束，被重新涂刷的墙面回归空白。

这个展览中，关伟的实践是从展览的整体逻辑出发，将壁画作为展览的重要组成部分，并且使之成为“另一种历史”的首要叙述力量。与此同时，他也充分地注意使用悬挂在其他墙面的，与大幅壁画相互独立的屏装纸面作品，以强调距离与自然空间的试验性设计，积极地创造场景和情绪的转换，激起观众不断拥抱新场景的欲望，更主动地联系博物馆环境。

合作：艺术家与博物馆

作为与博物馆全体人员有关的项目，“另一种历史”为我们提供了一个特殊的机会。它引起了我们对于博物馆所承担的角色，不论是管理或者历史文物说明的进一步思考。与关伟共同工作，使我们的脚步有可能远离严肃和日常展览的经验与教条，对什么是博物馆环境可能完成的或已经接受的，活跃地提出了挑战。与这个项目有关的每个人，包括作为策划人的我自己、展览设计者、图像设计师、展览协调人，以及展品登录人员、藏品保管员、教育项目人员等等，都联合在关伟的想象力周围，快乐地承担着各自的专业角色，共同建筑关伟的这个传奇。

关伟从这个项目的启动就开始设想装置的构成和画面的呼应，以及实物和文本内容的整合。到最终方案，关伟对在装置作品中他所希望包括的实物类型概要提出了具体描述，例如陶器、佛像、硬币、航海装备、以及关联到中国与澳大利亚历史和贸易的实物，比方茶叶和中草药等等。这些实物和标本来自博物馆的收藏，以及关伟所提供的，难以逐一确定原始来源的实物。

博物馆方面为关伟编制了在装置中可能存在潜在使用机

会的实物目录，以便他对我们的基本馆藏情况有所了解，并且共同参与对藏品的考察。然后，我们基于各种不同因素，经过全盘的综合考虑，基本决定了哪些实物可供构成装置进行陈列。对于参展实物，关伟注意的是表现作品观念所需的类型，然而我则有意识地从历史和文物来源的细节出发，关注该实物可能具有的特殊意义。我们的实物目录最终变得非常清晰，明确地集中于我们所期望的展览的魅力，围绕有助于建立探索真实与虚构之间的联系，并且和关伟的传奇叙述建立联系进行了精选。

展览所呈现的核心实物展品是动力博物馆征集收藏的，具有迷人外表的中国老寿星雕像。这尊矾石雕像于 1879 年在达尔文附近的一棵古老的菩提树下的洞穴中出土。因为它的发现的时间和特殊造型，引起相当多的猜测和学术探讨[11]。有作家和历史学家提出它可能是来自十五世纪的中国，因此显示出与郑和的航海事迹有所关联，而且在加义 · 孟席斯的著作中作为中国人比詹姆士 · 库克抵达澳大利亚海岸要早 350 多年的例证。但是博物馆方面的见解是，根据外观轮廓和雕刻风格等因素，这件文物很可能是 1800 年代的作品，它涉及澳大利亚北部的达尔文与中国的早期接触。在"另一种历史"中，关伟坚决地将这位老寿星认定为属于郑和的船队，在他的叙述里，老寿星是南十字星座的化身，引导着郑和的船队，以及更多的中国移民来到澳大利亚这片伟大的南方陆地。

从我们最初的讨论起，关伟一直急切并强烈地希望在构成装置的实物中包括澳大利亚特有的动物和鸟类的标本，以此暗示陌生的异国风情与郑和船队在澳大利亚的见闻。但是，在动力博物馆的收藏中很少这个门类的实物，我们为此向在悉尼收集和保护自然历史门类藏品的澳大利亚博物馆借来了袋鼠、无尾熊、负鼠和食火鸡的标本。关伟还为装置另外增添了更多的具有历史真实性的实物、赝造的文物和当代的商品，这类实物的添加，更加模糊了真实和虚构的边际。

壁画的创作过程

鉴于展览空间墙壁的巨大尺度，关伟在四位画家的协助下完成壁画创作。作为关伟助手的四位艺术家是侯松鹤、金沙、杨熹发和赵葆康。在过去的几年里，关伟曾和他们在其它项目中有过合作经验，他们都是在各自领域里非常熟练的艺术家，都是近年从中国移民到澳大利亚的，于是在感觉上和关伟的传奇叙述也存在着密切的关联。大型壁画的创作历时一个月。

作为壁画创作的主持者，关伟的工作不仅是绘制，还承担着协调和管理帮助他完成壁画创作的这四位艺术家的工作。他预先准备好包括布局和色彩细节在内的，精细的纸上小样，以供艺术家助手们遵循；然后，在关伟的指导下，每位艺术家承担着不同的壁画工作。根据壁画的题目和形式，关伟选择不同的艺术家承担可能发挥他们技能和兴趣最大值的内容，例如金沙擅长绘制海洋生物，杨熹发擅长水面波涛和花鸟，侯松鹤和赵葆康擅长风景。壁画的技术创作过程是先用炭条勾画轮廓，然后运用平涂方式多层使用不同色阶的丙烯颜料。在此时，未来的展览陈列空间变成了巨大的画室，到处分布着丙烯颜料罐和画笔。对于批次性重复出现的景物内容，为了形象和效果的一致性，他们使用了模版，比方郑和船队的宝船，以及富有毅力的杨熹发所承担绘制的大面积的海浪和一条又一条不断重复的稠厚的黑色浪迹线。

有众多著名的历史主题出现在关伟的画面，这类形象复制于相应的历史著作和航海著作，以及参照中国宫廷画家、殖民时代的澳大利亚画家和中国木版印刷古籍的图像。因此，在当时作为画室的展览空间里，堆积着供艺术家发掘的，可能提供视觉形象参考的书籍和杂志。关伟有意识地使用适当的主题与喜悦在他的历史中营造共鸣，借鉴得来的肖像很快地屈从他与众不同的绘画风格，直到变成细节，与巨大并且连贯的新的模式融合为一体。

随着博物馆展览空间中用于装置的实物日益增多，每天都可以在那里的墙壁上和陈列橱中可以发现再度更新的景象。展览创作的过程和非凡的感觉，因之成为这个富有演进性和启示性的项目的要素。在壁画创作的最后的三个星期里，我们邀请公众参观关伟和艺术家们的现场工作。参观活动通常从下午开始，观众站在隔开壁画绘制区域的栅栏后面。一位观众在留言中表达她的喜悦说："参观艺术家关伟和他的助手作画给了我异常的惊喜，他的作品是令人鼓舞和发人深省的，我为获得和他交谈的机会感到荣幸"。

在最后的几天里，新的壁画轮廓和陌生的标记出现在人们意想不到的地方，位于支柱、裙墙、天花板和防水壁的部分图形是从未在最初的提议中出现的。于是，不论你从哪个位置和角度观察，都会发现某些新的意外——澳大利亚本土的轮廓，来自英国和欧洲的探险家，早期的盎格鲁 · 撒克逊移民，破浪而至的船民；嬉笑人头，怪异的小妖、蜿蜒而行的蟒蛇，雷雨闪电和中国的印章；甚至还有富含幽默感的，毫无遮掩的圆胖的关伟本人的剪影。其中最为迷人的是最后添加的，由杨熹发完成的手绘花枝和鸟群画面，它用蓝色绘制在淡蓝色的壁面，为关伟提供了既自然又富有装饰性的舞台背景。在舞台表演的是关伟创作的一系列令人眼花缭乱的屏装纸面作品。这些纸面作品的形象灵感来自中国的古籍《山海经》，描绘着植物、动物和充满陌生感的大地。这些奇特诡异的，引人入胜的画面，更深远地将不同的单一成分综合为完全的整体，唤起并且举升了关伟起初即在追寻的神奥和秘密氛围。

我们在进入这个展览区域的过渡空间里构建了文字简介看板，提醒博物馆的观众们由此进入了这个展览的边界，也就是等于进入了关伟的世界，加入了他的旅行团队，成为他的发现活动的参与者。在展区内部的每一幅壁画前面有相关的文字说明，这些说明中的文本均使用引号方式表示这是关伟的声音而不是博物馆的言论。至于装置作品中的每块实物展品说明牌，都是使用两种字体来表达不同的层面：一种是关伟对装置作品中的实物的解释和定位，使用黑体字并加引号；另一种是在此之下的博物馆的藏品登录信息，包含着关于这件实物展品的科学解释和详细资料。采取这种以文字完成解答的方式，目的是为了让观众认清他们所参观的并不是传统意义的博物馆展览而是装置艺术作品，他们是在参与历史与幻想交织的，带有嬉戏成分的对话。观众因此变得活跃，富有活力地投入互动，积极地响应关伟的充满幻想的叙述，进入参与者的角色。

随同"另一种历史"发行的小册子，显示着关伟鼓励观众进行对我们人类共性的思考的急切愿望。他写道："我期望这个展览会引发观众们对有关我们生命的所有的惊喜的记忆，并且激励大家思索人类共同享有的经验。我们的世界到处都存在着美妙和令人惊叹的魅力。来自不同文化的背景的我们，需要更多的相互了解，彼此寻求友谊，为了未来的生存，我们必须找寻共有的价值"。

关伟自觉地认识到他作为艺术家的同时，又是建立在当今的生活与迷人的过去之间的活生生的链环。他运用个人经验和丰富的想象反思历史，并且对当代进行再思考，着眼于改善我们未来的探索。关伟的工作像侦探通过"证据"和寓言般的历史，将历史事件作为原料，展开封闭的知识，对其进行拆解和分离，以再汇编的方式加以改善。关伟试图重新书写历史的观念和行为的核心，浸透着乌托邦式的乐观精神。因此，我们所看到的并不一定是真实发生过的历史，但是它同样地可能发生过。在"另一种历史"中，关伟将他自己的角色造就为艺术家和传奇的讲述者。

翻译：桑晔

---

1. 约翰 · 麦克端纳，《联合文化的屏障》，刊《悉尼晨驱报》，2006 年 10 月 14 日— 15 日，艺术和娱乐版，第 17 页。
2. 瓦内萨 · 安纽，《什么是再设定》，刊《评论杂志》，2004 年夏季号，第 327 页— 335 页。
3. 关伟，罗清奇引用于《艺术家，同时是故事的讲述者》，刊《另一种历史：关伟为当代世界创造的寓言》展览图册，悉尼动力博物馆出版，2006 年，第 3 页。
4. 索南达 · 奎夫，《你能从我的作品看到政治境遇：这些身体没有眼睛》，刊《悉尼晨驱报》，2006 年 9 月 9 日— 10 日，艺术与娱乐版，第 5 页。
5. 见 2004 年 8 月 10 日的传真文件。
6. 关伟的展览方案，标题为《遗物的再创造：发现澳大利亚的中国先驱》，2002 年。
7. 关伟修订后的展览方案，标题为《在动力博物馆的展览—— 郑和，文化遗物展》，2004 年 8 月 24 日。
8. 向上的面容，澳大利亚的当代艺术展，班哈夫博物馆，柏林，2003 年 10 月 2 日 -2004 年 1 月 4 日；乌托邦的循环轨迹，澳大利亚当代艺术中心，墨尔本，2004 年 8 月 7 日— 10 月 28 日；另外的陆地，伊凡 · 多佛西画廊，悉尼，2004 年 8 月 20 日— 9 月 25 日。
9. 纳塔利 · 柯因，《中国私语：关伟的作品》，黛娜 · 迪萨特、纳塔利 · 柯因、侯翰如合著，《关伟》，悉尼艺舍出版社，2006 年，第 84 页。
10. 同上。
11. 悉尼动力博物馆藏品，编号 A4255。老寿星，矾石雕刻，据记载是 1897 年在靠近澳大利亚北领地达尔文港的博士溪谷发现于菩提树根下。1889 年动力博物馆获石膏复制品捐赠，1950 年购得原物。参阅约翰 · 威德《寿星佬：1879 年在达尔文出土的中国雕像》，刊《澳大利亚历史考古学会通讯》，1977 年 6 月号，第 13 页— 16 页。

行进在关伟的多宝阁

白杰明

引发这一切的是受欢迎的国际资本的挺进和激进地对它的历史上的很多阶段进行再设定，中国正在为此经历着前所未有并且如此清晰地重新演绎众多的往昔的过程。这些重新搬演的过去，多数是基于想象的报复性行为。于是，在经济开发者和机会主义者的喧闹中，真正的历史保存者只有微弱的声音。在这个重新发现的阶段里，在对中国历史的再想象与重述的时空里，关伟创建了他的"另一种历史"，展示给同时代人的世界的寓言。

除了来自这个复苏的环境，以及中国与他所定居的这个与旧大陆对距的南方国家间的文化张力，关伟创作"另一种历史"的动因也来自《1421 年：中国发现世界》中的一两个页码。加文 · 孟席斯的这本海上传奇，被许多评论认为是非学术而且有违学术准则的，并被各专业的学者嘲笑[1]。虽然如此，对于中国和新加坡等特定的对象而言，孟席斯的这本著作却仍旧被给以了显著的位置，它的特色在于创造了一个比事实更宏大的，处在现代世界边缘的中国如何与外部世界建立联系的行动过程。虽然每位严肃的读者都可能认为这本书是与阅后即弃小说别无二致的虚构作品，但它给予关伟想象他自己的另一种世界的动因，从而以历史的诡计将澳大利亚与中国融汇的灵感。

"另一种历史"是由关伟创造，在艺术家和展览策划人及展览团队的通力合作下实现的多宝阁，或者说奇珍馆[2]。多宝阁的历史起源于人类对自然科学与人文艺术间产生更加规范的逻辑分类之前。文艺复兴时代的多宝阁仿佛一个具体而微的博物馆，是兼有陈设与贮藏双重功能的房间。它发展于严格分类法之前的大光明时代，先于新的科学知识系统的奠立。这个时代的多宝阁就其性质而言是独立的，通常是基于个人特质与习性的陈列，藏品涉及稀罕的、奇特的、富有魅力的各种物件，以及诡异的技艺制品和生命短促的生物，因此它的收藏不仅包括真实的物品，也包括假想设定的物品。在这个时代里，多宝阁既是为了收藏家的研究，同时也是为了实现他的娱乐欲望而设置。这个拥挤空间的灵感，来源于人类知识的许多范畴，如同他们积聚因航海而发现的，通过海洋贸易和土地征服而来的物产。加百利 · 寇特马克便是这类收藏家中的一位，他曾指导萨克森公国奎斯钦一世在十六世纪末期建立了被称为"艺术房间"的多宝阁，他宣称在任何一个这类空间都需要收藏和陈列的，必须汇集要素项目包括"雕刻和绘画"、"来自本土和海外的新奇物件"、"鹿角，以及属于陌生或新奇动物的角、爪、翎毛和其它"[3]。关伟的"另一种历史"，以艺术多于奇技的方式，再造了如此的奇妙空间。

对于奇珍异物的收集，也存在于中国文化庄重且古老的历史之中。未可探知来源的物件，或者可能引发沉思遐想、喜悦和迷惑的物件，均被它们的偏爱者惊叹为天工非凡。因潮汐和波涛的自然淘洗而成的姿态万千的太湖石，因外形的古奥暗示着神秘来世的植物，可资追远而且联系到未知世界的占卜刻辞甲骨，似乎是四灵之首的天龙的骨骼化石等等，都被勤勉地加以收藏。但是，这些物品在集成后甚少共享，只提供给密友和鉴赏家朋友以为私娱清赏。引起最初看世界或者说接触文艺复兴后的欧洲文明的中国收藏家们惊叹，并且获得他们特别珍视的是时称"远西奇器"的物件。这种因为当时喜欢富有创造性的文化而被认为是伟大发明和奇技的物件包括机件擒纵复杂的时钟，使用明暗光线对比绘制人的面孔的奇特肖像，具有奇异的水力举升与造泉能力的水法装置。清朝的伟大皇帝之一乾隆（1736 年 –1795 年在位）异常喜爱这类妙不可言的物件和设施，并且在位于北京西北部的圆明园中给它们以特殊的显著地位[4]。

有人评述说西方的所谓"发现"中国和哥伦布的大航海有关，这个联系是通过马可波罗在元都的游记以及对遥远的古中国的想象而建立[5]。关伟用他特有的看法，或许会将他自己如何与澳大利亚遭遇的经验理解或视为新金山的发现，就像十九世纪末期从中国南部来到澳大利亚的许多人那样[6]。不论如何，他是以这里为现场，和活跃在国际艺术界的其他有中国文化背景的人们一道，经历了中国人在澳洲"发现"欧洲的大航海的航行。关伟以他自己在历史中的旅行，收集和陈列出一个现代要素齐备的，当代的多宝阁。在"另一种历史"的展览中，关伟用他的当代寓言制造了给澳大利亚的，给对跖地的人们和动植物的，给喜爱这一切的最初的访客以及后来的征服者的，充满事实与可能的庆典。它因此也是存在于关伟所说的"在历史和记忆中蜿蜒流动的诗廊，将事实和虚构交融并且模糊化"的作品[7]。

关伟围绕明朝永乐皇帝以及航海家三宝太监郑和与南海航行，编织出了这个带有假象成分的旅行故事，并且结合接触和寻宝等情节，生发为壮阔的壁画和装置艺术展览。罗清奇在本书提到："面对有关他所描述的历史事件真实程度的质询，尤其是关于概念上的真实与表层所呈现的神话的关系，关伟的回应是：郑和与他的船队所进行的大航海是千真万确的事实，参与航海的大约有 27,000 名船员，宝船在太平洋和印度洋总共行驶了大约 70,000 海里，先后长达 28 年左右，他们有可能先于库克船长 350 年抵达澳大利亚。至于是否真地抵达了，关伟说："这是无关紧要的，我是艺术家"[8]。

"另一种历史"的部分灵感来自小小的，有些神秘的老寿星雕像[9]。这件文物于 1879 年在澳大利亚北方城市达尔文附近被发掘出土，是悉尼动力博物馆的藏品。实际上没有人知道这个小雕像到底是怎样抵达达尔文的，于是有一些说法暗示或认为它是郑和与他的船队先于库克船长在澳大利亚登陆的证明。加文 · 孟席斯在他的书中即持此说，并且将这个小雕像作为支撑他过于奢侈放纵的主张的一个例证。在"另一种历史"中，关伟启动了他自己的想象进行探求，赋予老寿星以澳大利亚的象征南十字星座的一个组成部分的意义，让它引导郑和与他的船队，也引导着后来的移民由中国迁徙到这个岛大陆。

关伟的艺术创作轨迹，是通过一系列关联到这个小雕像和其它的物品的故事连缀而成的。这些物品包括博物馆的藏品，其中有些是翔实的，也有些是为了担任不同的角色进行过伪装改造的。此外还有廉价的，商业的成品，它们为关伟的历史叙事引进了歧义，使这个关于中国与南半球遭遇的，呈现在博物馆空间的关伟的"另一种历史"更加富有多样性。由于这个旅行并不仅在时间中经过，也穿行于阔大的空间，关伟给予他自己更多的想象与思考的机会，从容地移动和转换着他的艺术身份，以这种富有弹性的方法，他的叙述最初关于中国，然后关于澳大利亚，更远的则是关于中国在澳大利亚的位置和澳大利亚在世界的意义。

这个讲述给当代人的新寓言起于明朝的朱棣篡夺皇位成为永乐皇帝，使用有关长城、皇宫和贸易的因素作为始点。在此，关伟还为此后将要描述的永乐皇帝最伟大的作品——北京城的拓展创造了背景。朱棣摧毁首都南京，推翻他的外甥建文帝（1399 年 –1402 年在位）朱允炆之后，建文帝在这个被破坏的首都消失了，于是有谣传说他逃离了自己国家。因此，在一些人的说法里，郑和的远征的发动，部分是因着永乐皇帝希望追捕到他被废黜的这个外甥。

燕都北平是朱棣的根基，当他登基之后，便将王朝的中心转移到了这里，将它命名为北京，与原来的首都南京对应。北京不仅是王朝权力的根基，其地理位置也推动了皇帝为趋避来自东北方的入侵者广筑高城；与此同时，为了加强边界的防卫，开始续修长城。关伟所选择瞬间，即在燕王朱棣篡夺君权变为永乐皇帝的这个时代，他以此作为出发点开始了自己的叙述。他通过明版图中的南京城处于大火之中的巨幅的壁画，以及蜿蜒的长城、穿过广阔风景的长江、带来的离乱和迁徙的战争图景，呈现出靖难之变这一明朝历史的转折。永乐皇帝的统治中心转移到北京的历史事实，给予艺术家和他的博物馆合作者们以创造新故事的机会，即有关于永乐登基之后所发生的那些扑朔迷离的事件。"另一种历史"在此继续它的叙述，将壁画、玻璃橱窗和逼真的物件铺陈开来。关伟和他的画家助手团队创作了一系列壁画，讲述这个被细心选择的，被博物馆藏品陈列增援的故事。这类实物被艺术家的想象力重新赋予了新的含义，表现着纷纭复杂的历史正在由此展开[10]。

北京城和紫禁城的规划与建设，也同样地给予了关伟特别的灵感。北京和它的历史对于他至关重要，对于这位艺术家而言，这个城市的重要性并不仅仅在于可以因之运用丰富的想象再创作出"另一种历史"，而且在于这里和他的生命存在着密切的关系。关伟不仅出生在这里，而且和这个城市的历史有着血缘的联系。他是清王朝的后裔，目前所用的姓氏是满族姓氏瓜尔佳的汉语转写，他的高祖母苏完瓜尔佳是慈禧太后听政时期的军机大臣荣禄之女，是宣统朝（1909 年 –1911 年）的摄政醇亲王载沣的嫡福晋，末代皇帝的本生母[11]。

在他的作品中，关伟以新皇帝的新宫禁和北京城为背景表现永乐皇帝和太监郑和。艺术家随后勾勒出郑和船队的一次航行路线，郑和与他的船队在关伟所想象的航程中前行，穿过部分真实部分虚构的地区旅行到明朝所称的南海诸岛和南洋诸地，最后在魁伟的南方大陆的海岸登陆。这个以图示完成的旅行见闻，引导着我们抵达了澳大利亚。更为重要的是，关伟的这个航程始终引导观众或意向中的旅行者朝向他所关注的方向，他们所前往的是它的创造者所关心的，关于中国人的世界，关于与非中国人或者说非我族类的“他者”的接触，关于如何以非对抗的方式与域外平等交流相互感知的问题。关伟的文化冒险和海洋探险故事，创作于一个独特的，忧虑空气弥漫的澳大利亚历史时代。这是一个充满张力的，有关边界安全、种族划分与社会包容倾向的政治性辩论不断并且重复地威胁社会组织构成的时代。在这被保守势力控制的漫长的十年里，澳大利亚种族政治被用于制造国家洞察力狭隘化以及煽动公众的警戒。当这个国家正在更广泛更深入地进入与亚洲和太平洋区域经济体系，尤其是中国正在因为不断增加的能源与资源需求给我们的经济带来利益的时候，先前相对宽松的对澳大利亚本土以外的文化与人的姿态，反而受到了严重限制。

当这个国家洞察力狭隘化并且对外部世界感到极度忧虑的时代刚刚开始的时候，澳大利亚与中国关系的先驱者，著名的历史学家和外交官费斯芬曾经警告说：澳大利亚很可能会因此失去与正在崛起的亚洲沟通的道路。他当时即注意到世人因为仅仅关注亚洲经济的发展而忽视正在成长的亚洲可能给世界文化财富带来贡献的倾向。十几年前，费斯芬出版了他仅因书名所提出问题即引起人们的兴趣与遐想的著作《澳大利亚是否是亚洲国家》。在书中，他明确地指出了因为回应正在上升的中国和亚洲经济所发生的国家气质与精神面貌的变化。他警告说：

> 将亚洲的历史、文化和价值观念写入神话的行为……并不仅限于孔夫子的儒家。它是更多而且更普遍的。它是非历史的，包含着相当的危险。鉴于已经存在的一些征兆，那种已浮现的亚洲的“亚洲”，很可能像西方曾经的路径相同，也就是说他们会给自己创造关于自身的神话，并且会创造到连他们自己也相信这是唯一的善举和最后的德行所在。在一些地方，这已经有正统政治的味道。但是，如果联合的亚洲区域被这种正统所驱策，势必会形成联合区域的恐惧化，尤其是对澳大利亚而言，非常重要的是，我们的工作是为了维持整个区域性的多样化，保证非正统和独立自主[12]。

在这个正在扩大的亚洲经济和政治结构的背景下，关伟为当代的澳大利亚人创作了他关于中国人的冒险，并且在澳大利亚与“他者”遭遇的故事。关伟构思的这个作品是在一群艺术家助手的协助下完成的，因此“另一种历史”也是非凡的合作的结果，它的意义在于它就像费斯芬在他的著作中提出合作构想。在他的书的结尾，费斯芬所讨论的澳大利亚与亚洲间的新的约定是积极乐观的。他所预想的未来是在澳大利亚形成不同种族、不同思想观念和不同文化的融汇，这种融汇将造成社会与身份的多样性，而不是促成种族间的紧张和政治排斥的来源。他期望澳大利亚与外部世界的更广泛接触，期望与这个国家的近邻与远邦的相互了解，期望澳大利亚可能发展为包容并且融汇差异，因而引发出新的可能的国家，一个全世界的“他者”都可以在这里发现自己家园与祖国的国家。使他在竭尽全力后感到轻松的是他所设想的，在这个新千年与例如中国这样的国家进行丰富的、深入的、文化层面的交互式接触，这种互动式的接触将会成功，如果这种合作超越因民族国家概念的隔离和区域性排外的局限的话。所以，在至关重要的方面，关伟的这个作品对费斯芬所瞩目的新千年的家园做出了回应。

诗歌传统中的想象和来世，让“另一种历史”成为与精神世界也存在着陈述与对谈，运动与互动的故事。它通过一连串的，包括关伟与动力博物馆两者之间的，澳大利亚与中国之间的，强有力的与丰富远景之间的约定，不拘一格地提升和拓展了更多的可能，形成了富有成效并令人愉快的文化缠结。当中国经济的持续上升和澳大利亚因矿产繁荣所造成的景气可能导致形成一种信托关系之际，关伟创作的“另一种历史”提供了无拘无束的，更加丰富的，展望更广阔前景的可能，因此超出了相互间的利润追求和资源性消费增值的边际；与中国与亚洲的相互合作可以有更宽阔的天地，这使得这个地区的很多人走进澳大利亚，同时也空前地展拓了澳大利亚的外向途径，可以因此延伸到它亲近的和辽远的邻居，横越文化与时空的界限，达致充分理性的，个体与群体共同关心的人类共性的共享。基干历史的幻想和牛活经验的艺术化的再设定而创作“另一种历史”，并且使“另一种历史”成为我们所能够企望的，引人入胜的历史，而并非只是一个并未真地发生过的怀恋旧日的故事；它关联到被认为是狭隘的民族主义的表现的，但从未占领和支配被“发现”者的故事的观念在运动中与人际间生活历程的连接，是寻找在未来的领域里认定和解决人类共同忧虑可能以对过去的人们曾经如何试图努力超越自我为鉴的历史。

众所周知的关伟作品是具人形轮廓特征的，诙谐幽默地避开通常所见的那些带有反讽标志物的所谓北京当代艺术的，带有更慷慨更敏感的感性的作品。关伟的作品使用粗壮有力的色彩，创造着有吸引力的，直面而又不是相斥的，动人的世界。虽然如此，它又是倘若你逼近观察和内省会萦绕于心的见证。它是以表面的心情浮动为忧虑掩饰的作品，忧虑或者威胁被艺术家置于他可以轻盈触动的潜在之处。

被关伟轻盈触动的，也是阴沉所在。我第一次见到他的作品是在 1987 年的北京，经艺术家阿仙（现在以他非凡的彩绘瓷雕作品著名）介绍。此时的关伟正在创作一系列灵感源自针灸的作品。这些作品中的人形是没有特征的，灰暗并且缄默的。人形带有穴位，有些是真实存在的，也有些是关伟自创的，为了凸现这些穴位，绘有红色的圆环和标签；多数人形或者支离或者破碎，其中的一些还携带着斥责的警示。这些作品带有的幽灵的招唤和些微的诙谐，同样地令人难以释怀。在我们 1988 年出版的中国非官方作品文选《火种：中国良心的声音》中的〈穴位〉一节里，闵福德和我曾说到被我们称为“天鹅绒监狱”或“画地为牢”的情形。在那个时候，一位独立的文化艺术创作者，不论是艺术家、作家或知识分子，都“面对着两种选择，或者甘愿受到全面的文化排斥，或者顺服国家将他们纳入新的社会约定之中的做法。这个社会约定以默契取代了强制，并且通同合谋颠覆批评”。在评论关伟作品的时候我们谈到“他的作品同样地唤起艺术家作为囚人的噩梦世界”[13]。当这位艺术家南巡到南半球之后，南巡造成了引领他突破围困的新的路径，关伟因此想象并得以提供他关于与他相似的超国界的文化艺术创作者怎样在富有想象力的领域磋商的见解。所以“另一种历史”也提供给关伟以不同的领域，因而产生他对原本所在的出生地与现今驻足的新家园的新观念和前景进行观察的可能。

“另一种历史”是非凡的作品。这个作品是富有创造性的，经过在南半球的长期孕育的中国的智慧，在拥抱地方性期望与张力的同时议及更广阔的人类共同关心忧虑的，融汇创作者自身的作品。如同关伟这样的，在与他们的出生地保持密切联系的同时，在他们的定居地探寻意义的艺术家们，正在选择以谈及人类的现实与可能，赋予着世界性中国文化的范畴。

翻译：桑晔

---

1. 关于揭穿孟席斯此书的互联网专页，请阅 http://www.1421exposed.com/ 。
2. 此点亦在迈克尔·哥德伯格的《另一种历史：关伟给当代世界创造的寓言》展览评论中有所提及，刊《目标杂志》，2007 年 4 月 -7 月号，第 48 页。
3.B. 格佛雷斯和 J. 曼斯庄森，《多宝阁所必需的构成》，刊《历史与收藏杂志》，1989 年第 1 期，第 11 页，亦可参阅 http://en.wikipedia.org/wiki/Cabinet_of_curiosities 。
4. 见《中国遗产季刊》，第 8 期，2006 年 12 月，请阅 www.chinaheritagequarterly.org。
5. 彼得·胡拉姆，《殖民的遭遇：欧洲和原住民的加勒比海，1492 年—1797 年》，伦敦麦森出版社，1986 年，第 20 页—第 22 页。
6. 作为区别之对照，有助于追循自二战以来澳大利亚如何看中国的历史：请参阅蒂莫西·肯德尔，《鉴于中国之路：从红色危险到理想乐园》，费曼德艺术中心出版，2005 年。
7. 关伟，罗清奇引用于《艺术家，同时是故事的讲述者》，刊《另一种历史，关伟为当代世界创造的寓言》展览图册，悉尼动力博物馆出版社，2006 年，第 3 页。
8. 罗清奇，《关伟：艺术家和传奇的讲述者》，见本书。
9. 见罗清奇的《艺术家，同时是故事的讲述者》和关伟的《另一种历史》，刊《另一种历史，关伟为当代世界创造的寓言》展览图册，悉尼动力博物馆出版社，2006 年。
10. 实物展品的说明标签含有两种文字内容，一个显示该实物在博物馆的原始收藏记录，另一个是关伟和他的合作者们对该实物带有想象成份的创造性叙述。
11. 见我为关伟 1997 年 10 月 30 日 -11 月 22 日个人作品展撰写的评论《庄重的满人奇想：周边去来》，刊悉尼舍曼画廊为该展览出版的图录。
12. 费斯芬，《澳大利亚是否是亚洲国家？澳大利亚能否幸存于东亚的未来？》，悉尼艾伦和安温出版社，1997 年，第 145 页。
13. 白杰明和闵福德，《火种：中国良心的声音》，纽约希尔和王出版社，1988 年第 2 版，第 386 页和第 387 页。

雨燕可能谈到它的飞行，倘若故事不再……

阿里克西斯·莱特

在我的想象中，当灵鱼在浩瀚的大洋里创造故事的时候，它们会谈到那些盛大的日子，会有关于老寿星的塑像如何在几个世纪前抵达我们海岸的恢宏的传奇。

这个巨大的鱼群或许是我们这里特有的澳大利亚鲹鱼群，它们所形成的阵列一直延伸到海洋的尽头，随着飓风掀起的巨浪，一年又一年地进行着横过海洋的漫长旅行。在它们的旅行中，有时候会被大墙般高筑的潮峰围困，被不断高涨的狂暴波涛所造成的陷阱滞留，鱼群在浪涌的引导或者说驱动下逼近陆地，集聚在达尔文附近的海岸。

起初，老寿星的雕像大概是在其中的某条鲹鱼的腹中。这个神灵原本悬在渔民的颈上，每当出海，那位渔民都会将祂作为守护神挂在胸前，这一次却发生了意外，当渔民从小船上弯腰接近水面的时候，饥饿的鲹鱼飞快地越起，拉断了悬挂祂的绳索，攫走了这个神灵。但是现在又轮到这条大鱼失去祂了，当鲹鱼与岸边的激浪搏斗，试图从潮底洄游向背后的大洋深处的那个瞬间，这份宝贵的特殊财富随着它吐出的泡沫抛到了岸边。

在通常的情形下，这条巨大的鲹鱼恐怕很难逃离困境，注定会被海浪拍上沙滩。但是因着老寿星的保佑，这个勇敢的生命居然在这场搏斗中未受伤害，挣脱了死亡；它迅速地摆脱了困境，仿佛银色的闪电，飞快地回到了它背后的大洋深处。老寿星的雕像也没有受到丝毫损伤，只是被从水中抛向了沙滩，祂平静地卧在陌生的海岸；又经过了很长的一段时间，才被这片土地主人，澳大利亚的原住民们发现。这位手握陌生的水果，端坐在他的鹿上的老人的雕像从此再度回到了人群中来，归属于喜欢这位来自遥远异域的神灵的和祥面孔的人们。

神灵不可能永远地被人们所持有，更不可能成为人的仆佣，除了显示神秘与和祥的意向，老寿星的雕像对于人们似乎没有任何更实用的目的，因此最终被人们放置在树荫下歇息。百年过去了，这个在信仰祂的人们看来象征着永恒生命的老寿星一直留在菩提树下的这个洞穴里的角落里，被下垂如须的气生根围绕。这只是我的想象，或许那时候的人们会讲述与我的想象完全不同的故事——他们也可能以为这是远方老人的雕像，并且为这位老人的魂灵迷失在他们的土地感到遗憾，于是将他的雕像安葬在菩提树下的由海龟和野狗掘出的洞穴，让这位长者得到安息。不论如何，在与我们不同的另外一个信仰世界里，菩提树是神圣的，象征着人的长寿和灵魂的永恒。不论如何，在这片土地的原住民看来，呵护灵魂的最明智的办法是让灵魂与这片土地始终保持接触，让灵魂与树共生共长，直到永远，或者直到有一天……不论如何，是人们为来自鱼腹的老寿星雕像建造了这个小小的庇护所，然后从那个时候起，在漫长的日子将祂和这个渐渐被菩提树根缠绕的洞穴遗忘。

更可能的是在这里曾经有过另外一些人的梦境，因为有总是有很多到背井离乡寻求财富的冒险者在这里编织他们的梦想。这个人在漫长的航海中携带着他所拥有的财富，这个留着长长的胡须，身穿长袍和便鞋，一手捧着桃子，一手轻拍鹿头的乳脂色老寿星雕像。也许老寿星的雕像是这位驾驶小船来自中国的船员带来的唯一财富，也许他还带着指南针、钱币和一些衣服，也许他还带来了一些用于交易的土产和蔬菜种子。无论他带着什么，如果他能够安全地抵达他的向往之处，将会在布满露兜树和红树林的澳大利亚北部海岸登陆，而这片土地就是现今的城市达尔文。

我在想这个终于到达了这里的人是否在寻找关于他生命的答案，以及他孤独地在这片炎热潮湿的，被暴风雨吹袭的陆地寻找这个答案的时候是否遇到奇迹，或者接触到了神力。在他飞扬的思绪或者梦境里，他可能梦见了在中国大地奔跑的小鹿，或者正在森林和雪原自由飞翔的雨燕。在那片辽阔大地的夏日，桃树上成熟的果实会落到他的手里，在他自幼长大的家园，丹顶鹤的舞姿和澳洲鹳非常相似……通过这些回忆，以及另外的许多思索，这个来自远方的寻梦者是否渴念着他的祖国？我想也许会有些奇迹，比方这个人真地回归到了他的祖国，只是留下了他带来的神像，将老寿星和梦境埋藏在了菩提树下。

恐怕我们永远也不会准确地知道这个深藏在四英尺地下，并且已经被菩提树根缠绕的老寿星雕像在1879年修筑从古茹姆恩金伯[1]到接近现在的达尔文市的潘特埃莫瑞的道路时被发现的过程了。所以，我只能想象将这个雕像带到我们的海岸的中国水手大概是一位很普通的男人，在他的生命历程中肯定发生过一些故事，但是这个人的故事失落在了澳大利亚的北方海岸。毕竟还有老寿星的雕像，这个雕像不仅伴随他背井离乡一路前行，是世界上有过这个人，这个人在几个世纪前跨过大洋踏上我们这个世界的这一部分的证明。

他或许是一位水手。这位水手的老父亲为儿子被遥远的异域所吸引而闷闷不乐，对他在漫长的航海中可能遇到的危险而深感担忧。老父亲祈祷他所崇拜的神灵保佑他的儿子横过大洋，然后又平安地回来，于是小心翼翼地将老寿星的雕像放在丝绸口袋子里，用绳索悬挂在儿子的脖子上。祂可能是中国的老父亲赠予即将启程的孩子的唯一赠品，寄托着所有的期望，因为这个神灵在中国的神话中又被称为南极老人，是在南方的夜空中指点航向的星辰。

这个故事的真相留存在雕像的内部，如同祂所象征的长寿，自从发掘保存至今，并且继续延伸到永远。但是，假如我们由源远流长的本土文化传统出发，会从这个角度发现察看事实的更多途径。雕像的故事，祂和菩提树结合为一体的故事，祂如何发现的故事，都具有非常迷人的象征意义。这是一个绝妙的故事，它允许我们展开我们的关于奇迹的想象，让我们使用各种方式设想在我们的世界里可能发生的一切，让我们超越我们所感知的现实的边际，提供给我们所在的当代世界以引人注目的真实和连绵不断的故事。这是增加我们的经验与学识的机会，老寿星雕像带给我们不仅是中国的文化，也会引发我们关于如何通过多元文化的创立和完善，构建为我们全体所有的，具有多样性的澳大利亚文化的深入思考。目前，老寿星的雕像被保存在世界著名的悉尼动力博物馆，已不再仅仅是历史遗存的文物，无疑是虽然迟到了，却又非常真实的，关于在早年的殖民时代的澳大利亚很少受到关注与赞美的非主流文化的宏大故事的一个组成部分。

我相信中国水手的灵魂和他的故事，将会活在他的国家和他的人民之中；当他不论是在这里或者是在他的祖国面对死亡的时候，大概存在着同样的愿望。老寿星的雕像则是和另外的长寿象征菩提树，以及吃菩提浆果的鸟群在一起，和这个国家的神圣主人，同样具有悠久文明的原住民们永远地活在一起。这片土地的原住民当中的拉瑞凯部落有与大树的灵魂交谈的传统，他们会坐在菩提树的枝下与树对话，讨论部落中的重要事件。也许他们会在这时候谈到对于菩提树也同样陌生的，来自远方的人和雕像，并且问询大树如何将他们记载到拉瑞凯部落的律法，就象将另外一些生命记载进自己的律法相似。偶然还会有另外一些访客来到树下，他们将在那里庆贺关于大树的又一段神话归入这片辽阔的大地。

菩提树可能会发现它的生命是通过戴着黄色花冠的白色的大鸟的随意访问获得了传承。这些被称为美冠鹦鹉的大鸟携带着菩提树的种子远走高飞，将它们播撒在广阔的澳大利亚陆地。美冠鹦鹉在本土原住民的多种语言中有着不同的名字，在我的老家它叫巴若瓦，根据我的原住民祖先们的律法，巴若瓦的灵魂和中国神话中的老寿星相似，也关联着有关长寿传说。那些菩提树能够在澳大利亚的北方长久驻足或许并不仅仅是因为偶然，甘玛杰区域的尤卢古部落的长者穆古茹乌 · 尤茹宾古，也就是深受当地原住民尊重的领袖噶勒茹乌 · 尤茹宾古的父亲，曾经手握利斧和他年轻的儿子一道站在阿让赫姆兰地区的菩提树前，阻止澳加铝业公司的推土机为开采铝矾土矿在北部海湾地区毁坏植物。原住民的长者相信菩提树是神圣的，是自远古以来的雨林的灵魂家园的护卫者[2]。

我相信我们这个国家与中国的联系的历史将会因为这个小小的雕像发生令人惊异的巨大的事件。老寿星的雕像有助于人们了解长期缄默的，基本上没有获得文字记录的关于古代中国人在澳大利亚的历史，有助于我们认识将这个雕像和他们的文明携带到这里的人们。这个认识会沿着试图进一步打开这个古老的神秘雕像所隐藏的秘密的努力而发展，在本质上帮助我们与祖先的灵魂而不仅仅是自然世界建立联系，进而等到更多的关于其他人陆续登上在这片土地的历史。老寿星是一个活生生的神灵，具有为我们建立历史与未来之间的联系的能力；通过对关于这个雕像的想象，通过这位率直地望着我们微笑远古神灵，我们每个人都可能找寻到埋藏在自己头脑深处的美好的灵魂。

将老寿星的雕像埋藏在菩提树下，有可能是为了使雕像获得更妥善的保护，与我的家庭成员们也有将某些重要物件盛放在锡器中作为秘密埋藏终生，直至他们去世的习惯同样。假如这些家庭成员没有直系后代生存，我们很可能无从查找这个秘密的根底，传言中的这些宝藏只是在传言中埋藏在某处。于是，我们对于老寿星的雕像还可以有更多的想象余地，或许菩提树的气根带着这个雕像沉入到土壤的深处，直至神秘的黑暗之源，被气根的魔法纠缠的神灵直到 1879 年在达尔文港筑路时才被参加筑路的中国劳工们挖掘出来，倘若主持建设这条道路的澳大利亚殖民政府在设计道路时绕过这棵大树，它就会继续寄宿在树下，永远地拥抱着菩提树的灵魂，或者被菩提树的灵魂永远地拥抱。

我的曾祖父萨姆 · 阿邦是一名园丁。根据昆士兰州警察机关的记录，他 1883 年循陆路经达尔文移居到位于达卡奔塔利亚湾的拉温山地[3]。我无法进一步了解在这次由内陆到海湾的长途跋涉中他到底在达尔文停留了多久，也许他曾经有过一段时间工作在此时已经在当地建立的中国市场花园，而这个花园恰好就在正在筑路的古茹姆恩金伯范围之内，并且也正是在那个时候菩提树被砍倒，老寿星被发现。所以，他可能知道这个雕像在被砍倒菩提树下出土的过程，可能知道被雇佣在异常艰苦的环境中筑路的中国劳工的情形，可能知道为了保证这条道路的笔直而连根拔起生存在自然与精神双重世界的这棵菩提树的时候，当老寿星再次被暴露在澳大利亚的艳阳之下的时候，那些人们是否因此受到了祝福或者诅咒……

不论如何，老寿星毕竟是被发现了，并且继续地活着——在空中飞速掠过的雨燕回答说。雨燕归巢，天空留下了更多的空白，但是雨燕可能谈及它的飞行，还有更多故事要说……

翻译：桑晔

---

1. 现今通常被称为博士溪谷的这个地区，在拉瑞凯部落原住民的语言中被称为古茹姆恩金伯。2007 年 10 月 3 日，我在电话中与拉瑞凯部族的传统土地所有者，现任拉瑞凯发展有限公司董事长的克鲁皮埃亚提 · 理查德 · 巴恩斯先生对此进行了核对。

2. 噶勒茹乌 · 尤茹宾古曾在鲍勃 · 贝奥的著作《如果树能讲话：关于澳大利亚最伟大的树的故事》中讲述过这段故事的详细情况；见《如果树能讲话：关于澳大利亚最伟大的树的故事》，悉尼艾伦和昂温出版社，悉尼，2007 年，第 230 页。

3. 见 www.archives.qld.gov.au/downloads/Indexes/Asiatic_aliens/no_surname_ah_way.pdf 。根据这份档案的记录，萨姆 · 阿邦于 1883 年从格里高力丘陵地区到达路易小溪。然而这个记录也可能存在错误，因为他当时似乎是住在拉温山地，他在此前为当地的弗兰克 · 汉先生担任厨师。我祖母的出生证保存在我的堂姐菲利斯 · 阿杰的档案里，根据这个出生证，她出生于 1903 年，而她的长兄，也就是萨姆 · 阿邦的长子比她大十七岁，出生在 1886 年。

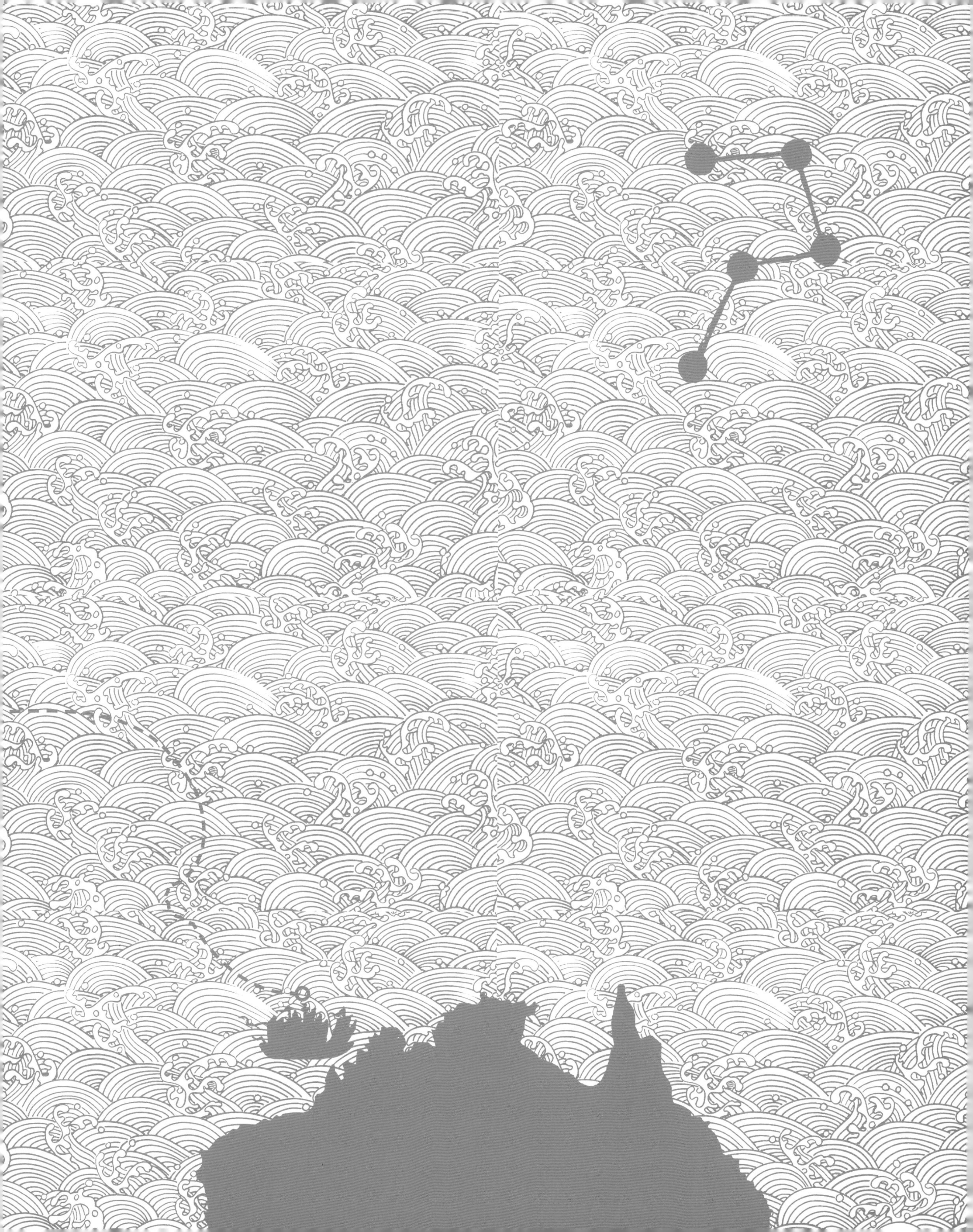

Artist Biography

Guan Wei (b. 1957, Beijing) graduated in 1986 from the Fine Arts Department at the Capital Normal University in Beijing. He migrated to Australia in 1990 and lives and works in Sydney and Beijing. Since his first visit to Australia as artist-in-residence at the Tasmanian School of Art in 1989, Guan Wei has had a fascination for narratives that connect China and Australia.

Selected Solo Exhibitions

2006 'Other Histories: Guan Wei's Fable for a Contemporary World', Powerhouse Museum, Sydney; 'Echo', Sherman Galleries Goodhope, Sydney; 'Unfamiliar Land', Contemporary Art Centre of South Australia, Adelaide

2005 'Guan Wei: Secret Histories', ARC One Gallery, Melbourne

2004 'Looking for Enemies', Sherman Galleries Goodhope, Sydney; 'Prediction—Reflection', Church Gallery, Perth International Arts Festival

2002 'Island', Sherman Galleries Goodhope, Sydney

2000 'Horoscope', Red Gate Gallery, Beijing; 'Looking for Home', Earl Lu Gallery, LASALLE College of the Arts, Singapore

1999 'Guan Wei: Nesting, or the Art of Idleness 1989–1999', Museum of Contemporary Art, Sydney

1998 'Revisionary', Australian National University Drill Hall Gallery, Canberra

1997 'The Last Supper', Tokyo Gallery, Tokyo; ' ex/inspire ', Sherman Galleries Goodhope, Sydney

1996 'Magic Garden', Hanart TZ Gallery, Hong Kong

1995 'Treasure Hunt', Sherman Galleries Goodhope, Sydney

1992 'Living Specimens', Plimsoll Gallery, University of Tasmania, Hobart

1989 French Cultural Centre, Beijing

Selected Group Exhibitions

2008 'Handle with Care: 2008 Adelaide Biennial of Australian Art', Art Gallery of South Australia, Adelaide

2007 'De Overkant/Down Under—Den Haag Sculptuur 07', The Hague

2006 'Between River and Lake', Jack Tilton Gallery, New York

2005 'In-Between Realities …', Three on the Bund, Shanghai

2004 'Cycle Tracks Will Abound in Utopia', Australian Centre for Contemporary Art, Melbourne

2003–4 'Face Up: Contemporary Art from Australia', Hamburger Bahnhof Museum, Berlin

2000 'Man and Space', Kwangju Biennale, Kwangju, South Korea; 'Inside Out: New Chinese Art', National Gallery of Australia, Canberra

1999 'Beyond the Future: The Third Asia-Pacific Triennial of Contemporary Art', Queensland Art Gallery, Brisbane

Recent Residencies

2007 Cité International des Arts Studio, Paris (Australia Council)

2006 Artists' Camp, Gunbalanya (Oenpelli), Western Arnhem Land (Australia Council, through 24HR Art, Darwin)

2005 Taipei Artist Village, Taiwan (Australia-China Council)

2003 Greene Street Studio, New York (Australia Council); Canberra School of Art, The Australian National University, Canberra

2002 Casula Powerhouse Arts Centre, Sydney

2000 LASALLE College of the Arts, Singapore

Selected Commissions

2004 'Feng Shui', mural painting for the main entrance foyer of the Bureau of Meteorology, 700 Collins Street, Docklands, Melbourne

2001 *Sydney Morning Herald*, cover artwork to celebrate Australia Day

1997 One of eight artists commissioned to produce limited edition prints for the Sydney 2000 Olympics poster program

Guan Wei's work has been collected by national and state galleries and museums in Australia and East Asia and is included in many private and corporate collections in Australia and overseas.

Selected Bibliography

Books

Barmé, Geremie and John Minford (ed.), *Seeds of Fire: Chinese Voices of Conscience* (New York: Hill and Wang, 1988), pp. 387–407.

Chiu, Melissa, *Breakout: Chinese Art outside China* (Milan, New York: Charta, 2007), pp. 159–203.

Clark, John, *Modern Asian Art* (Sydney: Craftsman House, 1998), pp. 198, 232, 268–269.

Dysart, Dinah, Natalie King and Hou Hanru, *Guan Wei* (Sydney: Craftsman House, 2006).

Lu Peng and Yi Dan, *Zhongguo xiandai yishu shi, 1979–1989* (A History of Chinese Modern Art, 1979–1989) (Changsha: Hunan Fine Arts Publishing House, 1992), p. 278.

McCulloch, Alan, Susan McCulloch and Emily McCulloch Childs, *The New McCulloch's Encyclopedia of Australian Art* (Melbourne: Melbourne University Publishing, 2006), p. 102.

Murray Cree, Laura (ed.), *Twenty: Sherman Galleries 1986–2006* (Melbourne: Craftsman House, 2002), pp. 20, 24, 30, 58, 108, 261–5, 293.

Smith, Karen, 'The Story of Guan Wei', in *Brought to Light II: Contemporary Australian Art 1966–2006*, edited by Lynne Seear and Julie Ewington (Brisbane: Queensland Art Gallery Publishing, 2007), pp. 292–9.

Turner, Caroline (ed.), *Art and Social Change: Contemporary Art in Asia and the Pacific* (Canberra: Pandanus Books, 2005), pp. 21, 468–9.

Wang Yiyan, 'Settlers and Sojourners: Multicultural Subjectivity of Chinese-Australian Artists', in *Alter-Asians: Asian-Australian Identities in Art Media and Popular Culture* (Sydney: Pluto Press, 2000), pp. 107–122.

Wu Hung (ed.), *Chinese Art at the Crossroads: Between Past and Future, Between East and West* (Hong Kong: New Art Media, 2001), p. 210.

Hart, Deborah, *Australian Art in the National Gallery of Australia* (Canberra: National Gallery of Australia, 2002), p. 389.

Deng Pingxiang (ed.), *2006 nian: Zhongguo dangdai yishu wenxian* (2006: Chinese Contemporary Art Documents) (Changsha: Hunan Fine Arts Publishing House, 2006), pp. 99–101.

Exhibition Catalogues (listed in reverse chronological order)

Roberts, Claire, 'Guan Wei: Flight Mode', in *Handle with Care: 2008 Adelaide Biennial of Australian Art* (Adelaide: Art Gallery of South Australia, 2008), pp. 64–5.

Roberts, Claire, 'The Artist as Storyteller', in the exhibition booklet *Other Histories: Guan Wei's Fable for a Contemporary World* (Sydney: Powerhouse Museum, 2006).

Jose, Nicholas, 'Fantastic Cosmographies', in *Unfamiliar Land* (Adelaide: Contemporary Art Centre of South Australia, 2006).

Engberg, Juliana, 'The Follies of History: Guan Wei's New Perspective', in *Guan Wei: Secret Histories* (Melbourne: ARC One Gallery. 2005).

Chiu, Melissa, 'Seriality as Survival: The Art of Guan Wei', in *Face Up: Contemporary Art From Australia* (Berlin: Hamburger Banhof Museum, 2003).

Cho Sung-kwan (ed.), *Kwangju Biennale 2000* (Kwangju: Kwangju Biennale, 2000), pp. 276–9.

Eastburn, Melanie, 'Reincarnation', in *Inside Out: New Chinese Art* (Canberra: National Gallery of Australia, 2000).

Gao Minglu, 'Gazing into Deep Space from a Zen Garden', in *Zen Garden* (Sydney: Sherman Galleries, 2000).

Cramer, Sue, 'Guan Wei: Storyteller', in *Guan Wei: Nesting, or the Art of Idleness 1989–1999* (Sydney: Museum of Contemporary Art, 1999).

Seear, Lynne, 'The View from the Master's Chair: Guan Wei's Feng Shui', in *Beyond the Future: The Third Asia-Pacific Triennial of Contemporary Art* (Brisbane: Queensland Art Gallery, 1999).

Wright, William, *The Rose Crossing* (Sydney: Sherman Galleries, 1999).

Chiu, Melissa, *Culture Graft* (Sydney: Gallery 4A, 1998).

Girard-Geslan, Maud, 'Guan Wei: An Adventure, From East to West', in *Revisionary* (Canberra: Australian National University Drill Hall Gallery, 1998).

Barmé, Geremie, 'Serious Manchu Whimsy: What Goes Around Comes Around', in *Guan Wei [ex/inspire]* (Sydney: Sherman Galleries Goodhope, 1997).

Huangfu Binghui, *In & Out: Contemporary Chinese Art From China and Australia* (Singapore: Earl Lu Gallery, LASALLE College of the Arts, 1997).

Chang Tsong-Zung, *Magic Garden* (Hong Kong: TZ Gallery, 1996).

Williamson, Clare, *Above and Beyond: Austral/Asian Interactions* (Melbourne: Australian Centre for Contemporary Art, 1996).

Murphy, Bernice, 'Fabulous Engagements: Recent Work by Guan Wei', in *Treasure Hunt* (Sydney: Sherman Galleries Goodhope, 1995).

Jose, Nicholas, 'A Breathtaking Balancing Act', in *The Great War of the Eggplant and Sausage* (Canberra: Australian National University Drill Hall Gallery and Canberra School of Art, 1994).

Murphy, Bernice, *Localities of Desire: Contemporary Art in an International World* (Sydney: Museum of Contemporary Art, 1994).

Li Xianting and Nicholas Jose, *Mao Goes Pop: China Post-1989* (Sydney: Museum of Contemporary Art, 1993).

Downie, Chris, and Nicholas Jose, *Chinese New Wave* (Hobart: Chameleon Contemporary Art Space, 1992).

Hull, David, *Six Contemporary Chinese Artists* (Sydney: Space YZ University of Western Sydney, Nepean, 1992).
Guan Wei (translated by Linda Jaivin and Geremie Barmé), '"Wo" de Yishu: Nesting, or the Art of Idleness', in *Guan Wei: Artist from the People's Republic of China* (Canberra: Photospace, School of Art, Australian National University, 1991).
Parr, Geoff, 'Introduction', in *Guan Wei: A Contemporary Chinese Artist* (Hobart: Plimsoll Gallery, University of Tasmania, 1991).

Articles and Reviews (listed in reverse chronological order)

Barmé, Geremie R., 'Telling Selves and Talking Others', *Art Asia-Pacific*, 52 (March–April 2007): 72–5.
Bolton, Ken, 'Guan Wei: Unfamiliar Land, *Eyeline*, 62 (Summer 2006–07): 67.
Devenport, Rhana, 'Beauty Shadow-play and Silhouettes', *Art & Australia*, 44. 2 (2006): 242 –251.
Eastburn, Melanie, 'Guan Wei's Perilous Journeys', *Art Asia-Pacific*, 50 (2006): 70–71.
McDonald, John, 'The Barrier That United a Culture', *The Sydney Morning Herald*, Spectrum (14–15 October 2006): 16–17.
Scheibitz, Thomas, 'Jiang Hu at Tilton Gallery', *New York Times*, Art in Review (23 June 2006).
Smee, Sebastian, 'Artist in a Floating World', *Pol Oxygen*, 14 (2005): 36–44.
Hill, Peter, 'Shock of the Real', *The Sydney Morning Herald*, Spectrum (2–3 October 2004): 19.
Grishin, Sasha, 'The Art of Conscience', *Australian Art Review* (November 2003–February 2004): 47–48.
Eastburn, Melanie, 'Method for Eggplant Cultivation', *Heat 5*, New Series (2003): 129–153.
Hart, Deborah, 'Looking for Home: The Fables of Guan Wei', *Art & Australia*, 40. 4 (Winter 2003): 618–625.
Kelly, Philippa, 'Thinking about Guan Wei', *Artlink*, 23. 4 (2003): 48–9.
Ouyang Yu, 'Guan Wei: Interview Horizontal and Vertical', *Meanjin: Read Their Lips*, 62. 1 (2003): 186–194.
Jaivin, Linda, 'Paint Me', *Australian Art Collector*, 20 (April–June 2002): 54–6.
Guan Wei (translated by Ben Donaldson), '10 years in Australia', *Postwest*, 19 (2001): 12–17.
Jose, Nicholas, 'Asian-Australian Dialogues in the Visual Arts', *Art & Australia*, 38. 4 (2001): 592–9.
Lee Weng Choy, 'The Rose Crossing', *Art Asia-Pacific*, 28 (2000): 95.
Low, Morris, 'Hybrid Transplants', *Artlink*, 20. 2 (2000): 56–7.
Chiu, Melissa, 'Asian-Australian Artists: Cultural Shifts in Australia', *Art & Australia*, 37. 2 (1999): 254–60.
Chiu, Melissa, Duplications Dialogue', *Art Asia-Pacific*, 27 (2000): 25.
Eccles, Jeremy, 'The Eye of a Banner Man', *Asiaweek* (2 July 1999): 38–9.
Genocchio, Benjamin, 'Enrichment From a Chinese Wave', *The Australian* (30 June 1999): 10.
Green, Charles, 'Guan Wei', *Art/text*, 67 (1999): 94.
Roberts, Claire, 'What Goes Around Comes Around: The Art of Guan Wei', *Art Asia-Pacific*, 1 (1999): 58–65.
Shao Yi Yang, '"Wo" de Yishu' (The Art of Nesting), *Yishujia* (Artist) (September 1999): 476–9.
Clark, John, 'Dilemmas of (Dis-)attachment in the Chinese Diaspora', *Visual Arts and Culture*, 7 (1998):14–45.
Pai, Maggie, 'Complex Cycles', *Asian Art News* (March–April 1998): 40–43.
Smith, Karen, 'Guan Wei at Red Gate Gallery', *Asian Art News* (May–June 1998): 80–81.
Zhu Dake, 'New Asian Artists in Australia', *Asian Newsweek* (29 June–5 July 1998): 60–61.
Rooney, Robert, 'The Cultural Revolution Shifts West: Guan Wei's Efficacy of Medicine', *The Australian* (15 August 1997).
Findlay-Brown, Ian, 'Guan Wei at Hanart TZ Gallery', *Asian Art News* (March–April 1996): 75.
Juers, Evelyn, 'Spirit-man: Guan Wei', *Art & Australia*, 33. 3 (Autumn 1996): 431–2.
Terrill, Ross, 'The Curtain Between Us', *The Australian* (9 October 1996): 14–15.
Annear, Judy, 'Juggler of Systems', *Asian Art News* (September–October 1995): 54–5.
Jose, Nicholas, 'My Search for a Shaman: Art In and Out of China, *Art Asia-Pacific*, 1. 2 (1994): 82.
Jose, Nicholas, 'Brokering a Space: New Chinese Art 1989–92', *Art Monthly* (September 1992): 9.
Jose, Nicholas, 'Notes from the Underground: Beijing Art', *Orientations* (July 1992): 53.
Jose, Nicholas, 'Guan Wei: A Contemporary Chinese Artist', *Agenda* (March–April 1992): 17.
Bernstein, Roslyn, 'China', *Contemporary* (September1990): 83.
Guan Wei, 'Nesting: The Art of Idleness', *Island* (Spring, 1990): 8.
Jaivin, Linda, 'Blowing His Own Trumpet', *Far Eastern Economic Review* (24 March 1988): 84–7.

List of Works

China and the Ming Dynasty

'Zheng He and Columbus', mural painting by Guan Wei, 2006. 200 x 308 cm.

'Kangaroo Kingdom', six panels, acrylic on canvas by Guan Wei, 2005. 137 x 300 cm.

'The Ming Dynasty: A Battle for Power', mural painting by Guan Wei, 2006. 246 x 650 cm.

'Yongle Emperor: The Maker of Beijing', mural painting by Guan Wei, 2006. 254 x 500 cm.

'Zheng He: The Eunuch Admiral' mural painting by Guan Wei, 2006. 270 x 310 cm.

Chinese Ceramics

• Covered jar, porcelaneous ware with cloisonné-style decoration, Fahua ware, Ming dynasty, Hongzhi reign (1488–1505). Purchased 1956. A4935

• Stemcup, porcelaneous ware with celadon glaze, Longquan ware, Longquan, Zhejiang, Yuan dynasty (1271–1368). Purchased 1953. A4422-3

• Plate, porcelain painted in underglaze blue with stylised Arabic script, made in China for the export market, late-Ming or early-Qing dynasty (1600s). Said to have been found in a tomb in East Africa. Purchased 1922. A2453

• Plate, porcelaneous ware with celadon glaze and incised decoration, Longquan ware, Ming dynasty, Yongle (1403–24) or Xuande (1426–35) reign. Purchased 1976. A6558

• Vase, stoneware, painted in brown on a tea-dust glaze, Cizhou ware, made in the Yaozhou kilns in Yaozhou, Shaanxi, Yuan dynasty (1271–1368). Purchased 1955. A4669

• Jar, stoneware with incised and cut-away design of phoenix and peony flowers, made in the Gangwa kilns in Chifeng, Inner Mongolia, during the Liao (907–1125) or Song (969–1279) dynasty. Purchased 1956. A4721

• Bactrian camel, glazed earthenware, Tang dynasty (619–906). Purchased 1956. A4719

• Bowl, porcelain with yellow enamel glaze, made in Jingdezhen, Jiangxi, during the Ming dynasty, Zhengde reign (1506–21). Purchased 1955. A45321

Buddhism

• Two figures from a Vajrabhairava group, gilt-bronze, Sino-Tibetan, Gelugpa school, Ming dynasty, Yongle (1403–24) or Xuande (1426–35) reign. An imperial commission, probably from a Tibetan Buddhist temple in Beijing or Chengde. Purchase sponsored by Edith Walker 1927. 231A

Roof Tiles and Coins

• Two architectural tiles, porcelain with incised dragon and cloud pattern under a yellow and green glaze, Ming dynasty, Zhengde (1506–21) or Jiajing (1522–66) reign. Purchased 1955. A4512

• Roof tile, in form of mythical animal, glazed earthenware, Ming dynasty (1368–1644). Said to have come from the Old Summer Palace in Beijing, souvenired during the Boxer Rebellion of 1900. Purchased 1926. A2622

• Roof tile, in form of mythical animal, glazed earthenware, Qing dynasty (1644–1911). Said to have come from the Old Summer Palace in Beijing, souvenired during the Boxer Rebellion of 1900. Purchased 1926. A2623

• Roof tile in the form of a figure astride a hen, glazed earthenware, Qing dynasty (1644–1911). From the Old Summer Palace in Beijing, souvenired during the Boxer Rebellion of 1900. Purchased 1926. A2624

• Coins (three), 'Currency of Hongwu', copper alloy, Ming dynasty, Hongwu reign (1368–98). Coins (three), 'Currency of Yongle', copper alloy, Ming dynasty, Yongle reign (1403–24). Coin, 'Currency of Xuande' copper alloy, Ming dynasty, Xuande reign (1426–36). Collection Hwong Ping Sing, 1862. Transferred from the Australian Museum 1961. N7602, N7611, N21249-46, N7618, N7619, N21249-47, N7620

Mirror

• Mirror, carved hardwood, Qing dynasty (1644–1911). Said to have come from the Temple of a Thousand Ages near the Old Summer Palace in Beijing, during the Boxer Rebellion of 1900. Transferred from the Australian Museum 1965. H7751

Voyaging

'Treasure Hunt', mural painting by Guan Wei, 2006. 224 x 1045 cm.

• Ship model, HM Bark Endeavour, 1:24 scale, made by Finecraft Scale Models, commissioned by the Museum of Applied Arts and Sciences for Captain James Cook Celebrations in 1970. Purchased 1970. H8855

Unfamiliar Land

'Medicinal Herbs': *Paeonia lactiflora, Eriophyton wallichii, Prunus mume, Rheum officinale.*

'People From Other Regions': Solomon Islands, Satanazes (known only from a 1424 map), Java, Tonga, Indonesia, Sri Lanka, New Zealand, Iran, Fiji.

'Animals': Crocodile, Possum, Emu, Platypus, Wombat, Koala, Kangaroo.

'Medicinal Herbs': *Zephyranthes candida, Aucklandia lappa.*

Works on paper by Guan Wei, 2006. Lent by the Museum of Australian East Asian Art.

'The Great Southern Land', mural painting by Guan Wei, 2006. 227 x 460 cm.

• Koala (*Phascolarctos cinereus*), Common Wombat (*Vombatus ursinus*), Common Wallaroo or Euro (*Macropus robustus*), Common Brushtail Possum (*Trichosurus vulpecula*), Cassowary (*Casuarius casuarius*). Lent by the Australian Museum.

'Island', mural painting by Guan Wei, 2006. 249 x 430 cm.

Tea

- Samples of Chinese black tea.
- Tea brick, made by the Zhao Liqiao Tea Brick Company, China, early 1910s. Gift of Narelle Jubelin, 2006.
- Tea bowl and saucer, porcelain painted in underglaze blue, with applied floral decoration, made in Jingdezhen, Jiangxi, for the export market, Qing dynasty, late-Qianlong (1736–95) or Jiaqing (1796–1820) reign. Gift of Miss D. Wentworth 1942. A3528-1:2
- Two cups and saucers, porcelain painted in underglaze blue, made in Jingdezhen, Jiangxi, for the export market, Qing dynasty, Qianlong reign (1736–95). Purchased 1911. A1266-1:2
- Teapot, porcelain painted in underglaze blue, made in Jingdezhen, Jiangxi, for the export market, Qing dynasty, Qianlong reign (1736–95). Gift of Nancy Wellerd 1977. A6669
- Hanging scroll, reproduction of painting by Ming dynasty artist Du Jin (1399–1474), with inscription 'Bringing tea', date and seals added by Guan Wei.

Chinese Medicine

- Contemporary plastic acupuncture models, glass cups and steel acupuncture needles.
- Medicinal herbs and glazed ceramic pot for brewing traditional Chinese herbal medicine.
- Hanging scroll, reproduction of 'Gazing at the Waterfall' by Ming dynasty artist Qiu Ying (1494–1552).

Map and Navigational Instruments

'Chinese Map of the World', drawn in the eighth year of the Xuande Emperor's reign (1433), based on the discoveries made on Zheng He's last voyage. Work on paper by Guan Wei. Lent by the Museum of Australian East Asian Art.

- Telescope, 3 3/8" refractor, metal, glass, used at Sydney Observatory, about 1875. H1025.7
- Telescope, leather-bound German silver telescope presented by the British Government to Ernst Kuhlman for saving the crew of the Hibernia in 1857, Troughton & Simms, London, about 1855. Gift of E. A. Watson 1983. B2514
- Eclectus parrot, female (red) and male (green), New Guinea/Northern Australia. The specimens were collected in New Guinea, about 1895, and prepared by the Australian Museum. Exchange objects from the Australian Museum 1895. E3102, E3103
- Magnetic compass, wood, glass, metal, made in China during the Qing dynasty (1644–1911). Purchased 1915. H3162
- Combined compass and sundial, wood, metal, glass, made in China during the Qing dynasty (1644–1911). Transferred from the Australian Museum 1965. H7728
- Surveyor's compass, made by Angelo Tornaghi, Sydney, 1860–70. Gift of A. McDonald 1938. B747-1-2
- Sextant, wood, metal, glass and inscription 'Presented by Richard Evan's Price Esquire to Captain George Johnston of the Barque Australia for his kind and unremitting attentions to me and my family', Troughton & Simms, London, about 1836. Purchased 1984. H10399
- Terrestrial table globe, made by Newton & Son, London, 1846–69. Transferred from the University of Sydney 1964. H7504

Maps and Ship Model

- Ship model, HM Armed Brig Supply, 1:24 scale, made

by Geoffrey C. Ingleton RAN for the Sesquicentenary of the arrival of the First Fleet, Sydney, Australia, 1937– 8. Gift of Australian Sesqui-Centenary Committee 1938. H4053

'Celestial Navigational Maps' (left to right): 'Western Jufu' Star, Southern Cross, Vega, Polaris. Works on paper by Guan Wei, 2006. Lent by the Museum of Australian East Asian Art.

China and Australia

'The God of Longevity', mural painting by Guan Wei, 2006, 296 x 430 cm, and installation of sand with fragments of ancient ceramic vessels, reproduction coins and objects.

God of Longevity

- God of Longevity, carved pinite, said to have been found wedged in the roots of a banyan tree in 1879 in Doctor's Gully, near Port Darwin, Northern Territory, thought to have been made in southern China in the 1800s. Purchased 1950. A4255
- Cast, God of Longevity, plaster-of-paris, made by the South Australian Commission for the Melbourne Centennial International Exhibition, 1888–9. Donated 1889. A1

Shrine to Zheng He

- Buddhist figure, wearing a Buddhist mantle, carved wood with lacquer and gilding, Ming dynasty (1368–1644). Gift of Katherine Jennings 1972. A6092
- Vessels for a temple altar, bronze, cloisonné enamel, Ming (1368–1644) and Qing (1644–1911) dynasties. Said to have been from the Old Summer Palace in Beijing. Gift of Christian Rowe Thornett. A6080

'The Southern Cross', mural painting by Guan Wei, 2006. 300 x 660 cm

Chinese in Australia

- Surcoat with silver pheasant rank badges, silk with silk floss and gold-wrapped thread embroidery, made in China in the late-Qing dynasty (1644–1911). The robe belonged to Margaret Tart (1865–1916), wife of Sydney merchant Quong Tart (1850–1903) who was awarded the rank of a fifth degree civil official in 1888. Gift of Ian Tart 1996. 96/361/1
- Kendi, stoneware with brown glaze, made in China in the late 1800s. Found in 1941 at Southport, Port Darwin, once home to a large Chinese community. Gift of W. J. Bellow. 92/185
- Family photographs. Reproduced courtesy of William Yang.
- Chinese property deeds, Qing dynasty (1644–1911) and early 1900s.
- Playing cards, made in China, before 1880s. Purchased from Messrs Sue Hing Long & Co., Chinatown, Sydney, in 1884. 7935
- Chinese lute, wood, ivory, made in Guangdong, China, in the early 1880s. Purchased from Messrs Sue Hing Long & Co., Chinatown, Sydney, in 1884. 7944

The mural paintings in the exhibition were created by Guan Wei and realised with the assistance of Frank Hope, Jin Sha, Yang Xifa and Zhao Baokang.

All objects from the Powerhouse Museum collection, unless otherwise stated.

Contributors

Authors and Translators

Geremie R. Barmé, Australian Research Council Federation Fellow and Professor of Chinese History at The Australian National University (ANU), specialises in the cultural and intellectual history of China. His publications include *In the Red: On Contemporary Chinese Culture* (1999), *An Artistic Exile: A Life of Feng Zikai 1898–1975* (2002), Sang Ye's *China Candid: The People on the People's Republic* (co-edited with Miriam Lang, 2006) and *The Forbidden City* (2008). He has participated in the film productions *The Gate of Heavenly Peace* (1995) and *Morning Sun* (2003). He founded The China Heritage Project at ANU with Bruce Doar, co-edits the e-journal *China Heritage Quarterly*, and he is also the editor of the journal *East Asian History*.

Guan Wei is one of Australia's leading contemporary artists. He was born in Beijing and graduated from the Department of Fine Arts at the Capital Normal University, Beijing, in 1986. In early 1989 he was invited to Australia as artist-in-residence at the Tasmanian School of Art. Since his migration to Australia in 1990 Guan Wei has held many solo shows, and in 1999 he was the subject of a ten-year retrospective at Sydney's Museum of Contemporary Art. His work has been included in many influential Australian and international group exhibitions. In 2003 Guan Wei was commissioned to create a large work for the foyer of the Bureau of Meteorology in Melbourne, said to be the largest painting in the southern hemisphere. Guan Wei's art works have been collected by major national and state art institutions in Australia. From 1991 to 2007 he was represented by Sherman Galleries, Sydney, one of Australia's leading commercial galleries. He is currently represented by ARC One Gallery (Melbourne), Kaliman Gallery (Sydney) and Redgate Gallery (Beijing). Guan Wei lives and works in Sydney and Beijing.

Claire Roberts is Senior Curator of Asian Decorative Arts and Design at the Powerhouse Museum, Sydney, and a Research Fellow with Geremie R. Barmé's Australian Research Council Federation Fellowship Project at The Australian National University. Her specialisation is twentieth-century and contemporary Chinese art, Northeast Asian art, decorative art and photography. Her exhibitions and publications include *New Art from China: Post-Mao Product* (1992), *In Her View: The Photographs* *of Hedda Morrison in China and Sarawak, 1933–67* (1993), *Evolution and Revolution: Chinese Dress 1700s to Now* (1997), *Earth, Spirit, Fire: Korean Masterpieces of the Chosôn Dynasty* (2000) and *The Great Wall of China* (2006). She was a curatorial adviser to the Queensland Art Gallery's Asia-Pacific Triennial of Contemporary Art (1993, 1996 and 1999). In 2006 she was awarded a Ph.D in Chinese art history from The Australian National University.

Sang Ye is a writer and oral historian born in Beijing and based in Brisbane. He is currently a Research Fellow with Geremie R. Barmé's Australian Research Council Federation Fellowship Project at The Australian National University. In the 1980s his publication (with Zhang Xinxin) of a series of oral histories made him a celebrity in China; the work published in English as *Chinese Lives: An Oral History of Contemporary China* (1987) has also been published in several European languages. His other books include *The Finish Line* (1994), *The Year the Dragon Came* (1996), *China Candid: The People on the People's Republic* (2006), and *La Danza Dei Vestiti* (2007), an Italian publication of stories originally commissioned by the Powerhouse Museum for *Evolution and Revolution: Chinese Dress 1700s to Now* (1997). Sang Ye's oral history interviews were also published in Claire Roberts and Geremie R. Barmé (ed.), *The Great Wall of China* (2006).

Alexis Wright is one of Australia's most important writers. She is a member of the Waanyi nation of the southern highlands of the Gulf of Carpentaria. Her book *Grog War* (1997), is a study of alcohol abuse in the outback town of Tennant Creek, and her novel *Plains of Promise* (1997) was short-listed for the Commonwealth Prize, the Age Book of the Year and the New South Wales Premier's Award, and has been published in French. Her most recent novel *Carpentaria* (2006), an epic set in the Gulf country of northwestern Queensland, won her the prestigious Miles Franklin Literary Award, the Australian Literature Society Gold Medal, and the Australian Book Industry Awards, Australian Literary Fiction Book of the Year. She is currently a Distinguished Fellow in the Writing and Society Research Group at the University of Western Sydney.

Photographer

Jean-François Lanzarone has been a staff photographer at the Powerhouse Museum, Sydney, since 2000. He studied photography at L'Ecole Louis Lumière in Paris, 1985–7 and has conducted photographic assignments in France, Romania, Portugal, Chile, Egypt, Australia and China. Prior to moving to Australia in 1999 he worked for 12 years as a freelance photographer in France where he held exhibitions including 'Portraits from Portugal and Romania' (1993); 'Portraits from Australia' (1993–4); 'Portraits from Chile' (1995); 'Students, Attitudes' (1996) and 'Public Transport' (1998). Since working at the Powerhouse Museum he has concentrated on exhibition, public program and object photography. In 2006 he was commissioned by the Powerhouse Museum to create an immersive installation, comprising a series of panoramic photographs taken on assignment in China, to accompany 'The Great Wall of China' exhibition held at the Powerhouse Museum (2006–7).

Assisting Artists

Frank Hope was born in China and graduated from the Department of Fine Arts and Design at Suzhou University in 1987, majoring in design. He worked as an art tutor at Shenzhen University, and later at the Suzhou Academy of Applied Arts, where he was also head of the fashion research studio. Since moving to Australia in 1997 he has worked both as an artist and designer, and as an art instructor at Hornsby Ku-ring-gai Community College. A participant in numerous exhibitions his works have been collected by national and provincial cultural institutions in China, and by commercial and private collectors in China and Australia. He lives and works in Sydney and in recent times his main focus has been three-dimensional works and video art.

Jin Sha was born in Beijing and graduated in 1992 from the Chinese Painting Department at the Central Academy of Fine Arts in Beijing. He is Secretary-General of the Beijing Institute of Traditional Chinese Painting and a member of the academic committee of the Zhejiang Research Institute of Traditional Chinese Painting. Jin Sha is also an active curator and has initiated many exhibitions in China and Australia. His recent exhibitions in Beijing include 'Face to Face: A National Portrait Exhibition of China', held at the National Art Museum of China (2007), and 'Spiritual-Material: An Exhibition of Work by Australian Artists Ian Howard and Michael Esson', held at the Art

Gallery of the Capital Normal University (2005). Jin Sha has won a number of art prizes and his work is in the collection of the National Art Museum of China. He lives and works in Sydney and Beijing.

Yang Xifa was born in Tianjin and graduated from the Chinese Painting Department at the Tianjin Academy of Fine Arts in 1989. He studied under Wang Xuezhong and was awarded his Master of Arts degree at the Art Research Institute at Tianjin University in 1996. In 1999 Yang was a visiting scholar at the Central University, Tokyo. He is currently Associate Professor in the Department of East Asian Arts at Nankai University, Tianjin, and a member of the Chinese Artists' Association. Yang Xifa has received numerous prizes and awards in China, including the bronze medal at the National Art Exhibition in 1992. In 2007 he held a solo exhibition 'Scattered Memories and Extinct Animals' at the Wollongong City Gallery and was included in 'Eligibility Options', the Third Beijing Biennial (2006). Yang Xifa lives and works in Tianjin and Sydney.

Zhao Baokang was born in Shanghai and graduated from the Department of Stage Design at the Shanghai Theatre Academy in 1978. He has participated in many exhibitions in China, Australia and elsewhere, including 'Sea Level: Painting and Sculpture', Liu Haisu Museum, Shanghai (2006); 'Alien and Illusion', Shanghai Art Museum (2005); 'Beyond Dimensional Space' Shanghai Duolun Contemporary Art Museum (2004); 'Fisher's Ghost Art Award', Campbelltown City Art Gallery, Sydney (2003); 'East-West: Chinese Contemporary Art', Artist's House, Vienna (2002); and 'Metaphysics 2002 Abstract Art Exhibition', Shanghai Art Museum (2002). Zhao Baokang lives and works in Shanghai and Sydney.

Acknowledgments

We gratefully acknowledge the support received from the Powerhouse Museum, Sydney; the assisting artists Frank Hope, Jin Sha, Yang Xifa and Zhao Baokang; Wild Peony Pty Ltd, Sydney; Song Ya Feng Culture & Art Center Beijing; Beijing Artron Colour Printing Co. Ltd; The Australian National University, Canberra; and the Project Team: Mabel Lee, A. D. Syrokomla-Stefanowska, Jin Sha, Sang Ye and Geremie R. Barmé.

The publication *Other Histories: Guan Wei's Fable for a Contemporary World* could not have been accomplished without the participation and assistance of many colleagues and friends.

Powerhouse Museum: First and foremost Guan Wei would like to thank the Powerhouse Museum, Sydney, for the opportunity to realise the exhibition and in so doing make this publication possible. We extend our thanks to the then Director of the Powerhouse Museum, Kevin Fewster, the Acting Director Jennifer Sanders and Associate Director Mark Goggin for their enthusiasm and support, and for allowing the publication of exhibition text and photographs. We also express gratitude to the Hon. Kevin Rudd, Prime Minister of Australia (then Leader of the Opposition) for opening the exhibition, Gene and Brian Sherman for their longstanding friendship and support, the Sherman Foundation for generously providing funds to produce the original exhibition booklet, and the Australian Museum for lending Australian native animal specimens from their collection.

We acknowledge and thank the professional staff at the Powerhouse Museum who worked on the exhibition: notably Ross Clendinning, the exhibition co-ordinator, who oversaw the development of the exhibition with care and thoroughness, and Tara Kita also in exhibition co-ordination; Paul Donnelly, Curator of Decorative Arts and Design who provided important curatorial assistance to the exhibition and helped Guan Wei with access to museum objects; Powerhouse photographers notably Jean-François Lanzarone who documented the process of the murals being painted and took the majority of the photographs that appear in this book, and Marinco Kojdanovski who took the final exhibition views; exhibition designer Donna Lopata who was patient, accommodating and inspired when it came to dealing with challenging requests; graphic designer Danny Jacobsen who was responsible for the typography used in the exhibition and designed the exhibition booklet; Melanie Cariss in the print media department who edited the exhibition text and booklet with patience and skill; Mandy Campbell in the media and marketing department who worked tirelessly to promote the exhibition; Helen Whitty in visitor services who invited Guan Wei to work on an animation about the God of Longevity figure for a children's program, and Jana Vytrhlik, Manager of education and visitor services, who responded enthusiastically to the idea of inviting visitors to view Guan Wei and his team painting on-site; and Kathleen Phillips for producing a short introductory film about Guan Wei and the exhibition. Special thanks are extended to the many staff who prepared and installed museum objects, notably Tim Morris and Gosia Dudek from the preservation department, and Stephanie Boast and Nicky Balmer in the registration department.

Assisting artists: Guan Wei especially thanks his friends, the four gifted artists who worked with him over a period of one month to complete the nine large murals that formed the basis of the exhibition: Frank Hope, Jin Sha, Yang Xifa and Zhao Baokang.

Wild Peony Pty Ltd: Guan Wei and I owe a special debt of gratitude to Mabel Lee and A. D. Syrokomla-Stefanowska, the directors of Wild Peony, for their tremendous support of this publication. Without their involvement the book could not have been realised.

Song Ya Feng Culture & Art Center Beijing: We extend special appreciation to Liu Zheng, Supervisor General of the Song Ya Feng Culture & Art Center Beijing, for overseeing the production of this publication, to Wang Zi and Zhao Fang for their handsome design, and to Jin Sha who has been instrumental in co-ordinating the project within China.

Beijing Artron Colour Printing Co. Ltd: Our sincere thanks are also due to the Beijing Artron Colour Printing Co. Ltd., without whose support the publication would not have been possible. In particular we acknowledge the cooperation and flexibility of staff to accommodate this project in an already full work schedule.

The Australian National University: Important support for the publication was provided by Geremie R. Barmé through his Federation Fellowship Project 'Beijing as Spectacle', funded by the Australian Research Council, and by Maxine McArthur who assisted with copy-editing and worked efficiently at short notice.

Project Team: A talented team of individuals has shepherded the publication from its inception and development in Sydney to its production in Beijing. Mabel Lee and A. D. Syrokomla-Stefanowska have been masterful copy-editors and overall co-ordinators on behalf of Wild Peony Publications, Jin Sha has liaised skilfully and effectively with Song Ya Feng Culture & Art Center Beijing and Beijing Artron Colour Printing Co. Ltd, key tasks that enabled the project to proceed, Sang Ye has translated the essays from English to Chinese, edited Guan Wei's essay and has overseen the copy-editing of all Chinese text, and Geremie R. Barmé has provided important institutional support of a moral and material kind.

Finally, we would like to thank Liu Liwen, Guan Qingying and Nicholas Jose for their support, and close friends who provided information and advice including Carrillo Gantner and Ziyin Wang Gantner, Linda Jaivin, Lisa Havilah, David and Margaret Williams, William Yang, Ning Zheng, Wang Yiyan, Zhu Dake, Cai Guo Qiang and Liu Yang.

Claire Roberts and Guan Wei
Sydney, March 2008

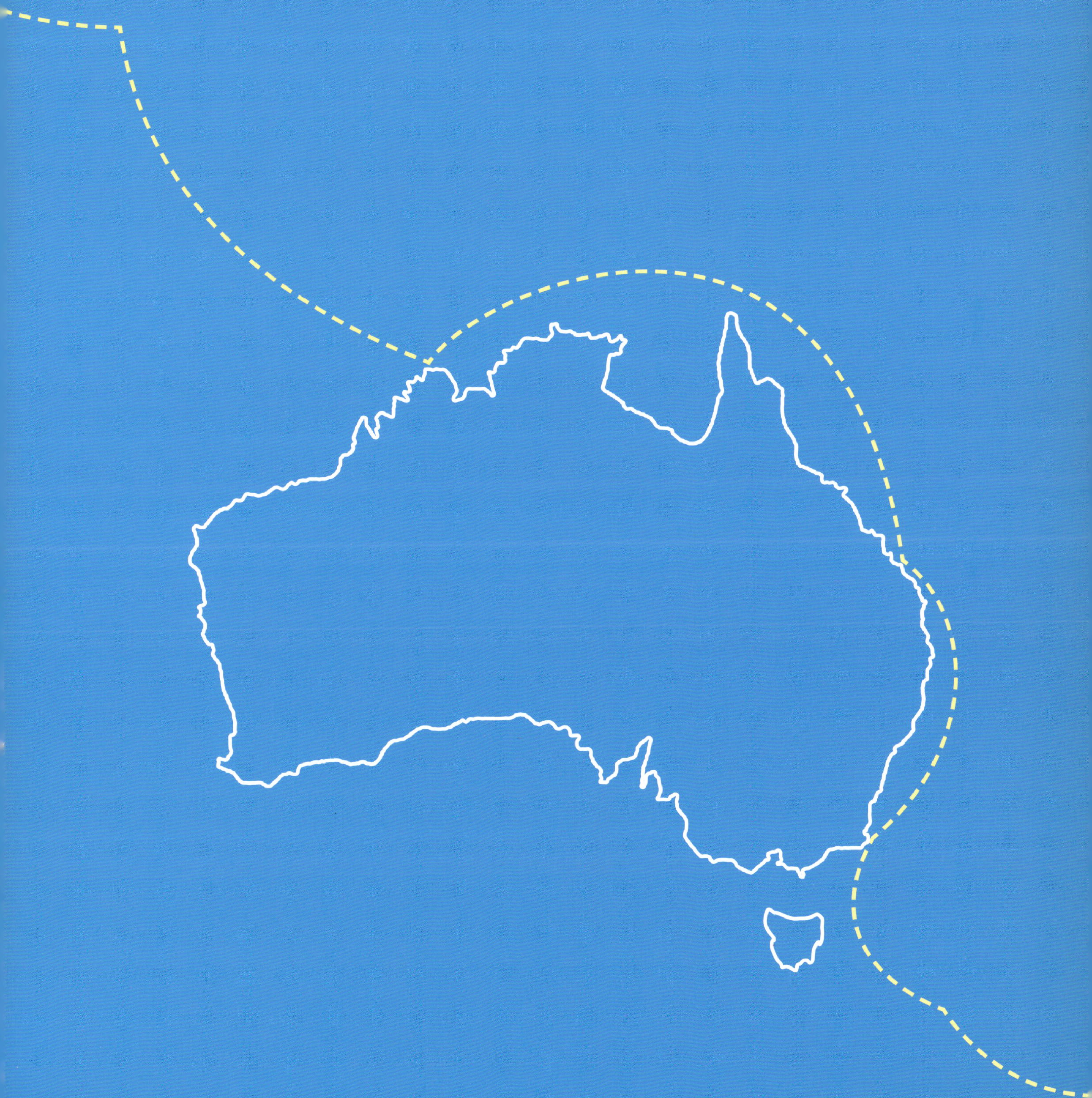

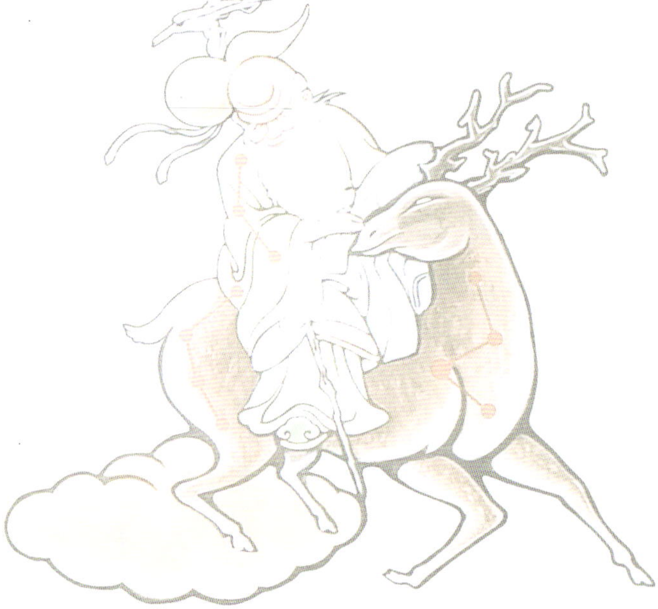

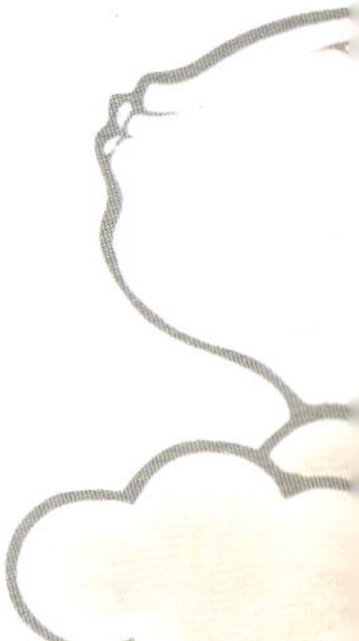